T0093996

Flexible Network Architectures Security Issues and Principles

Flexible Network Architectures Security Issues and Principles

Bhawana Rudra

CRC Press
Taylor & Francis Group
Boca Raton London New York

CRC Press is an imprint of the
Taylor & Francis Group, an **informa** business

CRC Press
Taylor & Francis Group
6000 Broken Sound Parkway NW, Suite 300
Boca Raton, FL 33487-2742

Printed on acid-free paper
Version Date: 20180306

International Standard Book Number-13: 978-1-1385-0543-8 (Hardback)

Library of Congress Cataloging-in-Publication Data

Names: Rudra, Bhawana, author.
Title: Flexible network architectures : security issues and principles / by Bhawana Rudra.
Description: First edition. | Boca Raton, Florida : CRC Press/Taylor & Francis Group, [2018] | "CRC Press is an imprint of Taylor & Francis Group, an Informa business." | Includes bibliographical references and index.
Identifiers: LCCN 2017057557| ISBN 9781138505438 (hardback : acid-free paper) | ISBN 9781351028301 (e-book)
Subjects: LCSH: Computer network architectures. | Computer networks--Security measures.
Classification: LCC TK5105.52 .R83 2018 | DDC 005.8--dc23
LC record available at https://lccn.loc.gov/2017057557

Visit the Taylor & Francis Web site at
http://www.taylorandfrancis.com

and the CRC Press Web site at
http://www.crcpress.com

Dedication

To my parents, who have guided me and given me inspiration to face challenges of life. This book and my education would not have been possible without their sacrifices and the encouragement they gave throughout to me and to my lovely sister and brother.

Contents

Foreword

The Internet is a remarkable catalyst for creativity, collaboration and innovation providing us today with amazing possibilities that just two decades ago it would have been impossible to imagine; and yet we are not amazed. Tim Berners-Lee invented the Web 20 years ago and immediately after two years, CERN publicized the new World Wide Web project. In today's world, even a child can access a free satellite image from any place and interact with others over the globe. This raised the issues of security. Our challenge is to solve the issues of security and make the architecture sustain from the patches. How do we sustain the Internet after 10 to 20 years?

Internet was never designed to serve massive scale applications with guaranteed quality of service and security. It is being used to transact the digital packets to each other through cyberspace, digital cash or any other sensitive information. Everything got changed to digital in the form of sequence of zeros which enabled broadcasting easily with Net as even our own dog wouldn't recognize it. Emerging technologies like streaming high quality video, other applications face severe constraints to run them from anywhere and at any time with good quality. If we want to support quality of services, then the new models have to emerge to survive for a long time.

The growth of connectivity, of viruses and hackers, of electronic eavesdropping and electronic fraud, security is paramount in current and Future Internet. Two trends have come together to make the topic of this book of vital interest. First, the explosive growth of the Internet connections for the exchange of information via networks increased the dependence of both organizations and individuals on the systems stored and communicated. To cope with the demands, researchers have come up with a set of solutions like Clean State, Revolutionary or Evolutionary approaches. As a result, many organizations like FIArch, GENI, IETF etc., have come up with new architectures based on one of the proposed approaches. This in turn has increased the awareness for the need to protect the data and add security as the chief ingredient in the newly emerged architectures. Second, the disciplines of cryptography and network security are mature and lead to the development of new techniques and protocols to enforce the network security in the Future Internet.

Preface

The Internet, as a worldwide communication network, has changed our daily life in many ways. It connects people from far-flung corners of the world. This evolution has created business dependency and developed security issues. The burden of various protocols to support the various applications along with security as a main ingredient on the architecture paved a path toward the Future Internet. The architectures along with security protocols allow us to communicate without security attacks. The most common tool which is available is cryptography, an old technique that has been revised and adapted to avoid attacks in emerging architectures. This book first introduces the reader to the limitations of the current Internet and then the various emerging architectures along with various principles of cryptography, applying those principles of network security protocols for the emerging architectures.

Features of the Book

Several features of this text are designed to make it particularly easy for readers to understand the importance of the Future Internet and network security. To structure this, the text uses an incremental form of teaching toward the importance of security.

Structure

As we cannot discuss network security without some background, we first discuss the limitations which paved a path for various new architectures and followed by the security issues and principles required for the Future Internet along with a case study.

Chapter 1 Putting The Internet Forward to the Next Level, explains the new demands that can be addressed to a certain degree through incremental infrastructure investment (i.e., more and more bandwidth in wire line, wireless and mobile networks) combined with over-dimensioning. The fundamental limitations of current

Internet architecture and some of the design objectives of the Future Internet are discussed. This is the next step, which contributes toward the specification of the design principles that will govern the Internet architecture. Design principles play a central role in the architecture of the Internet as driving most engineering decisions at the conception level but also operational level of communication systems. The architectures which are following these principles are explained in the next chapter.

Chapter 2 The Future Internet Global Standardization, delineates the relevant background information such as the Internet design goals and principles, initiative toward the OSI reference model, architectural principles, a rigorous critical review of Internet dealing with its limitations and issues, future research approaches, and the need of network architecture. Finally, we discuss the Future Internet architectures like RBA, AKARI, etc., along with the threats and attacks that may arise with lack of security followed by a summary.

Chapter 3 Security in Future Internet, places emphasis on the significance of security in the future Internet. The explanation is followed by various security threats and attacks, and how these impact the system. Finally, the chapter also provides a further discussion of the security services and the mechanisms that are required for the Future Internet architectures. Some architectures require all six principles of security whereas some others require more than that or less than the existing ones are explained. Service Oriented Network Architecture —Security Provisioning (case study), the case study of a particular architecture which uses the SOA structure as base explains the various threats which are possible in that architecture.

Chapter 4 Authentication —Future Internet Architectures, emphasis on the requirement of authentication, What are its objectives toward the future Internet architecture? Finally, it explains a secure communication model which authenticates the user and grants the permissions based on those certificate rules. The access permissions which are to be granted has been explained in the next chapter.

Chapter 5 Access Control Mechanisms Challenges —Future Internet Architectures, emphasizes the requirement of authorization, various mechanisms which have been used in the Future Internet architectures. This takes care of all the permissions granted to the specified users which use the system to access the pool (database) where the services are stored, etc.. Finally, it also discusses about convergence of services and composition of the various services which are to be used by several users.

Chapter 6 Detection Techniques continues the discussion of various security detection techniques by examining the concept of the intrusion, and the technologies necessary to prevent, detect, react, and recover from intrusions. Specific types of intrusion detection and prevention systems (IDPSs) —the host IDPS, network IDPS, and application IDPS with their respective configurations and its uses are presented. It even focuses on the discussion of DoS and DDoS attacks, and avoidance techniques which suits the Future Internet architectures. The chapter finally concludes with a summary.

List of Figures

List of Tables

Contributors

Prof. Dr. O. P. Vyas
Dean (R&D)
Indian Institute of Information Technology-Allahabad, India

Dr. A. P. Manu
PES Institute of Technology and Management
Shivamogga, Karnataka, India

Dr. A. Jagan
Dr. B V Raju Institute of Technology
Narsapur, India

Dr. Chiranjeevi Manike
Dr. B V Raju Institute of Technology
Narsapur, India

Mr. Karthik Kovuri
Dr. B V Raju Institute of Technology
Narsapur, India

Ms. Shaik Salma
Dr. B V Raju Institute of Technology
Narsapur, India

Symbol Description

N	Natural numbers, $(1, 2, 3, \ldots)$	e_r	Access grant categories
a_x	Applications	q_n	Classified applications
M	A set of mandatory information	m_x	Mandatory informations
K	A set of additional information	k_x	Additional informations
S	A set of principals/ entities	P	Set of protocols
Z	A set of security levels of the services	p_x	Protocol "x"
		F	Security function
		W	Secure state

Chapter 1

Putting the Internet Forward to the Next Level

1.1 Introduction

This chapter aims to provide a concept for Future Internet architecture while discussing the current Internet design goals and principles, A critical review of the present Internet-Open Issues, a Path towards the Future Internet which includes the seeds for new design principles, design principles of the Future Internet and their potential factors for the benefit of the society. Finally, guidelines are derived for use by researchers as well as practitioners.

The goal is to draw lessons from the history to the future of secure communications. Many new technologies such as ATM, Frame Relays, etc. emerged for the improvement of current network systems but could not succeed to get evolved and qualify as possible alternatives. Most of the approaches adopted a *patch-work* approach to cope with the need and aspirations of the network community in which it is desirable to have evolution and revolution of technology growth with acceptable cost and speed along with flexibility as a prerequisite for continuously changing scenario [203]. The view is broad, covering many technologies, and many issues, and not very detailed. The functionalities of today's Internet have been divided into several layers considering their abstraction level, but the experts in the networking community could not agree on a specific number of layers. As a result of this, the TCP/IP model has 5 layers and OSI has 7 layers, etc. Moreover, the placement of functionality in the layered approach is sometimes difficult to decide. In addition, the dependency among the protocols and functionalities is hard-coded making the architecture inflexible. However, this is remarkable in that the history considered here covers many services and its issues, including security limitations.

The proposed chapter is figure the future network architecture in which some of the current Internet functionalities are capaciously analyzed and the various limitations resulting mainly from the inflexibility of current architecture are identified while propounding the flexible network architecture with some network functionality implementations.

1.2   Ideas for Current Internet

J C R Licklider of MIT discussed the concept of a Galactic Network i.e., Internet in the year 1962 for accessing the data and programs from any site. Later DARPA explained the importance of networking concept. The concept of packet switching theory came into discussion in 1961 and the concept was applied in 1965 creating the first ever wide area computer network. DARPA developed the network concept and planned for publishing it in 1967 under ARPANET. Later as a development ARPANET developed switches, host-to-host protocol called NCP. The public demonstration of the Internet along with the development of electronic mail was done in the year 1972. From then onward, email took off as the popular network application used for a kind of people to people communication. This open architecture was developed based on four ground rules:

- No Internet changes should be required in order to connect to the Internet.

- If the packet fails to reach its destination due to any reason, it should be retransmitted to the source.

- Gateways and routers are used to connect the networks, gateways will know about individual flows of packets passing through them.

- There should not be a global control on the operations performed in the Internet.

The researchers worked more on NCP and came up with a modified protocol named it as TCP which can interface with existing operating systems. TCP provides a wide range of transport services. This worked fine for file transfer and remote login applications. The applications that do not want the services of TCP, UDP was introduced as an alternate protocol for direct access to basic IP service. In 1980s, the development of Local Area Networks (LAN), PCs and workstations allowed the nascent Internet to spread. Research by Vinton G Cerf and Bob E Kahn [43] led to the design of the TCP/IP suit in 1982. Though many researchers indicate that US DoD created ARPA or DARPA to regain a technological lead over the USSR in 1958 [80], but the first Internet connection, *ARPAnet* in 1969 was the outcome of the pressing necessity of a large number of computers spread over different locations in the United States and other places as well.

It came out of our frustration that there were only a limited number of

*large, powerful research computers in the country and that many re-
search investigators who should have access were geographically sepa-
rated from them* [23]...

– Charles M Herzfeld [1]

First time Network Control Program (NCP) ARPAnet successfully exchanged data
between UCLA and Stanford Research Institute computer systems by employing a
technique of *packet switching* over the telephone network system. Later on ARPAnet
involved with major innovations such as email in 1971, Telnet in 1972, and FTP 1973
etc., and thus allowed users to avail these application facilities. The inclusion of non-
military users to avail these applications over the same LAN compelled creation of
a separate dedicated military network (MILnet). This was the first modification that
ARPAnet experienced with their technology and that forced them to make a separate
network for their own defense research development purposes.

NSF is funded by supercomputer centers, public funds, private industry partners,
etc., for the development of Internet backbone and to support research and education,
instructional institutions, research arms engaged in open scholarly communication
and research. In 1986 NSFnet successfully linked fast supercomputers by replacing
slower ARPAnet computers. As a result of which ARPAnet was finally shut down
completely in 1990, and NSFnet became the backbone of today's Internet using the
technique of packet switching, where the packet is a fragment of IP and TCP and
together formed TCP/IP suite. This was redesigned to support a large number of
protocols in 1982.

DARPA initiated for successful development of network communication architecture [1] and evolved into TCP/IP network model with many modifications to share
web-based content across networks and thus initiated a new era of *Internet*. The
TCP/IP suite was developed with a goal to operate over a wide range of networks,
like long haul nets (ARPAnet and X.25), LAN (Ethernet, ring net, etc.), broadcast
satellite nets (DARPA ASN, I5, DARPA EWS Net, etc.), radio networks (DARPA,
British and amateur radio operators), a variety of serial links, and a variety of other
ad hoc facilities etc., for wide use of military and commercial application systems.
There are many papers and specifications to describe the working nature of protocols,
but it is difficult to deduce that, why the protocol is as it is like a connection-less or
datagram mode of service. The motivation for this was greatly misunderstood and
the researchers highlighted some of the early reasons which shaped Internet protocols [50]. It is clearly suggested that Internet architecture should provide wide flexibility in services that it offers. Different protocols are used to provide different types
of services and also different networks incorporated within this. Evolution phases of
the Internet along with its hindrances, future expectation of users and also factors
like heterogeneity are influencing for the development of the next generation Internet (for more details, please refer Chapter 2). The Internet architecture had reformed
several times to meet the demands of application developers, needs of the Internet
users, policies of network providers, rules and regulations of location, technological

---

[1] Director of ARPA, tenure 1965–67.

revolutions etc., gives a clear indication of drastic changes expected to be done in the upcoming days.

In 1990, ARPANET officially handed over the control of public Internet to National Science Foundation. With the help of its decentralized nature and support for multiple applications with different operating systems has increased the usage of Internet. In 1991, Internet Society has noticed the traffic passed is around 1 trillion bytes to 10 billion packets per month. In order to protect the packets over the network, within the same year, they came up with a popular encryption program, i.e., Pretty Good Privacy (PGP). This protocol was used by all the users in order to protect their data. All thesel users include even the criminals who wish to hide their Net identity and try to perform some anti-social activities. It means that the encryption can enhance privacy and anonymity of users but it may also undermine their own security. The Internet not only provided the communication safe but has opened new horizons for criminals. In 1992, there were almost 50 websites but there were nearly 1 million users. Within one year, the websites were increased to 623 and by the end of 1993 the users were increased to 2.1 million. This drastic increase was due to the result of technological creativity, flexibility, and decentralization. By 1994, the users were aware of more and more features of the Internet which bought more and more business to believe in innovation like shopping malls and so on which has increased the users up to 3 million. NSFNet has upgraded to OC-3 which has supported up to 155 mbps links and allowed the traffic of 10 trillion bytes per month. Worldwide Telecom companies announced the Internet services to its users which resulted in a drastic change in the year 1995. By this year, there were 30,000 websites and they were doubling every two months. Due to its maintenance like Internet addresses, directory and database services, Information services to the users has increased the Net usage to more than 6.6 million and this is doubling every year for various purposes like finding information, business entailment, research and essentially any need. From the mid-1990s, the Internet took a new turn for the exchange of information by running TCP/IP protocols via "Intranets" and "Extranets". Fiber Optic Link Around the Globe (FLAG) is the single-cable network, providing support for all the Internet applications from 1997. This has increased the usage of the Internet by its users. The development of the Internet and its architecture is not a grand plan but a means to exchange the data within a lab. The evolutionary growth from a private network to a public network increased the development of more protocols to overcome the architectural as well as security issues. As a result, the burden to support these protocols and more users is collapsing the architecture and raising the issues.

1.3   Internet Design Goals and Principles

David D. Clark has highlighted that *end-to-end* arguments are a set of Internet design principles which were first articulated in the early 1980s. It was also observed by many researchers including J. H. Saltzer *et al.* that end-to-end arguments served as the basis of architectural paradigm in Internet design debate for 20 years. Although it was believed by leading Internet researchers that the end-to-end arguments cannot support the application level function and preferably should not be built into the lower levels of the system.

1.3.1 Design Goals of Internet

The design goals of the Internet are very difficult to address as technology kept on changing over the past few decades. Some researchers have identified and broadly classified the Internet design goals into *main* and *secondary* goals as follows [50]:

Main Goal: Use the interconnected networks at its maximum utilization with the technique of the multiplex.

Secondary Goals: These consists of:

- Accommodation of a variety of physical networks,
- Allow accountability of resource usage,
- Allow distributed resources management,
- Allow host attachment with a low level of effort,
- Connection with existing networks,
- Cost effective,
- Support for a large number of services, and
- Survivability from its failure.

Not only these, but also a few other secondary goals are emerging as hidden patterns on the Internet that could not be recognized during its design; for example, issues like security, control and management, flexibility, and others [41].

1.3.2 Internet Design Principles

The principles adopted for the development of the Internet architecture for the fulfillment of the above-mentioned design goals are as follows [103]:

Layering: The concept of abstraction is adopted for making a communication protocol into different subprotocols of smaller sizes [102]. The Internet model used layer concept to define a framework for implementation of protocol stack. Layer is a logical collection of similar types of functions which provides a service for the next level of layer without any bypass of in between layers. The concept of last-on and first-off is used for the realization of layer headers stack. That is, layer N presents a service to layer N+1, and construction of service is performed based on the instruction issued by N-1 layer. The control of the Internet protocol is passed from one layer to its adjacent layers, starting from the application layer of one system to the bottom layer of another system by strictly adhering to the hierarchy. The modularity, information hiding, and abstraction helped in the creation of complex protocol interactions.

Packet Switching: The different modes of data transfer in a computer network are packet switching and circuit switching. In case of packet switching, a stream of message is split into a sequence of small packets, and each packet is transferred individually [21]. A packet can take the same ora different path to reach the destination. At the receiving side the gathered packets are reorganized to get the original information. Modern WAN protocols such as Frame Relay [208], TCP/IP [191], and X.25 [178] works based on packet switching principle which are efficient, robust for delayed tolerant data transmission and receiving applications such as email and Web pages.

Simplicity Principle: The Internet architecture follows *simple to control principle* with the help of layering concept, where there is no provision for overriding any layers and thus provides a very smooth and fine control over the packet flow.

Intelligent End System: As end systems are becoming more and more intelligent due to the advance in technologies, resource power, economy, etc., which helps for easy solving of routing problems.

Collaborating Networks: Internet is a collection of networks or networks of networks, and thus it allows for the collaboration of WAN, LAN and MAN for the support of users [181].

End-to-End Arguments: The principle of end-to-end communication never made intermediary nodes as responsible for the reliable delivery of data rather it did end hosts as fully responsible, such as identification of *completeness and correctness* of packet information. Thus, it helped in the reduction of intermediary network nodes load considerably. CYCLADES was the first end-to-end network designed by Louis Pouzin for research at IRIA in France by employing the concept of a virtual circuit to establish a reliable link between the end systems using connection-less, unreliable datagram services [163]. The clean separation of virtual circuit mechanism for datagram routing gave birth to a new concept of IP on TCP. The network never knows about the type of the applications for which it is used nor the knowledge about applications, still it needs to support for all applications irrespectively. The intermediate nodes will handle only communication specific functions, and other non-communication related functions such as reliable delivery, delivery control of the packet, check and cross verification capabilities, etc., are untouched by these intermediary nodes and which are handled by the end systems. The intermediate nodes and network are made to behave as dumb nodes and dumb network respectively to support for easy communication.

1.3.3 Initiative toward OSI Reference Model

In 1979 BSD Unix began to support TCP/IP protocol suit officially and in the same year ICCB was formed with the oversight of Technical and Engineering development of the Internet. Later on the ARPA converted all their machines to provide support for TCP/IP protocol suite. In 1980, DoD was expanded and on recommendation of ISO a model called *ISO OSI Reference Model* was created. Later on it became the official standard for the Internet, in the year 1996. At the same time different protocols were developed by many organizations such as ANSI, ITU (formerly known as CCITT), IEEE, etc., and started the concept of layers for the integration of communication protocols. Some of the standards defined by the OSI reference model consist of;

- Communication between devices,

- To inform when to send and when not to send data,

- Ensure correct data flow rate,

- Ensure data passed and received by recipient and

- Physical transmission media arrangement and connection.

The OSI reference model consists of 7 layers [102] of abstraction that are presented by stack format [46]. For network application, the data passes through all 7 layers where each layer performs a unique and very specific functions on data. Seven layers of OSI model are: Application (layer 7), Presentation (layer 6), Session (layer 5), Transport (layer 4), Network (layer 3), Data Link (layer 2) and Physical (layer 1) (Figure 1.1). The Internet Advisory Board was formed in 1984 for Internet standardization, followed by the Internet Activities Board in 1986. In 1992 the Internet Architecture Board was formed under ISOC to monitor the world Internet.

Ethics and the Internet: The IAB's 1989 *Ethics and the Internet* strongly endorse the view of the Division Advisory Panel of National Science Foundation Division of Network, Communications, Research and Infrastructure. Following are characterized as unethical and unacceptable activity [9] by the committee:

- ∗ Seeks to gain unauthorized access to the resources of the Internet,

- ∗ Disrupts the intended use of the Internet,

- ∗ Wastes resources (people, capacity, computer) through such actions,

- ∗ Destroys the integrity of computer-based information and

- ∗ Compromises the privacy of users.

1.4   Internet Architectural Principles

The current Internet architecture followed an approach of evolutionary for its development which made it technologically very successful [38]. The architectural principle of the Internet is broadly categorized into Fundamental and Secondary Principles and these principles are consisted for many specifications. These specifications are required to be fulfilled for the development of better services.

➤ **Fundamental Principles:** Some of the specifications used under this principle are as follows;

Multiplexing: A simple dictionary meaning of multiplexing is *the use of a common communication channel for sending / receiving two or more messages/data*. The data may be a simple text, or audio stream, or video stream, or error detection/recovery information and many more. The data is transferred with the help of packets, and these packets are of variable length in nature. Logically a packet is made up of header and payload. The Internet uses a universal approach for transferring any variable length of data using the concept of packet headers to multiplex the communication channel.

Transparency: It is the ability to access and work with data irrespective of where they are located or what application created them. It works with the principle of *If It Works, Don't Mess With It* [92]. The intended receiver gets the original sent data without any modification.

Connectivity: Internet uses direct and real time communication system with a minimal duration of time delay. In this structure, a system connected to any part of the subnet/class of network is also treated as attached to the same network. Due to this principle, any host can send/receive packets directly to any other host unless otherwise it is prohibited.

End-to-End Arguments: It has been already expounded in the previous section under the same subtitle. (Please refer to Section1.3.2 for more details).

Subnet Heterogeneity: Very few assumptions are made toward the functionality of subnet to support a variety of existing as well as upcoming technologies. Because of this nature, it made the Internet into highly flexible and universal for any kind of adoption/modification/changes/addition to new technologies.

Common Bearer Service: Internet protocol serves as the universal networking protocol by providing common bearer of service to E2E systems. It performs the functionality of packet forwarding through each subnet, and these sub-networks are interlinked with the help of routers. These services are loosely defined to handle diverse characteristics of the system at its *best effort* such as dropping of packets, duplication of packets, reordering of packets, and so on so forth.

Forwarding Context: Connection oriented and connection-less are the two distinct communication techniques used for the transfer of data in network. These techniques have their own advantages and disadvantages. The connection-less nature of the Internet (also known as datagram) allows senders to simply send/forward packets without establishing a connection between the recipients. The host simply drops

the destination addressed packet onto the network, that is, no step is required before sending/forwarding a packet and these packets are self-
contained in nature. It helps for burst transfer of data without maintaining any per-flow state information, for example, Ethernet, IPX, and
UDP.

Global Addressing: A universally accepted unique global addressing
scheme (IPv4 and IPv6) is used for identification of nodes in the network. This unique identification information is used in all IP headers,
and the routers utilize this information during forward operation of the
packet. The global address is also mapped with unique name known as
a *DNS name*. By knowing either the IP address or *DNS name* any node
can be easily identified on a network.

➤ **Secondary Principles:** Some of the specifications used under this principle
are as follows:

Routing: It is the process of selecting a definite path between the source
and destination in a network. The network consists of intermediate
nodes such as routers, bridges, gateways, firewalls, or switches. The
routing device performs computations to ensure loop-free, hop-by-hop
forwarding of packs without any single point of failure. Two different
methods are available for routing a packet such as *source routing* and
non-source routing. In case of source routing the application can decide the path of packet flow whereas in non-source routing the path is
not determined and it is of dynamic in nature.

Regions: The Internet supports a 2-level hierarchical routing for administrative purposes. The level-1 (L1) decides the area and that of level-2
(L2) decides the backbone region. The domain of routing is partitioned
into areas. The L1 type of routers has information about their area and
the L2 type of routers knows the address of the very next reachable
nodes.

Protocol Layering: It has been already expounded in the previous section
under the subtitle *Layering*. (Please refer to Section 1.3.2 for more details).

Minimal Dependency: The service of the Internet follows E2E communication with a very minimal interval of network facility. By knowing
each other's IP addresses the end nodes can successfully communicate
among themselves and there is no need of knowing the system DNS,
thus provides robustness to the system. With the help of symmetrical
interface hosts can directly communicate with each other without the
intervention of routers.

Security: The Internet is architected for E2E security mechanisms to provide application privacy and integrity. There is a need of a mechanism
to control excessive traffic and self defending against any type of attacks.

Congestion: The collision of packet forms congestion in network. The Internet has sufficient buffering space to get a place to play with the different congestion adaptation algorithm. The congestion algorithm works based on the round-trip network latency. The control plane of the Internet architecture has an explicit signal for the adaptation of algorithms. There is no central and standard model for the measurement of network performance which is forced to measure the performance at the host.

Resource Allocation: The Internet allows its resources to get controlled by the applications on the basis of request. With the help of explicit mechanism Internet QoS can be controlled. The individual flows of the Internet can be controlled by the mechanism of *int-serv*, similarly the *diff-serv* mechanism provides the controlling facility for resource allocation and aggregation, and MPLS mechanism allows for deciding the *virtual path* for traffic engineering.

Mobility: The current Internet architecture is optimized for stationary services. With the advent of new wireless communication technologies such as MANET, VANET, mobile IP, etc., made architecture rethink to provide support with additional cost.

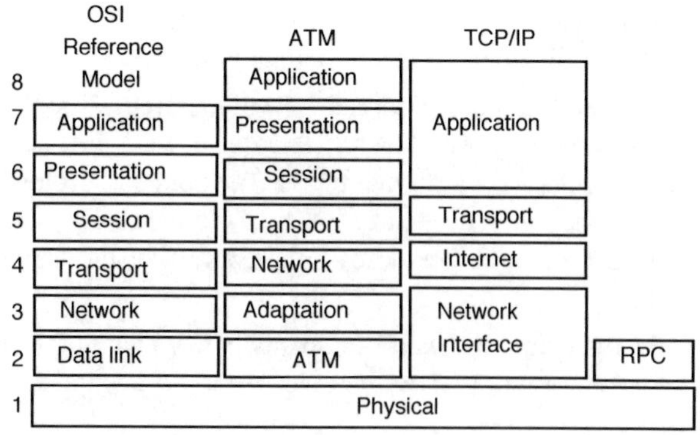

OSI Reference Model		ATM	TCP/IP	
8		Application		
7	Application	Presentation	Application	
6	Presentation	Session		
5	Session	Transport	Transport	
4	Transport	Network	Internet	
3	Network	Adaptation	Network Interface	
2	Data link	ATM		RPC
1	Physical			

Figure 1.1: Different layers comparison.

1.5 The Internet of Today

The Internet was originally started with the design principle of strict layering to make implementation simple but, in recent years it has been found violating the original design principle. As a result of this severe problems are being faced, and one of the ideal ways of solving these problems could be a modification of existing protocol or changing protocol interaction or introducing a new protocol for requirements satisfaction. The gigantic size of the Internet made any changes at a global level practically unsuitable and impossible. As the roots of the Internet had been deepened overthe past four decades, so there is no easy practical way out for changing all available protocols or type of interaction or their functionalities. The mechanism of future Internet architecture should support for easy build up of protocols, version's of protocols, easy to add, remove or modify, automatic communication, so on and so forth.

Internet became an important medium of information exchange and communication environment. There are many organizations to address various issues of the Internet and also independent organizations to develop protocols related to the Internet functionalities. The ISOC and its affiliated organizations are responsible for the development and support of the Internet protocols, while RIRs and the ICANN administers the Internet addresses and domain names. A network protocol development that relates to Internet protocols is being done by organizations ranging from the ITU and the IEEE to the W3C and the ATM Forum [125]. Twenty-First century technology is coalescing and increasingly embedded with our social and cultural fabric. Understanding and leveraging of these are essential for future success.

The current Internet was designed as a simple network service used to connect intelligent system universally. The focus is on a network layer which is capable of selecting a path dynamically from source to destination. The simplicity of the network is due to the end-to-end argument and has pushed the complexity to the end points which made the Internet to have interconnected systems. A point has come where the Internet is reaching its capability limits and capacity limits. It has been observed that it is good at delivering the packets, a level of inflexibility is seen in network layer and no support for non-basic functionalities like self management functionality, capability of activating a new service on-demand, large-scale provisioning, orchestration of security, mobility, service support, etc., common resources and services. Other issues like addressing, mobility, need for security, energy awareness, etc., are to be addressed.

1.6 "Patch-Work" Approaches for Current Internet Conflicts: Critical Review

Due to the complexity of the network, the computer network softwares follow a hierarchy of protocols and create a kind of communication service abstraction that follows P2P communication. There is a debate in the network community that, *What is the right number of layers?* From then [151], the ISO community claims as seven layers, TCP/IP community argues as five, OS research community implemented by just a single layer (RPC protocol), X.25 reference as three, G.hn has got three, etc.(Figure 1.1). In fact, layering results in inefficient network code and poor performance no matter how good the OS is [60]. Some of the current Internet hindrances are as follows:

☞ TCP/IP was originally designed and implemented for WANs, even though it is usable on LAN, but it is not optimized for this domain. In TCP/IP, checksum is used for E2E reliability check, in spite of the CRC mechanism which performs checking per-packet basis.

☞ IP uses *Time-To-Live* which is relevant only in the context of WAN environment. It also supports packet fragmentation; inter network routing and reassembly features are not useful in a LAN environment.

☞ TTL has the maximum number of seconds that a packet can exist within the Internet [103]. However, this field allows only integers (with values from 0 through 255), and as every node takes some non-negative, non-zero amount of time to process so the TTL behaves almost exactly like a hop counter. As an 8-bit field, the maximum possible TTL is only 255 [32]. Requirements for Internet hosts communication layers suggests that the default value for new packets should be set to at least big enough for the Internet *diameter*; which is the longest possible path. A reasonable value is about twice the diameter, to allow for continued Internet growth. Current figures suggest a default of 64, and which is unchanged since 1994. RFC 1122 requires that this value be configurable on all Internet hosts so that the value may be changed as and when necessary.

☞ Internet will do the best what it can, but there is no standard specification of how good that is. Packet delivery may go out of order or get delayed or even drop out based on several conditions. This approach burdens the application designer to cope with the variations with the intention of *poor* service is better than no service at all [50].

☞ TCP/IP round-trip latency is poor, which affects the communication performance.

☞ The assumption of the TCP/IP model is that it communicates between autonomous machines which cooperate minimally. But machines on LAN frequently share common file system, administrative service, etc.

☞ The TCP/IP protocol suite and socket separate interfaces and protocols stack into multiple layers and the transitions can be costly in terms of effort put to program and amount of time. This focuses on message throughput rather than latency of protocol. There are only a small number of protocols (TCP/IP and UDP/IP) and interfaces (System V Transport Layer Interface and Berkeley Sockets) in widespread usage so the generality of forming the multi-layer concept is made questionable.

☞ The implementation of TCP/IP is complex with the memory management mechanism which reduced the system performances.

☞ The outer header identifies the inner protocol header. Thus in advance, the outer protocol must be defined by a set of possible inner protocols which is a hard-coded selection. Because of this during development phase, the developer has to know the pool of protocols that exist in the system, which made induction of new protocols almost impossible.

☞ The TCP/IP protocol suite was developed under the sponsorship of DARPA, despite there being a number of serious security flaws inherent in it. Some of the security-based flaws are authentication attacks, sequence number spoofing, source address spoofing, and routing attacks, trivial attacks, etc. [25].

☞ TCP/IP assumes a fairly simple and predictable notion of the E2E communication, that is, minimum one permanent path availability between source and destination with a small E2E delay and packet loss, but this does not always hold well in a dynamically varying mobile environment. The TCP/IP has been designed for wired networks, but not for wireless network so handling data link layer in wireless media requires a different approach.

☞ Implementation of QoS, QoC, mobility and other sub-services comes in the form of accessories and these were not considered as design issues at the time of TCP/IP architecture design.

☞ Simultaneous use of IP security with quality of service, Mobile IP and multicast is completely infeasible in TCP/IP paradigm, and also failed in providing Simplicity, Efficiency and Trust (SET).

☞ The functionality of locating circuit switching technology of MPLS lies above the link layer and below the network layer. As a result of this Internet got speed up, however, it duplicates many roles of network and link layer. In the same way SIP reserves resources between network providers. However if the transport layer reserves the resources then this protocol will be unnecessary, hence it shows that there is a limitation in the layer mechanism.

☞ The reduction in the price of the memory increased the buffer size considerably to a large extent. A buffering provides a space for packets to wait during a transmission while minimizing the data loss. But a problem that needs more attention is *bufferbloat* [42] and it is due to the excess of buffering inside a network resulted in defeat of the TCP's congestion avoidance mechanisms. Transmission of more packets even after reaching a checkpoint starts and lengthens the queue to reduce the packet drop. The queue length drains after the occurrence of flood and it is slow in response. Some of the applications such as VoIP, network gaming, chat programs, etc., are working with latency constraints and with the increase in demand the problem would likely to worsen due to bufferbloat.

☞ Apart from the above-mentioned issues, other factors which are also held equally responsible for the development of new architectures are multitude of application growth, protocols needed to perform congestion control, loss recovery, no universally approved model for traffic engineering, busty nature of traffic, and so on.

In spite of the above-mentioned issues some more limitations of current Internet are as follows:

1.6.1 Multicast Routing Limitations

The concept of multicast routing followed by unicast and broadcast to suppress the growth of the routing table for the better performance of domain routing. Many types of routing protocols are available for identification of host through message advertisement. CBT, DVMRP, PIM-DM, PIM-SM and MOSPF are some of the examples for routing protocols to handle the problems that arise during the increase of the number of sizes of groups to a large extent or the growth of connected domain to very big volume.

In case of unicast routing, the same routing table is used for all distinct locations whereas multicast routing destination is a set of hosts. Hence, separate routing tables are required for multicast routing which is made impossible to aggregate multiple multicast groups. This limitation has come from the start of inter-domain multicast routing. BGMP was proposed to aggregate routes [193] but could not accomplish its goal at the end. In the case of PIM-SM numbers of advertisements remain the same even if the domain gets larger, but it is limited to only one domain. Although RSVP was designed to support all types of multicast protocols, but the same problem of the table continues in it.

Introduction of IGMP made multicast routing method understandable by only router which complicated the network and in the meanwhile violated the E2E principle.

1.6.2 ATM Limitations

There was hype in the Internet community that the ATM would be the foundation for future telecommunication network. However, providing a guaranteed QoS on ATM was very complex than that of the Internet. And the average packet size of ATM cell is $\frac{1}{10}^{th}$ of that on the Internet as a result the speed of the ATM dropped down by 10 times.

Point-to-multipoint communications using ATM are realistic and are observed in a pure ATM network [97]. But the coexistence of ATM network as a data link layer on the top of Internet is not realistic which is being equivalent to IP multicasting, and resulted in more expectations from multicast. This resulted in unwanted IGMP traffic generation which delayed the response time.

The current Internet does not support direct implementation of ATM technology on the existing infrastructure, which requires heavy infrastructure investment. Due to some of these limitations it is hardly used anymore as one of the Internet technologies.

1.6.3 Inter-Domain Routing Limitations

BGP is an inter-autonomous system, used for the exchange of network reachability information with other systems of BGP [47]. It is also known as inter-domain routing protocol that selects a path between systems and performs identification of alternate paths during recovery when there will be a failure of an existing path. This recovery process takes a long time for the identification of an alternate path. For a mission-critical system it will be a limitation of inter-domain routing.

Due to a provision of multi-homed sites, on the Internet, the number of entries in global routing table is exceeding more than 300,000 entries [97]. And that is expected to continue in the future, which is an alarm. Attempts are also made to use the BGP to perform inter-domain routing, for example, in MPLS path assignment, which will increase significantly the BGP advertisement volume.

1.6.4 Network Layer-Specific Time Interval Limitations

Transport and data link layers rely on the time stamp of packet delivery. The time stamp functionality facility identification of packet loss or lack of response in a network. The time-stamp time starts when that packet leaves that layer, whereas in the architecture of IP the network layer follows the concept of connection-less for the function of networking; which is free from the concept of time factor, and any introduction violates the original architecture of IP. In IPv4, TTL indicates the time elapsed (in seconds), but it lost its meaning as it is actually a number of hops [186]. The concept of time officially dropped in IPv6. The timeout must differ with data link layer, but routing protocols use fixed timeout value, which is not the case in reality.

1.6.5 Long –Term Problems

For solving the problem of IP addressing some alternatives were found like CIDR, NAT which result reduced the problem but found easy hack due to their ubiquitous nature. With virtually unlimited address space, the IPv6 was designed for many deployment scenarios, starting with an extension of the packet technology and supporting the transition models of IPV4 and keep it working even forever and allow new uses and new models which require a combination of features that were not tightly designed like IP mobility, E2E connectivity, E2E services, and ad hoc services [198]. A universally accepted unique global addressing scheme (IPv4 and IPv6) is used for identification of nodes in the network. This unique identification information is used in all IP headers, and the routers utilize this information during uninhibited operation of the packet. The global address is also mapped with a unique name known as a DNS name. By knowing either IP address or DNS name any node can be easily identified on a network. But the link broadcast is not supported by IPv6 for the neighbor discovery and started using multicast functionality which is made to depend on the functionality of IGMP [84]. To overcome these limitations, IGMP protocol got directly inherited to IPv6. IPv6 is introduced to overcome the limitation of exhausted IPv4 address resources as well as some other causes of limitations. Nonetheless, these limitations are getting hastened like in the case of a sensor network, packet switching. But the avoidance of the limitations of packet switching technology lies with the new generation network and its surrounding technologies, which should be reconsidered [87].

1.6.6 Medium –Term Problems

Some of the issues of the Internet are not impeding stability, but trends to show that they effect in the future. Problems like inter-domain routing, congestion control, mobility, architectural ossification, etc., fall under the category of medium-term problems with the current Internet architecture. Border Gateway Protocol (BGP) is an inter-autonomous system, used for the exchange of network reachability information with other systems of BGP [47]. It is also known as inter-domain routing protocol, that selects a path between systems and performs the identification of alternate path during recovery when there will be a failure of the existing path. This recovery process takes a long time for identification of an alternate path. For a critical system it will be a limitation of inter- domain routing. Due to a provision of multihomed sites, on the Internet, the number of entries in the global routing table is exceeding more than 300,000 entries [97]. It is only expected to continue to increase in the future. Attempts are also made to use the BGP to perform inter-domain routing, for example in Multiprotocol Label Switching (MPLS) path assignment, which will increase significantly the BGP advertisement volume. Multicast routing concept followed by unicast and broadcast for the suppression of the routing table growth and for the better performance of domain routing. Many types of routing protocols like CBT, DVMRP, PIM-DM, PIM-SM and MOSPF are available to handle the issues that are raised due to the increase in group size and for identification of the host through message advertisement. In case of unicast routing, the same routing table is used for all distinct locations whereas in multicast routing the destination is a set of hosts.

Mobile traffic is increasing unprecedented beyond the capacity of today's networks and is estimated to consume 7 GB or more of traffic per month by 2014 [58]. The current network is optimized for stationary services but with the advent of wireless communication made the architecture rethink to provide a support with additional cost. The increase in number of services as well as the users is generating tough challenges which need to be met by the research community.

Congestion is one of the issues which were found after TCP/IP systems took over the Network Control Program (NCP) in 1983. And the first congestion collapse was found in 1986 which was caused by TCP's reaction to packet loss. This was solved by using *"congestion bit"* in IP datagram header. Many congestion avoidance schemes were found like binary feedback, but it was found that the packet loss is due to damage in transit or due to insufficient buffer capacity. The collision of packet forms congestion in the network. The Internet has sufficient buffering space to get a place to play with the different congestion adaptation algorithm. The congestion algorithm works based on the round-trip network latency. The control plane of the architecture has an explicit signal for the adaptation of algorithms. There will be a significant drop in performance due to congestion which needs to be solved [74] [87].

1.6.7 Short –Term Problems

The issues that can be solved with adequate solutions within a short period of an attack are treated as short-term problems. Security of the Internet architecture is a problem for which there is no magic bullet. At best, the short-term problems are related to the spams, viruses [55] [185], phishing [68] and spyware [140] which sometimes leads to a drastic destruction to the companies that results in critical situations [87]. Many defense techniques were found, even these can be misused by making the servers busy for fulfilling the request as with DoS attacks [87] [206] .

1.6.8 Avoiding New Generation Packet Network Limitations

IPv6 is introduced to overcome the limitation of exhausted IPv4 address resources as well as some other causes of limitations. But these limitations are getting accelerated as described above. In the case of a sensor network, packet switching could be required for a new generation network. But the avoidance of the limitations of packet switching technology lies with the new generation network and its surrounding technologies, which should be radically reconsidered with serious.

1.6.9 Security Hitches of Current Internet Architecture

In the 1990s the Internet was available to the public and several events contributed to the birth of network security [39] [40] [64] [120]. The threats toward the information and the networks raised drastically with the evolution of the Internet. The huge gap between the security technology developers and network developers which existed in the past made the architecture to result without security. Later when they realized the importance of security, they started adding security protocols into the present architecture. Design of a network does not contain the same advantages of secure network design as the breaches may result in monetary issues. Several security protocols were introduced by IETF at various layers of the Internet protocol suite [137]. Internet has a reputation of not having security even though several mechanisms exist. In spite of its importance, some portions are fragile where the entire network suffers with the unceasing attacks that range from software exploits to denial of service. The main reason for these threats is that the architecture was designed primarily for a trustworthy environment with supporting protocols but no consideration of security issues. The assumption of trust no longer exists in today's Internet as millions of people connect all over the globe via computers for the communications and this has increased the level of attacks. The growth of connectivity is due to the communication protocols by which the threats also increased in a network. The network attacks seen today are because of the loopholes which exist in the protocol of the Internet. There exist a number of serious security flaws that are inherent in the protocol design or most of TCP/IP implementation. Addressing space, routing, security, etc., problems associated with IPV4 [103] [112] are addressed in IPV6. The security architecture of IPV6 [66] [106] [113] [144] has become interested as IPSec [77] [148] [159] was embedded and this IPSec [93] that was introduced for encryption and authentication was similar for both IPV6 and IPV4 but still attacks occur in the networking code [24]. The difference is that the IPV6 utilizes the mechanisms of security forthe entire route. After studying IPV6, it is emphasized that it is not necessarily more secure than IPV4 but it is slightly better that is not a revolutionary improvement [64]. In sequence number attacks a surfer can predict the round trip time accurately even if the clock varies with 4μ seconds clock time [25] [26]. The predecessor attack in which a cracker tracks an identifiable stream of communication over the multiple communication and logs the next node on the path [135]. One more problem is how to design, implement and deploy key management according to the security contexts existing all over the world as it is based on unicast and is driven by top-down operational models [19]. RIP is used for generating routing information on local network especially broadcast media. This allows an attacker to send bogus information to the target host. This attack can yield more subtle and more serious benefits to the attacker as well. There are many other network attacks like port scanning, DOS, etc.[212]. The compromises of security still exist by the protocols of the Internet [24]. It is difficult to analyze and model and understand the security implications due to the increase of the patchwork of the security protocols for the services which indirectly increased the system load [36].

The rigidity of the architecture not only raised the architectural problems but also unable to solve the issues related to security. Several other factors which are equally held responsible for the development of new architecture are multitude of application growth, protocols needed to perform congestion control, loss recovery, no universal approved model for traffic engineering, busty nature of traffic, lack of data integrity, methods of dependability, lack of originality of the architecture, flexibility, etc. [81] [128]. Some security limitations of the present Internet due to the rigid structure are as follows.

1.6.9.1   IPSec Limitations

IPSec provides a common security mechanism by the concept of authentication and encryption during communication of various protocols. However, the required functionalities vary in accordance with the applications and during the process of standardization these applications are ignored [214]. The standardization of security is not fixed to any one layer; rather, it is application dependent and appropriate layer dependent. Theoretically it is impossible to share secret information between specific parties, and this problem is trying to solve by using a mechanism of public key encryption. The sharing of public key accomplished with the involvement of trusted third party/mediator called CA. Although CA can be equally trusted as that of the ISP, in that case, use of IPSec is unnecessary.

1.6.9.2   IPv4, IPv6 and ND Limitations

IPv4 is a 32-bit addressed protocol that uniquely identifies 4 billion devices in approximation. As these IP addresses are exhausting, that forced for the creation of NAT which violated the E2E transparency of the Internet [65]. One of the ways of solving this problem is to increase the length of address and which is seen in IPv6.

As IPv6 inherited many features from IPv4 so it also acquired some of the problems of IPv4 by inheritance and due to this there is an alarm for collapse of the Internet [97].

Various RFCs are available defining the specifications of IPv6 such as RFC 2460, RFC 4861, RFC 4862, RFC 4443, RFC 4291, RFC 4301. IPv6 is the next version of IPv4 protocol, hence it has followed most of the conventions of IPv4. Some of the limitations of the IPv4 are overcome as improvements in IPv6 such as Neighbor Discovery (ND). IPv6 can link a variety of lower layers due to its simplicity and hence it became a standard protocol for linking lower layers. Currently ATM, PPP and Ethernet are considered as some of the lower layers on which the implementation of IP is very well supported. Although neighbor discovery was designed as a universal protocol over lower layers, the problem of adopting to new lower layer requirement is uncertain and a new kind of limitation is expected in due time. As the link broadcast is not supported by IPv6 so for the neighbor discovery it uses multicast functionality. This made IPv6 completely depend on the functionality of IGMP [84], due to this, all the limitations of IGMP protocol got directly inherited to IPv6.

IPv6 uses timeout specifications of neighbor discovery as well as IGMP. The timeout value will be denominated in terms of seconds and it is unjustifiable as it ignores the characteristics of data link layer, especially in the case of high-speed handover of the wireless medium. Congestion causes a significant drop in the performance of packet processing which still has not been solved in IPv6 [74]. An attempt was made to increase the performance of the system by reducing terminal functionality to a larger extent, for this a mechanism of uni-cast routing is used, but it completely relies on the performance of the router. This is one of the violations of E2E principle in TCP/IP network.

The architecture of the Internet is trying to enhance the header specification of IP by attaching a meta-data or with the concept of state mechanism as an *optional*, example, XCP [111], IP trace-back [177]. However, the measurements of wide-area paths for with and without the IP header specification options are tested on PlanetLab planetary scale network test bed [49]. The outcome of the results showed that these options are not well supported on the Internet [76].

The increase of addressing space from 32 bits to 128 bits develops a significant barrier for the attacker avoiding the port scanning attacks. The concept of cryptographically generated address adds an additional security by discovering "neighbor" in the network using neighbor route discovery mechanism which provides a proof of ownership for an IP address. This concept avoids spoofing attacks and does not require any modifications to overall network architecture. ARP is not required in IPv6 because IPv6 address directly derived with the help of the interface identifier of L3 and MAC address of L2. ARP protocol was replaced by Neighbour Discovery(ND) protocol [57] [66] [90] [113] [145] [194].

1.6.9.3 Common Attacks in IPv4 and IPv6

Regardless of the fact that many improvements were developed, still there exist some attacks which are common for both IPv4 and IPv6. Application attacks like buffer over flow, virus, malicious codes, etc., attack on authentication modules like brute force, password guessing, unauthorized access, DOS etc. [94]. The improved security protocols for the protection of the information over the network were implemented at some higher layer of the protocol stack like SSL works at the transport layer and HTTP for application layer which leaves many problems unsolved. The architecture still consists of the problems like encryption performed at the application layer allows an intruder to gather information about the systems involved in communications over the network. Spoofing attack, sniffing, application layer, man in middle attacks and flooding are very common in both IPv4 and IPv6 [37].

The introduction of IPV6 was to overcome the limitation of the address resources of IPv4 and also some additional causes of limitations. Nonetheless, these limitations are getting accelerated as described above. In the case of a sensor network packet switching will also be required for a new generation network. Nevertheless, the avoidance of the limitations of packet switching technology lies with the latest generation network and its surrounding technologies, which should be reconsidered more seriously.

1.6.9.4   Security and Trust Limitations

Security and Trust were not considered at the beginning phase of the Internet architecture. Because of this, many tussels were raised which influenced the life of the network. The tussels which were found are broadly categorized as conflict and malicious. *Conflicts* occur between the interests and the principals. *Malicious tussle* occurs between the principals and the adversaries. To overcome these problems, some trust and security mechanisms were introduced as add on, but the Internet still remains untrustworthy and unsecure.

The information warfare and network security of today raised its importance with its own reasons. Many attacks are taking place day by day as the whole world is depending on the Internet by its usage. Security is required for the protection of information and the networks. It can be referred with hardware, software characteristics, operational procedures, access controls, feature accountability measures and the required policies for providing the level of protection for the services. The main problems that raise the importance of security are the information and the networks.

■ Information security: Information loss can be devastating for the users whether it is generated by a company of public or private sectors or government. Information assets refer to documents that contain vital data related to your business. This includes, but is not limited to, research reports, financial disclosures, and legal correspondence. These may exceed the financial arena or much more. Confidential information can be stolen by the competitors and can be used for other purposes such as for blackmailing or for patents and the list goes on without an end. One typical example that raised the importance of information security was Operation Desert Storm where the United States prevented Iraqis from obtaining the critical information which enabled the military of U.S. to get control over Iraqis by destroying the troops of Iraq [100]. All these reasons made the information security essential. Security must be provided for the prevention of the information loss. Information security deals with the policies related to security, information control, procedures for identifying and protecting the information from different attacks. The protection comprehends how the information is distributed, stored, processed and destroyed. Information can be passed through a paper, a disk or via a network which must be protected. The classification and limits of the information are to be clearly specified and different levels of security to be provided [171] which is a necessary step for securing information. Throughout the existence of the information, it must be monitored, tracked continuously and consistently. Securing a network is also an important issue of information security. For securing the information services is essential for all the aforementioned measures and network security is the key for securing the information.

■ Network Security: The history shows clearly that network security is an afterthought concept, leading now into numerous threats to the information of the network. It is one of the important components for securing all information that is passed on over the network. Network security threats range from a harmless cracker to the critical destruction of information. The security breech can be from an internal entity or an external entity. The three fundamental principles it has to follow to provide security for the prevention of the information loss are integrity, confidentiality and availability. The other features which are treated as heart of security and to be considered are authentication, authorization, detection and recovery, privacy, access control, non-repudiation for the protection of the information over the network. These principles evolved from a long time back which makes network history [100].

Adding a security layer to the protocol stack is not a feasible approach for securing the Internet as single layer security will allow the cracker to attack other layers that are unsecured. The best example to illustrate this is BGP protocol but this could not secure the semantic of exchanging information, malicious routers can still send malicious information. It is not sufficient if we think of the securing semantics of routing information then the attacker can exploit the vulnerabilities of TCP/IP for tearing down the connection between BGP hosts. Therefore, it is required to consider security at every layer of the protocol stack but the security being implemented at the link layer, network layer, transport layer, session and application layer are sometimes based on the same algorithm without specific benefit [27]. The flaw of using the same algorithm at every level leads to security breaches and repetition of the same algorithm at all levels is unnecessary and inefficient. Providing security to current protocols seems good, it is also important but has its own drawbacks. The primary challenge is to provide security to individual protocols which is a complex task as the interaction between multiple protocols is unanticipated. A change in one protocol introduces an incompatibility with others or some desirable functionalities gets limited results in highly restrained design problems. Complexity increases if security is added to individual protocols and assumptions to operate them in a valid manner. This additional complexity may increase system vulnerability further by the introduction of new attacks. The major problems of security are because of the ossified and fragile nature of the architecture. Observing all these fundamental problems, it is sought by the researchers to redesign the Internet architecture from the grounds by considering security and robustness as the main fundamental requirements. In short security should be no longer postponed. Networking community also considered it as an important issue [71]. It has to be better understood preferably before a compromise occurs. A plan has to be established to incorporate the basic security requirements into the emerging Internet architecture.

1.7   Summary

The goal is to draw lessons from the history to the future of secure communications. Many new technologies such as ATM, frame relays, etc., were emerged for the improvement of current network systems but could not succeed to get evolved and qualify as possible alternatives. Most of the approaches adopted *patch-work* approach to cope with the need and aspirations of the network community in which it is desirable to have evolution and revolution of technology growth with acceptable cost and speed along with flexibility as a prerequisite for a continuously changing scenario [203]. At the same time patch opened a way for creation of some new problems. This is not due to the inherent problems of protocols rather it is an issue of the architecture of the protocol [167]. The view is broad, covering many technologies, and many issues but not very detailed.The functionalities of today's Internet have been divided into several layers considering their abstraction level, but the experts in the networking community could not agree on a specific number of layers. As a result of this, the TCP/IP model has 5 layers and OSI has 7 layers, etc. Moreover, the placement of functionality in the layered approach is sometimes difficult to decide. In addition, the dependency among the protocols and functionalities is hard-coded making the architecture inflexible. However, this is remarkable in that the history considered here covers many services and its issues, including security limitations.

Chapter 2

Future Internet Global Standardization—State of Play

2.1   Introduction

Academician, scientist and technologist are attributing many problems and limitations to the rigidity of the layered approach of the current Internet and therefore many of the existing efforts are found toward the design and development of a network architecture which is flexible in nature. As the future has many unforeseen demands and continuously changing scenarios, therefore the flexibility in the future network architecture assumes much more significance. This chapter deals with the need and vision of flexible network architecture, research issues and challenges, network advancements in this field along with significant issues are explored.

2.2   Architectural Review Approaches for Current Internet

In the 1960s, DARPA supported the successful development of network communication architecture and in the 1990s, the same network architecture was reused with a modification to share web-based content across the Internet. Researchers believed this development initiated the era of Internet. By 1996, it was estimated that around 13 million systems were connected all across the world. It is a worldwide collection of loosely coupled systems that are accessed by the individual hosts using a variety of tools like routers, dial-up connections and gateways which helps in reaching any point on the network without any restriction of national and geographic boundaries [181]. Many limitations and bottlenecks are chronicled by researchers worldwide and efforts for improvement in technology were also made to catch up with the dynamically evolving Internet. Some of the limitations of Internet architecture were chronicled by David D. Clark *et al.,* [51], Tim Moors [139], Subharthi Paul *et al.,* [161] and AKARI architecture [97] design projects to name the significant ones in their successive research papers. Most of the researchers in the past four decades have criticized the Internet architecture with its limitations to meet rapidly changing requirements and encouraged for the development of new architectures which are flexible, loosely coupled, scalable, robust and secure.

M.Handley gave the historical perspective of the Internet highlighting the era of 1970–1993 as *a history of change* and 1993 to the publication of his paper (2006) as the *era of failures and stagnation* [87]. As the Internet is not designed for any specific purpose so the future network is expected to host much more than today's applications in an efficient manner. At the same time, researchers predicted rigidity of Internet architecture as one of the momentous failure factors for meeting these demands. Many researchers also believed that the commercialization of the Internet has given birth to many diverse interest groups in the Internet ecosystem. These diverse and contrasting set of requirements from the Internet have resulted into the so called *Tussle in Cyberspace* [51] which describes the ongoing contention among parities with conflicting interests. It is opined by some that the Internet is shaped by this controlled tussle. Tim Moors [139] also argued that the end-to-end arguments are insufficiently compelling to outweigh other criteria for some functionality such as routing, congestion control etc., therefore, the end-to-end argument should be adopted intelligently with a great deal of information about system implementation.

Technologies evolve and mature with time and every stage requires structural and procedural changes. As the technology changes, process repeats and time shrinks [150]. The last generation technology maturity becomes the foundation for the next generation technology and the same cycle recurs (Figure 2.1). Hence, the success of the Internet forced for the creation of new applications and services with higher hopes and expectations. New applications and its demands can be temporarily addressed to a certain extent through *over dimensioning* of existing Internet capabilities [73] and to support for these functionalities, there will be a need of many more new protocols and those protocols should be supported by the Internet. Unfortunately, transparent use of enhanced or newly generated protocols cannot be used by applications or middleware without performing any modification, such as the middleware code successfully providing complete support for TCP/IP protocol suite may not provide the same support for SCTP/IP protocol suite without any modification. E2E arguments are insufficiently compelling to outweigh other criteria for certain functions such as routing and congestion control [139]. This is due to the fact that the Internet architecture evolved by incremental and reactive additions over a period of the last 50 years [38]. The architecture defines necessary conditions for better performance of the Internet, but defining only sufficient conditions made to demonstrate limitations of architecture by scientists and researchers world-wide for the development of

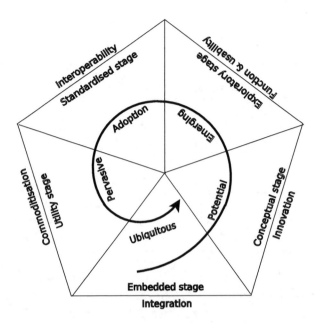

Figure 2.1: Cyclic evolution of technology.

future Internet architecture [123]. That is, the architectural problem of the Internet failed to estimate future needs and demands of the user, and it is limiting the growth of deployment of new applications.

Some of the above-mentioned issues and other factors like thin waist of IP (Figure 2.2), the gigantic increase of numbers of Internet users, diversified applications and application developers, fast technological advancement, an unjustifiable need of layer concept, nonunion about the exact numbers of layer, etc., motivated to think of convergence of multiple layer technologies and E2E mechanisms during the design and development phases.

In this regard, AKARI has done noteworthy work in identifying the strengths and limitations of the current Internet and has highlighted that the architectural expectations can be stipulated as capabilities for *integrating existing communication technologies and satisfying all user communication requests*. The AKARI group has observed that the main factors contributing to the success of Internet protocol were:

* Conglomeration of various technologies of lower layers into the network layer. Communication technologies that are newly developed could be easily converged on the IP layer, minimizing the effects on the upper layers.

* Network layer functions are held to a minimum level so that new application request can be flexibily supported.

It was also agreed by many that the current Internet design principles also conform to the KISS principle (Keep It Simple, Stupid) [101], and for the Internet this

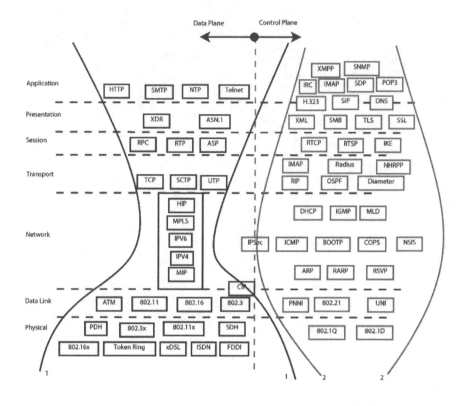

Figure 2.2: Patches of TCP/IP suite.

means that the network layer is kept as simple as possible and that services or applications are implemented at end hosts or edge nodes. Having designed its architecture using these principles, the Internet could adopt new technology while accommodating various services over the years [36]. Leading Internet researchers agreed that the simplicity of the network carries the tendency to optimize or functionally maximize one technology without considering its consistency with other technologies or other layer functions [97].

The ideal way of solving these problems could be the modification of the existing protocol or changing the protocol interaction or introducing new protocols for requirement satisfaction. The gigantic size of the Internet made any changes at the global level practically unsuitable and impossible. As the roots of the Internet had been deepened over the past four decades, there is no easy practical way out for changing all existing protocols or type of interaction or their functionalities.

Although the Internet was designed originally for education, the usage patterns were changed by expanding for various purposes like medicine, public, private, and business along with its openness for malicious entries for tampering of the information [15]. It is a client-server model and facing challenges for supporting content oriented functionality in a secured fashion. To solve these problems, patch work was adopted by including the protocols as add-ons by lacking its approach and the architecture was overloaded by the functions. The current architecture implements the security functions as a piecemeal such as SSL protocol that works under application layer and IPsec below network layer. Even though many protocols were included into the architecture it couldn't solve the emerging demands for wireless services. The Internet has created a tremendous impact over society and its values. This will cause enhanced growth in the Internet and takes a new form known as *Future Internet*. There are many hidden expectations that are covered under the umbrella of future Internet which are required to be uncovered during upcoming days. The researcher articulated these issues as improper set of vision during the design phase of Internet architecture.

2.3   Need of Network Architecture

The network architecture is an architecture which effectively supports working of different application programs that exist on the same/different networks. It provides abstract design principles for making a decision about alternatives as a fusion of science and technology. There is no general methodology to satisfy all the requirements in a network [97].

The conceptual architecture of the flexible network is positioned in between the network technologies and user applications as an intermediate. The responsibility of the network architecture is to identify and satisfy the user specified requirements considering all constraints of the system. The network architecture should consider the evolution and revolution changes of the technologies (addition of upcoming technologies or deletion of obsolete technologies) and the user needs and demands (launch of new applications or up gradation of existing applications or take-off the old applications) to fill up in-between gaps to make the stable architecture (Figure 2.3).

The architecture of the Internet is designed to connect sensors to supercomputers, based on the principles of modularity, layering and E2E arguments. In the research thesis of Barbara van Schewick, it is clearly highlighted that there are many ways for the Internet development which are guided by its use, production, and development environments. The structure of the Internet continues to change based on the goodness of the network providers, while neglecting the application developer, organizational/corporate users, individual, etc. There is a need of realization of Internet structure with full economic, social, political, and culture [202].

The future Internet architecture has a disagreement with the incorporation of a wider range of stakeholder value as network neutrality. Ian Brown *et al.* highlighted the impact of network neutrality over the design of architecture [34] along with framework design having a greater understanding of the socioeconomic analytic model embedded with the Internet [190].

The flexible network architecture should help in establishing a connection and exchange of application data that are interconnected with networks. The design and

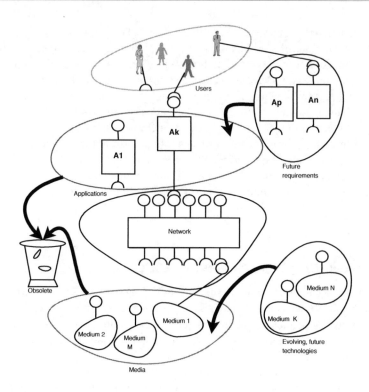

Figure 2.3: Role of network architecture.

development of a flexible network architecture should meet the long-term as well as a short-term change in the requirements of the user as well as the system satisfactorily.

2.4   Future Internet Research Issues and Challenges

Though this seems to be a too simplistic and vague proposition for the future Internet but FI research issues and challenges are broadly classified into two categories such as *network foundation* and *pillar* challenges [25],[162].

2.4.1   Network Foundation Challenges

It is one of the challenges of the future Internet research and is further categorized into nine broad categories as follows:

Routing and Addressing

The routing and addressing system are facing a very serious problem of scaling due to increase in the traffic, multihoming, business events and non-aggregate address allocations. Apart from this, the size of the routing table has already grown up to 300k and it is estimated to reach an order of 10^6 active route records in the next 5 years. Side by side there are other equally important systems of networks which are also expanding, such as mobile devices, urban traffic management and SCADA. The current Internet has excluded these networks but it is expected to be getting served in the future [221]. This not only increases the records of the route table, but also the constraints of growing-up and functionalities of route records becoming an issue for researchers.

Diagnosis and Manage

Reconfiguration of system resource is a common practice and human errors are quite frequent; sometimes this may lead to fatalities. The ad-hoc nature of the Internet infrastructure made very complex to diagnose the system and to give any solution. Two methods are identified to overcome the above problem, such as *data mining* and *static analysis*. The former method deals with the analysis of statistical performance of the system and the later deals with the detection of critical problems with requisite prior specifications. A technique of software engineering can be adopted to address the issues such as network configurations, validation of network, auto configuration and self healing mechanism, etc.

Security, Availability and Adaptability

Security, Privacy and Trust (SP&T) are closely interrelated with each other and become very important in all digital dimensions of the environment. The Internet is working on the basis of mutual trust, where each party protects themselves against outside the world. The future Internet is required to provide services with trust to protect the privacy of users. Strong drive behind implementation of SP&T is business which requires the flexible mechanism facility to design, change, evolve and adapt.

Maintainability is defined as the probability of a system or component that will be retained in or restored to a specified condition within a given period of time. Reliability concern to a design parameter and must be incorporated at the design stage as an inherent characteristic of the system that emphasizes on quality of product and services. System reliability is a function of its component reliability. For any Internet user service availability is a prime concern, particularly the IP connectivity and availability of the system [10]. Improvement of availability implies the improvement of maintainability by the technique of resiliency. Resiliency is the ability of system recoverablenes and is maintained at an acceptable level of functioning in spite of failure of one or more of its components due to attack, accident or failure.

Some of the open issues related to the future Internet are mechanisms of self-healing, technique of fast recovery, fast rerouting, enhanced resiliency against distributed attacks, load balancing, multi-path routing, etc. Some of the security researches challenges need to be addressed in the arena of the future Internet are trust architecture, credential management architecture, seamless user authentication etc.

Operating System Mobility

Cloud is a dynamic innovation of software engineering. The policy of *pay and use* or vice versa is adopted for the service usage [6]. The services are mainly classified into PaaS, SaaS and IaaS (Figure 2.4) and the characteristics as *essential* and *common*. The *essential* services deal with broad network access, rapid elasticity, resource polling, on demand self services, etc., and that of *common* services deals with scalability, reliability, open access, interoperability, sustainability, privacy, virtualization, economies of scale, etc.

On-demand Self Service: The service provider provides the service to the service consumer after satisfying the desired credentials by the system. It decreases the capital expenditure (CAPEX) and at the same time one can avail the domain experts' service by paying the operational cost (OPEX) only.

Broad Network Access: A large number of capabilities can be accessed either by thin client or by thick client. This transcends CAPEX to OPEX issue of simple and easy reachable type and it creates a healthy competition among small, medium and big enterprises.

Resource Polling: The resources are dynamically polled on demand basis. It provides location transparency and data security for the user.

Rapid Elasticity: The stretch and shrink property of cloud resource reduces the effective cost of the service considerably.

Measured Services: This provides the automated control and optimized resources to customers [18].

A Web browser could act as an interface between the service consumer and cloud. Amazone, Gmail, Yahoo, etc., are some of the examples of cloud operated service providers. The issues required to be addressed in the arena of the future Internet are data security, reliability, green computing, standardization, etc.

The *layer fusion* is a kind of network embedded OS paradigm which is beyond today's Cloud or grid computing. It separates the information and process logic from the execution. It is in the budding stage and extensive research to be carried out for its suitability.

Energetic Sustainability

The data rate of communication channel is exponentially increasing. There is a need of long-term energy efficient and sustainable communication technique for the reduction of carbon footprint. The energy consumption is independent of data rate, but directly proportional to the volume of traffic data (migration of 2G to 3G has multiplied the power consumption by a factor of 5). The ICT focused mainly on increase of

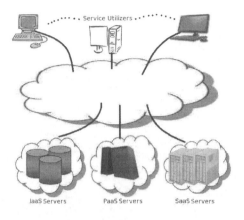

Figure 2.4: Cloud computing architecture.

data transportation capacity, but not on energy efficiency. For significant reduction of energy consumption special attention is required in energy efficient radio transceivers and protocols. To address these problems optimization of each communication layer like physical, MAC, network, modulation, coding schemes, cross layer optimization technique, etc., should be restructured.

Localization

IP dominated its presence in communication. As it is simple, routers are meant to be simple, but with all added functionalities, routers actually became more complex, especially for high data rates. As in telephony, per flow QoS is not reached on the IP Internet. Method of packet switching would continue in the future, but the core of the network will be circuit switching to provide good reliability and performance. A serious think should be made for promotion of non-IP networks to improve the performance of the Internet[136].

Beyond Digital Communication

Increase of availability of bandwidth made to think of expecting more and more animated and virtual reality applications. However, some of the issues like how 3D behaves with other physical properties, intelligence, 3D rendering, fabrication of interacting hardware devices, regulatory issues, standardization, convergence of standards (COLLADA, VRML, X3D), economical, social and political issues, etc., are to be addressed.

2.4.2 Pillar Challenges

The Internet Foundation has identified four pillars of the future Internet and the challenges associated with these pillars are as follows[56]:

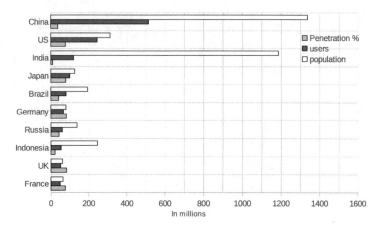

Figure 2.5: Top 10 countrie's Internet statistics.

Internet by and for the People: Only 32.7%[1] of users are availing the facility of the Internet all over the world (Figure 2.5). In spite of such a low percentage of users, the CI could not be able to fulfill the expectations of the user satisfactorily. In the coming days, the FI is expecting to host an unanticipated amount of applications beyond the expectations of users as follows:

1. Bridge between consumer and producer,

2. Facilitate day-to-day activities, and

3. Irrespective of size, domain and technology allow for business.

The FI is also expected to be equipped with an unprecedented level of interactive tools for creation of high-quality content within no time or at almost no expense. The evolution of the Web in a new dimension such as knowledge exchange, processing, semantic technology and generation of machines are becoming significant for the future Internet. The semantic Web provides intelligent access, right information and helps in filtering unwanted information at better extent[117].

Internet of Things: A precisely unidentifiable object is referred to as *things*. The current Internet is simply a collection of uniform devices. The *Internet of things* is referred to as a network of objects that can *talk* to each other and worldwide identifiable with a standard communication protocol. The *things* are uniquely identifiable at anytime, anywhere with universal addressing. The ubiquitous computing capability with sensors of RFID creates a set of novel, cost-effective and robust applications. This is expected to change the CI usage completely from a request-and-retrieve to a push-and-process paradigm

---

[1]As of December 2011, http://www.internetworldstats.com/stats.htm

[170]. New innovative applications are expected to emerge out of this social and technological context which is expected to increase the overall quality of life.

Internet of Contents and Knowledge: The cognitive society is going beyond the information. The local and global levels of knowledge dissemination involved with the accumulation of intellectual activities such as learning, thinking, reasoning and remembering, which forced the development of multimedia search engines. The journey has already begun on its way such as YouTube (asynchronous video), Zattoo and Joost (Digital TV channels), etc. Sharing of human knowledge with machine was introduced in Web 3.0 by semantic tags. These tags also cover functional and non-functional properties of services. In the coming days the future Internet is expected to render these information with the support of adequate processing power to provide beyond information access intelligibly.

Internet of Services: These are the services serving as applications in the domain of financial/ePayment/eBusiness, pervasive/immerse/ambient etc., and are classified into following categories:

Contextualized proactive and personalized services support for reactive as well as the proactive type of service access and empowered to personalize by the user. The term *context awareness* stands for the context interaction, personalize and suite.

The *emergence of Internet-scale SoC* has the potential to change the way of Internet applications. It is the next evolutionary step after component-based software, which treats everything as a *service*, such as physical compute resources, software functionality or data.

Service orchestration integrates core and isolated services especially in the field of business.

These four pillars are considered to be the deciding factors of FI and many organizations are exploring the impacts of these factors, in that Network Infrastructure Foundation (NIF) is one such example[155].

2.4.3 Vision of Future Internet

The generalized vision of the future Internet is to develop a flexible architecture which provides facilities for addition or deletion or exchange of protocols irrespective of any changes in communication media or technologies. And it should also support a wide range of applications that are flexible enough to the user, creator as well as for administrator.

2.5   Future Internet Initiatives

Many researchers have outlined the influencing factors of future Internet as SPET, which is described as follows:

☞   **The influencing factors of future society are[2]:**

$$\left.\begin{array}{l} \text{◆ Society (S),} \\ \text{◆ Politics (P),} \\ \text{◆ Economics (E), and} \\ \text{◆ Technology aspects (T).} \end{array}\right\} SPET$$

The progress of SPET changed world education, social interaction, trends as well as the living style of the society. The world informational and non-informational data are rapidly transferring into digital form, as a result of this the Internet became an important means for the exchange of these data/services at the same time it is opening many new challenges such as availability, mobility, presentation, performance, reliability, scalability, security, and trust. Similarly the need and expectations are progressively reaching toward the architectural fundamental technological limitation of the Internet. As a result of this, the original characteristics of the Internet such as simplicity and transparency got deteriorated and to address these challenges many organizations are formed worldwide and showed their interest on networking architectures which may or may not be based on TCP/IP. Some projects such as G-Lab, SONATE, GENI, Internet2, National LambdaRail, FIND, AKARI,NDN, JGN2plus, FIRE, SOA4ALL, OpenFlow, 100x100 to name a few are already started as an initiative measure with the objective of defining a vision and to provide recommendations and come up with a technology which can sustain the next generations needs and demands.

2.6   Network Architecture: Recent Advances

Since the beginning of ARPAnet the concept of layering became a fundamental design principle of network communication protocols. Current Internet communication works based on packet format and that are organized into layers [131] and it is a great success. The data which controls the delivery is called headers. In spite of its importance, some portions are fragile where the entire network suffers from the unceasing attacks that range from software exploits to Denial of Service (DoS). The main reason for the vulnerabilities is that the architecture was designed primarily for a trustworthy environment with supporting protocols with no consideration of security issues. The assumption of trustworthy environment no longer exists for today's Internet where millions of people connect across the globe via computers for communications. This increased the level of attacks, many researchers and industries are working to counter them, yet they are facing difficulties for significant gains. The most critical security problems are present in depth in a highly ossified and fragile network architecture.

---

[2]Beyond the scope of this book.

At a glance, adding a security layer to the protocol stack is a feasible approach to secure the Internet. But it is not sufficient to secure a single layer as the intruder can attack other layers which are unsecured. The best example to illustrate this is BGP protocol which could not secure the semantics of exchanging information. Malicious routers can still send malicious information. It is not sufficient to think about securing semantics of routing information as the attacker can exploit the vulnerabilities of TCP/IP for tearing down the connection between BGP hosts [27]. Therefore, it is required to consider security at every layer of the protocol stacks but the security being implemented at the link layer, network layer, transport layer, session and application layer are sometimes based on the same algorithm without any specific benefit [27][83]. There exist a number of serious security flaws that are inherent in the protocol design or most of TCP/IP implementation. Addressing space, routing, security, etc., problems associated with IPV4 [112][147] are being addressed in IPV6 also.

Providing security to current protocols appears to be a good idea. It is also significant but consists of its own drawbacks. The foremost challenge is to secure the individual protocols which is a complex task as the interaction between multiple protocols is unanticipated. A change in one protocol introduces repugnances with others or some desirable functionalities gets limited resulting in a highly restrained design problem. If the security is added to each and every protocol, the complexity to operate them will increase. This additional complexity may increase vulnerabilities as well and decrease the network speed. There are many network related threats like port scanning, spoofing, sniffing, denial of service attacks [25][138] which are yet to be solved. The solutions provided for these are not completely successful and the compromises still exist by the protocols of the Internet [24]. Observing all these fundamental problems, it is sought by the researchers to redesign the Internet architecture from the ground by considering security and robustness as the main initial requirement [180] The fundamental limitations of the present Internet architecture (Please refer to Section. 1.6 for more details) forced the research community to work in the direction of the future Internet [19]. Three alternative ways were identified to address the above-mentioned limitations, which are as follows [81]:

1. Design a new Internet reference model from scratch by repealing the *laws of Internet physics* (Clean slate approach [61]),

2. Redesign of current Internet architecture by letting *market forces prevail* (Evolutionary approach [91]) and

3. Re-engineer of today's Internet protocols [164].

The growing demands and heterogeneity of applications are continuously challenging, making it necessary to devise an architecture which is flexible in terms of any modification or updating of applications or protocols. It should be free from any revolutionary technological changes while addressing the issues of the present Internet and support for the future Internet. The present Internet's inability to accommodate the innovations force for the development of a framework [115]. A multitude of projects are going on under the world of the current Internet, which is focusing on evolutionary [156][174][179], revolutionary [27] or clean state approaches for the development of future Internet in order to solve the architectural problems.The *evolution* versus *clean-slate* approaches debate on biological metaphor and argues that it is less costly and more robust than that of clean-slate approach. The evolutionary approach also argues that the architecture is not ossified rather core protocols play a major role. That is, complexity and diversity emerge at higher and lower layers, and it is applied at every level of system design [70]. For solving various issues, many funding agencies of the European Union, United States, China, Korea, Australia, Japan, India and other countries showed their interest on networking architectures which may or may not be based on TCP/IP.

There is discrimination between methodical design at one end and desire of the community at the other end. This difference led to a design and development of a new framework in accordance with the need of society; such as scientific approach forced to develop distributed systems in the field of network [63] [195]. While economic approach forced to introduce economic models into the network [201]. To overcome some economic issues many projects are offering the testbeds in more realistic way to evaluate the various infrastructural ideas are Planet Lab [99], GENI, FIRE [79] [98], AKARI, G-Lab, JGN2plus [96], SOA4ALL, Open Flow, 100x100 to name a few. They have already started as an initiative measure to come up with a technology which can sustain next generation needs and demands. This allows a flexible and spontaneous creation of virtual networks. This opens an opportunity for many architectures to work in flexible environments without making them depend on a single architecture for the avoidance of various issues [4] [161].

There are numerous hidden expectations that are covered under the umbrella of future Internet which needs to be uncovered during the upcoming days. The researcher articulated these issues as an improper set of vision during the design phase of Internet architecture. The future Internet architecture should be flexible, accessible, accountable, manageable, scalable, reliable, robust, stable, simple, cost-effective, secure and so on. Some of the recent advances in the field of network architecture to deal with architectural as well as the security issues are as follows:

2.6.1 RBA: Role Based Architecture

Overthrow of the principles of layering concept made an investigation of non-layered approach for the design and implementation of network protocols leads to non-stack network architecture, which is also called Role Based Architecture (RBA) [33]. RBA uses roles to communicate, and these roles are not hard coded in nature. These roles are modular in nature and the packet headers form a protocol heap rather than a protocol stack. Hence these are more richly interconnected than that of current Internet protocol layers. Rethink of packet communication without protocol stack shed new light on architectural principles. It follows heap instead of stack as followed by TCP/IP for the flow of information.The permissions are assigned based on the roles the users play for that session and the user assignment. The permissions are assigned based on the constraints and the role hiearchy. In this, encryption and authentication are treated as one role. Encapsulations reserved and has a special building block which takes care of forwarding and packet processing.

2.6.2   ANA: Autonomic Network Architecture

Architectural stress of the Internet made a large number of dynamically attached devices to suffer from integration, security and management problems. This is forced to design and develop a novel, autonomic future Internet network architecture which performs autonomic formation and adaptation of whole networks and network nodes [30]. The outcome of this research work is Autonomic Network Architecture (ANA) that works based on the existence of *network compartments* [105] by following disruptive research principles, without backward compatibility. It gives an idea of separation of mechanics from networking logic and it is an example of network meta architecture. It extracts and refracts core networking concepts to support heterogeneous addressing and naming of network nodes and networks. It is neither protocol centric nor address centric, but the system has evolvability and dynamic reconfiguration capability. It supports inter and intra compartment communication. The outcome of this method emerged as Generic Autonomic Network Architecture (GANA) a holistic reference model [45] used in a network environment for the management of functions and services (refer to the appendix for more details).

2.6.3   RNA: Recursive Network Architecture

The architecture of the network and the layering of the protocols tried to relate using a method called Recursive Network Architecture (RNA) [195]. This is a new approach developed based on the combination of the above-mentioned two methods which examine the dynamic service composition, cleaner cross-layer interaction, and the impact of layers of architecture as a goal [204]. A single, tunable protocol is made to implement discrete layers protocol stack to avoid reimplementation. With the help of a selection algorithm, it gets the capability to create and run diverse network architectures in parallel.

Extended work of RNA came out as the Dynamic Recursive Unified Internet Design (DRUID) which is basically designed to support the future Internet. The security, management, control and data of conventional layered network architecture are unified to get trustworthy network. The architecture of the DRUID is made up of a single recursive block, like that of RNA, this block adapts itself to provide functions like congestion control, fragmentation, compression, etc., [130] which is basically designed to support for the future Internet. A translation table is used to develop a graph which helps in identification of spaces and compartment of functions. The graph also helps in optimizing the discovery process and organizes persistent states [196].

2.6.4   SILO: Service Integration and controL Optimization

It is another architecture with an abbreviation of Services Integration controL and Optimization which works based on the concept of vertically arranged micro-protocols [72]. The architecture differs from the current philosophy & practice by compartment / separation of things with the design prototype of just-in-time. The architecture of SILO resembles a structure of an inverted tree and the data transformation methods are totally responsible for delivering data between nodes. The methods of SILO implement services, and these services are of ne grained. The goals of SILO framework is to provide flexibility, extensibility, smooth integration of security feature, an increase of performance, cross service interaction etc. A new connection can be built a SILO dynamically. It does not use different management and control interfaces for routing as used by contemporary devices and focuses on explicit cross layer optimization. The services and their interfaces may be defined, but their methods are not by which they are implemented. It provides security according to the services by using policies and is limited to embedded capabilities of control agent inside the node of a network and allows runtime adaptation.

2.6.5   CCN: Content Centric Network

This technology of networking deals with the establishment of connections between hosts, whereas use of network deals with the content distribution and retrieval [3]. A perfect mapping of *What users care about?* To *Where it is required?* In network is required to access content and services. The Content Centric Networking (CCN) is a new approach that retrieves the content based on named data. The packet contains the name of the *address* but not location. It does this by replacing *Where* with *What*, to provide a better abstraction for communication as well as to achieve scalability [104]. It provides security to its contents but not in the network channel and aims to encrypt the content for private instead of providing security at hosts or communication links. The concern of the network is to concentrate on distribution of data and security control of data is taken care by publishers is itself instead of like existing in a traditional network. It looks very conventional and provides trust with the public key.

One of the outcomes of the CCN approach is content-centric inter-network (CONET) that provides users with network access to remote named resources, rather than to remote hosts [67][153] [218]. It is a novel integrated approach and to provide the facility of content-awareness the header of the IP is extended. The data or service access points are identified by the network identifier (a name). It supports a clean slate and overlay approaches with stateless content delivery mechanism.

2.6.6   AKARI Future Internet

Japanese initiative is based on evolutionary architecture and also takes care of not repeating the crisis of CI. The architecture role is to select and integrate that guide toward more simplicity. Its implementation is on a virtual space of the network which solves the problems of security. The security is provided using the concept of Authentication, Authorization and Accounting (AAA) as in (Figure 2.6). It explains the importance of AAA in the next generation networks for providing the services like identity management, confidentiality, integrity, privacy, non-Repudiation, access Control and resilience. The six principles are common which have been covered and Accountability is used for billing and correct charging, Resilience is to recover the network from the attack and the last one is identity management which is concerned with the user identities as well as the policies associated with them. In this architecture, the user's information will be managed in a distributed manner by contacting the individual ISPs [97].

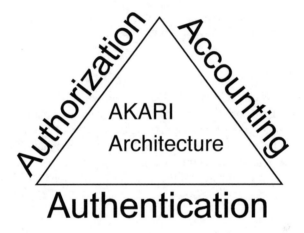

Figure 2.6: AKARI Architecture.

2.6.7   NDN: Named Data Networking

The basic idea of this architecture is similar to CCN. This architecture tries to secure the content through a security-enhanced method rather than securing the transmission channel or the data using encryption techniques. The main goal of this architecture is to build a narrow waist around the content chunks instead of IP. It uses a network TAP-Tunnel which creates an ethernet tunnel between the two nodes using the NDN communication channel. The TAP-Tunnel collects the packets and the TAP interface convert these into NDN packets. It gains the connectivity by connecting to NDN forwarding Daemon (NFD) as in (Figure 2.7).It works on issues related to security of data and trustworthiness. It proposes to secure the data directly using the concept of public keys instead of securing the "containers" as of in the current architecture [154][220].

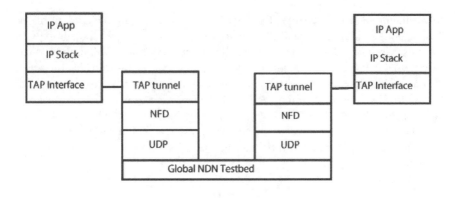

Figure 2.7: Named Data Networking Architecture.

2.6.8 Mobility First

Today's architecture was designed to connect xed endpoints but failed to support mobile devices. The rising demands of the Internet usage are a key driver for the development of future Internet to support wireless networks. It concentrates on providing security for the data that is accessed by wireless systems. It adopts a clean state approach by building a "narrow waist" for the protocol stack. It is trying to provide high security and privacy for the wireless information [154] [183].

2.6.9 NEBULA

It envisions the future Internet as highly available and extensible network of services interconnecting the data centers. The architecture of NEBULA is based on cloud computing centric network, provides services by fetching them from cloud for the fulfillment of the user requirements. Cloud services are embedded with security, high availability of the services, integration of the data, reliability, security for both access and transit information. It offers a control plane security using the policies that are selected using network abstraction [16][78].

2.6.10 XIA: eXpressive Internet Architecture

This architecture supports communication between various entities of the system. The various principals of the system are content, host, and service which communicates for the fulfillment of the user request. Each and every principal is specialized to define the minimal function required for interoperability. The significance of security was realized by analyzing the current Internet architecture and tries to provide intrinsic security such as self certified identifier etc.[13].

2.6.11   PONA: Policy Oriented Naming Architecture

It is a two-part protocol stack with a virtualization layer between them. It envisions the next generation Internet to be dynamic, secure, heterogeneous, flexible to support innovations and implementation of policies at the end and core of the system. It considers three features for providing security such as well-defined context, separation of management control and data plane, and policy servers. It uses realms or zones with well defined gates for providing security. The separation of the planes is logical by which the packets of one plane cannot penetrate to the other. The concept of policy servers helps in achieving security easier than in the CI. This architecture uses advanced mechanisms of security like biometrics, larger key size, tokens etc.[160].

2.6.12   RINA: Recursive Inter Network Architecture

This architecture is based on the clean state approach and considers IPC alone for its development. It is secure and resistant to the attacks like port scanning, data-transfer and connection opening. It focused on developing the security modules for access control, data transfer, etc., to overcome the vulnerabilities. It decouples various functions of security like authentication, confidentiality and integrity [29].

2.6.13   GENI: Global Environment for Network Innovations/ FIND: Future Internet Design

One of the major project of the U.S. National Science Foundation is GENI. It is a Clean Slate approach project aiming at design, development and implementation of a realistic, large scale, open experimental facility for the evaluation of new network architectures, services and applications. A typical networking component of GENI [5][20] comprises of storage capacity, compute nodes, backbone links, customizable routers, tail circuits, and wireless subnets. Design ideas of GENI made up of the virtualization, programmable, seamless opt and modularity of components. It partitions the overlay network as a slice. The functional complexity of the Internet architecture was nicely reduced by following a mechanism of layers which resulted as the inflexibility of the current Internet architecture. Meanwhile many applications are developed based on cross-layer functionality to optimize the performance of the system; such as audio and video streaming. And some protocols are also designed by introducing intermediate layers such as IPSec and MPLS, and middle boxes like NAT etc., which made communication very complex by corroding the functionality of layer boundaries [188]. Many solutions are proposed by researchers, among them modularity in protocol design approaches and single common network architecture approach are considered to be the most prominent ones.

It focuses on the network that consists of optical access, wireless access network, security, network management, economics but not limited to conventional technologies. While GENI focuses on constructing a network architecture for the global facility of the users where FIND aims to develop a comprehensive network architecture design. GENI works on various topics of the Internet like work flow service group, operation management, integration and security working group, instrumentation and management group. It is focusing on federation, trust and security.

2.6.14 ChoiceNet

It is one of the future Internet architecture projects of U.S. National Science Foundation. It is a clean state approach which aims to develop a new network architecture of the Internet by supporting the innovation in the core network by following the economic principles. The design idea of this architecture is to adapt to the emerging solutions of current and future Internet challenges. The purpose is to expose the choices throughout the protocol stack for the support of business transactions over a wide range of time. The three principles of the architecture for performing the functionalities are *Encourage alternatives, Vote with your wallet and Know what happened.* Encourage alternatives states that the Building Blocks (BB's) must provide for the creation of various services and helps in development of alternative services for the fulfillment of user needs. Vote with your wallet states that the superior services are to be allowed to provide for the users if they are ready to pay for the providers. It provides service composition for the services to be composed and deliver simple to complex services. It provides a roll-your-own alternative between the network connections. It creates a dynamic ecosystem between technical and economic choices. Within the network users are allowed to verify the services they are paying for. And finally, know what happened states that the network must allow Building Blocks to exchange information that allows users and providers for the determination of the performance of the system by knowing the exact location of the faults [209].

2.6.15 SOA: Service Oriented Architecture

Another approach used for the design and development of a system is SOA [133]. It is an abbreviation of Service Oriented Architecture and works based on the principles of services [157]. These services are loosely coupled, highly cohesive in nature and perform certain actions. A domain specific set of principles and methodologies are used for the development of the system. During the design phase of applications, many requirements of software engineering such as interoperability, reusability, composite applications, flexibility, standardization, abstraction, etc., can be incorporated easily by the use of SOA.

The methodology of SOA fails to address some of the overarching concerns like service orchestration, transaction management and coordination, security, etc., and these were tried to address by Service-oriented Computing (SoC) [157] . A methodology of SOA is used for the development of SoC, which identifies the software application and infrastructure as a set of interactive services. As an extended SOA, it has been tried to address the above issues by making separate tiers to manage services, compose and coordinate services, etc., which resulted in developing Service-oriented Software Re-engineering (SoSR) [172]. The legacy systems are not directly getting supported by SOA software. As these were not designed and developed with the concept of service components, a total re-engineering is required to make the same system operable by making loosely coupled services. For this, the authors [172] proposed SoSR to make legacy systems compatible with SoC. SoSR uses the methodology of model driven, architecture centric, role specific and best practice. And it is conceptualized with 4+1 view model, RACI chart and three-service-participants model.

SOA supports any specific type of technologies and has already emerged as one of the candidate approaches of software development, which adheres to the software engineering principles of flexibility, maintainability, interoperability, fast development and deployment at low cost. SOA allows to solve the problem by treating the user/system needs as a service and it is good for the development of massively distributed applications/systems. These service entities are autonomous, platform independent and can be discovered, published and described in a loosely coupled way [157]. Service oriented computing allows the developers to develop application portfolios to grow dynamically by:

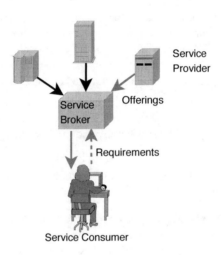

Figure 2.8: SOA service model.

➤ Creating solutions which use organizational internal software assets, enterprise information and legacy systems, and

➤ Combining these solutions with other external components which are possibly available in networks.

SOA (Figure 2.8) provides an easy assembling of a network of service application components along with loosely coupled nature. It can create any sort of dynamic business process applications for any type of organization. This is not an architecture rather it leads to a concrete architecture/paradigm philosophy. It neither provides a robust tool nor is a framework to buy, rather it is an approach or a way of thinking that leads to cover materialized decisions for designing software architecture. However, it is agreed that SOA is a paradigm for flexibility improvement, and it never says to design everything from scratch. It rather makes available for large distributed systems which are legacies in nature necessitates the changing structure of an existing system that are in use will remain in use by providing backward compatible. SOA is an approach of system maintenance which is part of different platforms, programming languages, paradigms and even middleware. Fundamental functionality of computer networks using SOA paradigm has three major elements [157]:

- **Services:** Represents the self-contained functionality of business and that can be a part of one or more processes, or can be implemented by any technology on any platform with fault tolerant, flexible and scalable. It aims to: *Interoperability:* services should be able to connect easily in a heterogeneous system, services should able to connect easily in a heterogeneous system.

  Loose coupling: minimizing dependencies among others and its different forms are asynchronous communication, heterogeneous data types, mediators, weak type checking, binding platform dependencies, interaction patterns, compensation control of the process, logic deployment and versions. All these goals are consummated with the help of a loose coupling concept.

  Other factors: like interfaces and contracts, self-contained, coarse-grained visible/discoverable, stateless, idempotent, reusable, composable, technical interoperable, vendor diverse are also required to be considered while building services.

- **Specific Infrastructure:** It allows for the combination of any services in an easy and flexible manner.

- **Policies and Processes:** This deals with a fact that the distributed systems are heterogeneous, under maintenance and have got many owners. The way to maintain flexibility in large distributed systems is to support decentralization, heterogeneity, and fault tolerance.

A *Service Broker* plays a role of negotiator to establish communication while accounts the following factors for obtaining an optimized service.

- ➤ Availability of very large numbers of services,

- ➤ On demand self-organizing capable services are required for Service Providers, and

- ➤ A small tolerable amount of additional time for composing a service (i.e., add a delay in the decision making process).

A *Service Consumer* plays a role of utilizing the services of the provider. The consumer defines its requirements to the broker.

In short, the SOA entities can be defined as

1. A user defines it's requirements to the broker,

2. Service Provider defines offerings describing communication services, and

3. A broker matches user requirements and offers service provided by a set of Service Providers.

All the principles and characteristics of SOA are incorporated in SONATE that is, Service Oriented Network Architecture, respectively. The motivation behind the development of the architecture of SONATE is more than just a switch replacement.

2.6.16   FIA: Future Internet Assembly

Many funding agencies of the European Union - Future Internet Assembly (FIA) [82][162], other countries showed research interest on networking architectures which may or may not be based on TCP/IP. Some projects of the European Projects that are working on the security issues related to the current and future Internet are

Managing Assurance, Security and Trust for Services (MASTEr[3]): It is an integrated project with the objective of assuring security and trust levels in business scenarios like centralized, distributed and outsourcing by regulatory compliance of dynamic SOA.

PRIMELIFE[4]: This integrated project aims at sustainable control and management of privacy and identity of user's personal data in future networks and services.

Trusted Architecture for Securely Shared Services (TAS3[5]): This is an integrated project and its objective is to develop a generic architecture for trusted services in the healthcare and employability platform.

Trusted Embedded Computing (TEC[6]): Provide trusted computing standards to embed computing platform is the main objective of this integrated project.

AVANTSSAR[7]: The aim of this specific targeted research project is to develop and implement a new language for specifying trust and security properties of services and dynamic composition with algorithms and tools to validate those using SOA.

Ad-hoc personal area network and Wireless Sensor Secure Network (AWiS-SeNet[8]): The specific targeted research project aims to implement and validate secure, trusted scalable networking protocol stack data from self configuration and secure roaming over multiple domain like heterogeneous, adhoc PANs.

---

[3] www.master-fp7.eu

[4] www.primelife.eu

[5] www.tas3.eu

[6] www.tecom-project.eu

[7] www.avantssar.eu

[8] www.awissenet.eu

Infrastructure for heTerogeneous, Resilient, Secure, Complex, Tightly Inter-Operating Networks (InTeRSeCTION[9]): This specific targeted research project aims at enhancing heterogeneous networks and infrastructure security by focusing on vulnerabilities at different interoperating network providers intersection points.

Privacy and Identity management for Community Services (PICoS[10]): It is a specific targeted research project that aims to develop, build and manage a state-of-the-art platform for providing privacy, identity and trust in the application and community services on mobile communication and inter networks.

Privacy-aware Secure monitoring (PriSM[11]): This specific targeted research project aims at setting a new guaranteed de-facto standard traffic monitoring and delivering tools for legal compliance.

Secure Widespread Identities for Federated Telecommunications (SWIFT[12]): This is a specific targeted research project that aims to integrate transport infrastructures and services for the benefit of providers and users by developing a standard aligned model.

Worldwide Observatory of Malicious Behaviors and Attack Threats (WOMBAT[13]): The specific targeted research project aims to provide a new means of understanding emerging threats targeted to Internet economy and the citizens.

eCRYPT II [14]: It is a network of excellence coordination and action project on cryptology continued as eCRYPT-II.

FORWARD[15]: It is a network of excellence coordination and action project aimed at the partnership and promotion collaboration of researchers from industries and academia involved in the protection of infrastructures against threats such as spam, phishing, viruses, spyware, etc.

THINKTRUST[16]: This is a network of excellence coordination action project that deals with regard to trust, security and dependability issues under ICT Security Research Action Board bringing together the requirements and opinions of stakeholders.

100x100 to name a few are already started as an initiative measure to come up with a technology that can sustain the next generation needs and demands. The functional complexity of the Internet architecture was nicely reduced by following a mechanism of layers which resulted as the inflexibility of the present architecture. Meanwhile, many applications were developed based on cross-layer functionality to optimize the performance of the system; such as audio and video streaming. And some protocols are also designed by introducing intermediate layers; such as IPSec and MPLS, and middle boxes like NAT, etc., which made communication very complex by corroding the functionality of layer boundaries [188]. Many solutions are proposed by researchers, among them modularity in protocol design approach and

---

[9] www.intersection-project.eu
[10] www.picos-project.eu
[11] www.fp7-prism.eu
[12] www.ist-swift.org
[13] www.wombat-project.eu
[14] www.ecrypt.eu.org
[15] www.ict-forward.eu
[16] www.think-trust.eu

single common network architecture approach are considered to be the most prominent ones.

2.6.17   SONATE: Service Oriented Network Architecture

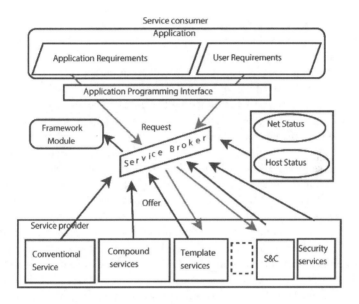

Figure 2.9: Service Oriented Network Architecture.

SONATE (Figure 2.9) [167] uses a paradigm of SOA to overcome some of the issues of the current Internet [157]. SOA works based on the service. A service can be either atomic or composite. An *atomic service* is a service of unbreakable functionality. On the other hand, composite service consists of a number of atomic services to constitute a complex service. Services are the fundamental design elements of SOA. The SOA paradigm is prominent in addressing issues of rigidity by providing the flexibility, which was used in the development of a flexible network architecture [88].

This architecture is being designed by considering the limitations of current TCP/IP architecture and support integration of disparate systems like the support for TCP/IP. The use of the concept of SOA helps for the access and communication for both the existing systems like the current Internet and the emerging ones. SOA can facilitate communication by coordination among the different systems by the services for the fulfillment of the requirements of the user. It is flexible, loosely coupled, scalable, maintainable, economical, allows integration of disparate systems.

The concept of Service Oriented Architecture (SOA) approach is an emerging, feasible and can be used for implementing the levels of security in the management of the emerging threats. One such architecture which is emerging using this concept is SONATE [141] [167]. The services that are provided by the SONATE architecture are developed using the SOA concept. SOA is an architectural prototype that can be used as a base for enabling the services to fulfill the needs of the user. Several new trends are relying on SOA as an alternate foundation for its flexible, scalable, maintainable feature.

Service Oriented Network Architecture project i.e., SONATE, is being developed by G-Lab provides flexible Internet architecture by introducing the concept of building blocks. It considers the Internet as a largely distributed software system. For its development, it envisions a fresh inter-network architecture by utilizing service oriented architecture paradigm and software engineering methodology. A collection of nodes in a network is enabled with SONATE framework. Different levels of network functionalities are implemented at each node. In SONATE, the Building Blocks (BB's) are recognized as a single protocol or a service composed of different protocols. All the services have self-contained functionality and a well-defined interface. SONATE hides internal data structures and internal mechanism. The services are granular enough to perform an action which can be called micro protocols, for example, a service which ensures "reliable transmission" can be implemented using separate retransmission strategies. Complex functionalities can be constructed by orchestrating several interacting services. It is also possible to use traditional mechanism i.e. TCP/IP itself as a service in the service pool. It makes possible to decouple the logic from implementation with the help of standardized, open and generic service interfaces. By decoupling, a straightforward consolidation of the innovative technologies is enabled. The orchestration of services is done at run-time means at the time of fulfilling a request of the user and it also enables the architecture to adapt to the changing requirements of the user. By this, it can be concluded that SONATE can also be seen as an evolutionary approach. Services (protocols) are loosely coupled and provide service autonomy.

Entities of SONATE

The prototype of this architecture follows the SOA paradigm, which contains the three components. They are the *Service Provider*, the *Service Consumer* and the *Service Broker*, which are visualized with respect to the SONATE architecture (Figure 2.9). The *Service Provider* is treated as a passive entity which produces and supplies the service, the *Service Consumer* is treated as active entities utilizes the service and the *Service Provider* provides the facility to advertise, search and discover the desired services and treated as passive entity. The entities may increase in number as there is no restriction for the entities that may be active or passive. When an entity role is treated as vigorous, that entity can be constrained by the principals of the system. A detailed description of all these principals is discussed in the following.

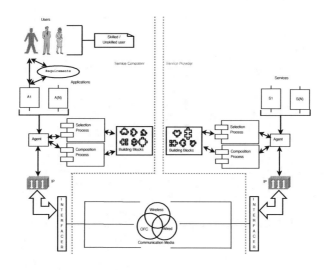

Figure 2.10: Schematic model of Service Oriented Network Architecture.

Service Users

The functioning of SONATE begins with the request of the user by selecting a suitable requirement satisfying application. Acquaint levels are categorized based on their skills on the network as *Non-Technical user* and *Technical user* (Figure 2.10).

- **Non-Technical User**

    When the user plays a role of a normal user it means that the user lacks the technical knowledge then the application is used with default settings. The user is given minimum rights like to read or execute with no technical changes to the applications. The demand of the user is forwarded to the broker and the requested applications are fetched from the provider and delivered to the user by the broker. In this, the user is not allowed to connect to the provider for the utilization of the services (Figure 2.11).

- **Technical User**

    The requested applications are tuned to the desired levels of needs based on the technicality of the user. If the user plays a technical role in the system, then it performs additional actions such as modify, update, delete other than the normal user. The request for an application by the user is based on the knowledge of the user and this request is forwarded to the broker. The broker verifies the role of the user and if the user plays a technical role and registered with the broker then the broker connects the user to the provider (Figure 2.12). The technical role of a user is for the development of static services and to store them in the provider's pool and these services are utilized by the users accordingly.

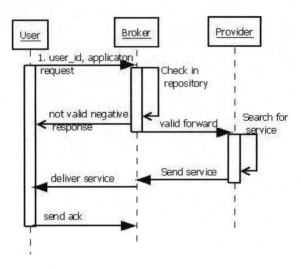

Figure 2.11: Sequence diagram for a Non-Technical User Process.

Service Broker

The following three types of functionalities must be performed by a broker for the successful communication in the distributed environment of SONATE.

Protograph Generator A very composite service can be made by the combination of simple services. A definite combination pattern/sequence is called a protocol-graph. The graph description specifies the definite interaction pattern required for getting a specific service of a consumer. Each node should have the capability for generating the protograph. The creation of protograph is performed by service Selection and Composition Algorithm. The application requirements and network constraints are used for the dynamic creation of a protocol graph. The dynamic information like How to combine? What do they do? And etc., are addressed with the help of the BB descriptions.

Message Translator There are some messages which need to be composed of more than one message and which is done using a messageList (with the use of TLV formats). A BB can create/add messages or reads/removes messages from a received mesageList to make it compatible. Transformation of messages is done with the help of special BB, that is, an application BB which bridges the gap between application and the work flow.

Message Transmission The intra and inter message transmission involves Application BB and Network BBs respectively.

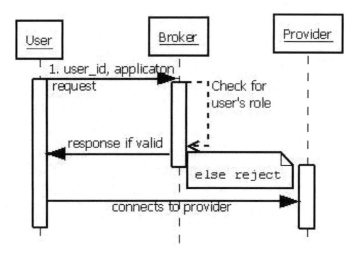

Figure 2.12: Sequence diagram for a Technical User Process.

Message Formats for Communication

The following abbreviations and their corresponding information / messages are used in explaining the inter and intra communication of SONATE system.

msg1 & msg4: An XML file name in string format.

msg2 & msg5: It is *msg1* built in messageList format.

msg3 & msg6: A tagged message with file name and fragmented data to be transferred.

Communication Broker's Operation

After getting a request from the user, the agent creates a list consisting of unavailable BBs and which will be in XML format. This information is sent to *Application BB* as *msg1* (Figure 2.13). The *Application BB* sends *msg2* to up-port of *Transmission BB* after the translation. *Transmission BB* sends *msg3* to Data port of *Network BB* after making a data chunk. So received *msg3* by *Network BB* will be communicated to the other *Network BB* of the network with the same message format. At the receiving side *Network BB* sends *msg3* to down-port of *Transmission BB*. The data extracted from *Transmission BB* will be copied in the form of an XML file and the above procedure is repeated until all the packets get over. And the above-mentioned procedure is repeated for a return message with appropriate message formats.

The broker starts functioning after gathering the required information from the point of the user, and at the same time it also gathers other information such as BBs availability in the local repository, network status, etc., from the point of the network.

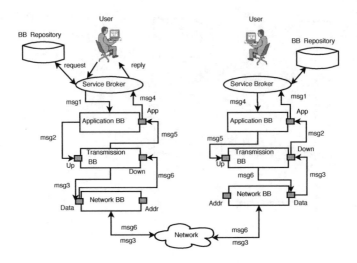

Figure 2.13: Broker's Communication.

If a service S(N) is made up of 3 subservices (s1, s2, & s3) and these services are made available with the local provider, then it is provided to the user by the broker else the broker plays the role of requester for requesting the services from another brokers that reside in the network (Figure 2.15). Once the requester knows the exact location of the service availability it fetches the service from other broker of the network and delivers it as an agent to the user (Figure 2.14). And thus a service gets fulfilled by the broker of the system. The broker plays a role of the selector for the selection of services, as a requester for requesting services from other principals in the network.

Service Provider

The *Service Provider* produces and supplies the service, the *Service Consumer* utilizes the service and the Service Broker provides the facility to advertise, search and discover the desired services. The *Service Provider* provides services, and these services may be the type of conventional, compound, template or dynamic.

➤ A *Service Provider* may provide different types of services. Many flavors of a service with the same or different *Service Providers* are made available for the purpose of backward compatibility of conventional systems.

➤ The new services are made available on the basis of pre-compiled, predefined and precomposed methods. And with the help of these methods, a compound service can be easily formed. As an example of this, a pre-self-organization approach is followed in the creation of Netlets.

➤ Another type of *Service Provider* is a template. In this, some built-in formats

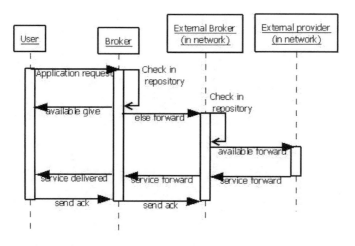

Figure 2.14: Sequence diagram for a Broker Communication in a network.

are made available to the customers. The customer can tune the functionalities of these templates by the addition or deletion of modules.

➤ Another type of *Service Provider* is who instantly develops the requested service and makes it available to the user on requirement basis. Two methods are available under this type of service provider: static self-organizing (the developer develops the service and interfaces manually with the other services) and dynamic self-organizing (the runtime self-organization of a service). The factors such as requirements of developers / end user, constraints of local hosts, networks etc., are considered for the dynamic self-organization of service and the whole operation is known as service Orchestration & service Self-organization (O&S). The database of a *Service Broker* holds all the information about the system, and this information will be used at the time of dynamic self-organization of a service. A protocol graph is the outcome of a service self-organization.

Flow of Phases in SONATE

The following are the three Phases planned and identified at the initial level to explore Service Oriented Network Architecture functionalities suitable for the distributed environment (Figure 2.16).

Phase–1: Implementation of SONATE framework for standalone systems: During this phase of action a framework for Service Oriented Network Architecture is installed over the standalone TCP/IP box. The various functionality providing

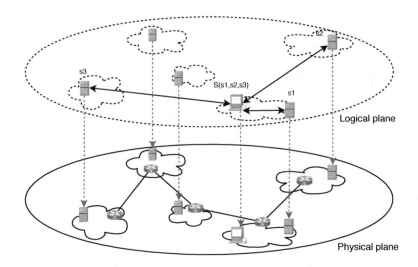

Figure 2.15: Service selection and composition process in a network.

BBs for standalone systems are created and deployed in accordance with the paradigm of Service Oriented Architecture.

Phase–2: In this phase of action the current networking facility is planned to use for the interface of Phase-1 equipped boxes with TCP/IP boxes. The existing framework functionality is trying to upgrade as a middleware for communication, and it supports to install a local repository consisting of basic functional BBs. The additional BBs that are necessary for providing these services are included in the repository. If the requested service is not available or not possible to compose using locally available BBs, then only the request is sent outside the system.

Phase–3: During this phase of action a SONATE box is trying to interface with another SONATE box utilizing the networking facility of TCP/IP protocol. The additional BBs that are necessary for this service are included in the already existing repository according to the need.

Phase–4 (P4): This is a challenging task where there will not be any support from the TCP/IP protocol for the establishment of a connection. The additional BBs that are necessary for providing this service are required to be developed, implemented and added to the repository (during Phase-4 to 6, Type2 packet format could be used for communication).

Phase –5 (P5): The framework of SONATE can be planned to make use as a middleware.

Phase –6 (P6): The SONATE framework and TCP/IP protocol systems can be planned to connect with the help of SONATE middleware software.

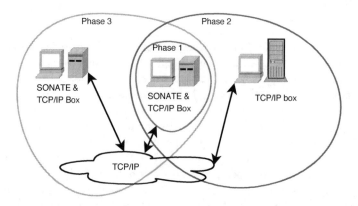

Figure 2.16: Phases of Flexible Network Architecture.

Phase –7 (P7): In this phase SONATE system can be planned to connect with the help of SONATE middleware. This setup resembles that of a current TCP/IP Internet connection (during this Phase Type3 packet format could be used for communication).

Phase –8 (P8): This phase is the Phase of ultimate expectation that can be expected from this research work, where the complete Internet system will be developed in coordination with the above-mentioned all 7 phases to form a new flexible Internet architecture and to provide compatibility with other existing protocols. This phase could use all the packet formats for connectivity establishment (Figure 2.17).

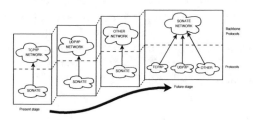

Figure 2.17: Future scope of SONATE.

2.7 Summary

In recent years, it was noticed that the usage pattern of the Internet has been changed, as the emerging architectures are concentrating on the contents, data seems to be promising in the future. The demands and expectation of future is unforeseen and key to handle this can be flexibility in Network Systems to accommodate the rapid changes. The design goals of any architecture change the design principle. The clean state design imposes no restriction on the assumptions for the architectural design. If the infrastructure of the Internet is following the revolutionary approach, it's implementations also need to be evolutionary. There is no unique answer for the requirements of the future Internet as it changes from time to time but it is expected to be highly dynamic, flexible, secure and efficient mobility. The architecture must be compatible with the present Internet applications and support the demands of the future. It must provide the facilities to adapt newborn to old architecture for the services. The necessary features that are to be considered for the development of future Internet are security, mobility, self-organization of the services, tolerance of the errors, provide extensibility, flexible interfaces to allow interaction among users, providers and enforcement of the policies along with societal and economic features, etc. It takes a continuous rounds for achieving a comprehensive architecture between the theoretical improvement and the practical experience. Although various projects have different accents, it is always useful to integrate the different architectures for the fulfillment of the demands. Several new trends are relying on SOA as an alternate foundation for its flexible, scalable, maintainable feature. For solving various problems of TCP/IP protocol stack, many architectures were developed using the clean state approach and SONATE is one of the architectures, among many which is considered as a case study, where orchestrating of loosely coupled services is done in this flexible open network architecture. The architecture makes it possible to decouple the logic from implementation with the help of standardized, open and generic service interfaces as it uses SOA paradigm. By decoupling, it enables a straightforward consolidation of the innovative technologies. The orchestration of services is done at run-time and it also allows to enable the architecture to the changing requirements of the user. The flexibility of the architecture is good for the strategical plan of the system but it opens serious security issues like the authentication of the entities, authorization of the entities, confidentiality of the services, etc.

Appendix—2A

Chapter 2 is aimed to discuss various Internet architectures which were into existence after the emergence of TCP/IP. The recent advances are discussed along with the limitations of the current Internet architecture. The chapter does not discuss the arcitecture of current Internet which has been discussed in this along with OSI model.

Open Standards Interconnection Model

The Open Standards Interconnection (OSI) model is a model developed by the International Standards Organization for defining different networking protocols and distributed applications. This model consists of seven layers, namely:

Layer 1: *Physical Layer*–Defines the mechanical, electrical, and procedural events that take place when the data is being physically transmitted as electronic signals on the wire.

Layer 2: *Data Link Layer*–Defines data format (on the network)and facilitates a reliable and errorfree transfer of data (in the form of frames) across the physical layer.

Layer 3: *Network Layer*–Transmits packets of information from the sender to the receiver. It provides establishment, maintenance, and termination of connections.

Layer 4: *Transport Layer*–Provides reliable, transparent transfer of data between end points. The transport layer is considered at the top of the lower layers of the OSI model physical, data link, network, and transport layer.

Layer 5: *Session Layer*–Provides services such as data exchange, dialog control, synchronization, and error reporting for connections (sessions) between users.

Layer 6: *Presentation Layer*–Provides services such as data compression, encryption/decryption, and protocol conversion. In this layer, data transmission is standardized such that the computers using different data structures can communicate.

Layer 7: *Application Layer*–Provides services (such as network management, transaction server) and protocols (such as Telnet, FTP, and SMTP) to the different network applications

The designers of OSI assumed that this model and the protocols developed within this model would come to dominate computer communications, eventually replacing proprietary protocol implementations and rival multivendor models such as TCP/IP. This has not happened. Although many useful protocols have been developed in the context of OSI, the overall seven layer model has not flourished. Instead, the TCP/IP architecture has come to dominate. There are a number of reasons for this outcome. Perhaps the most important is that the key TCP/IP protocols were mature and well tested at a time when similar OSI protocols were in the development stage. When businesses began to recognize the need for interoperability across networks, only TCP/IP was available and ready to go. Another reason is that the OSI model is unnecessarily complex, with seven layers to accomplish what TCP/IP does with fewer layers. Figure 2.18 illustrates the layers of the TCP/IP and OSI architectures, showing roughly the correspondence in functionality between the two. (For more details refer to Appendix 3A.)

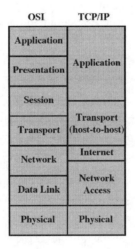

Figure 2.18: Comparison OSI and TCP/IP Architectures.

TCP/IP Procotol Architecture

TCP/IP is a result of protocol research and development conducted on the experimental packetswitched network, ARPANET, funded by the Defense Advanced Research Projects Agency (DARPA), and is generally referred to as the TCP/IP protocol suite. This protocol suite consists of a large collection of protocols that have been issued as Internet standards by the Internet Activities Board (IAB).

TCP/IP Layers In general terms, communications can be said to involve three agents: applications, computers, and networks. Examples of applications include file transfer and electronic mail. The applications that we are concerned with here are distributed applications that involve the exchange of data between two computer systems. These applications, and others, execute on computers that can often support multiple simultaneous applications. Computers are connected to networks, and the data to be exchanged are transferred by the network from one computer to another. Thus, the transfer of data from one application to another involves first getting the data to the computer in which the application resides and then getting the data to the intended application within the computer.

There is no official TCP/IP protocol model. However, based on the protocol standards that have been developed, we can organize the communication task for TCP/IP into five relatively independent layers, from bottom to top:

■ Physical layer

■ Network access layer

■ Internet layer

■ Host-to-host, or transport layer

■ Application layer

The **physical layer** covers the physical interface between a data transmission device (e.g., workstation, computer) and a transmission medium or network. This layer is concerned with specifying the characteristics of the transmission medium, the nature of the signals, the data rate, and related matters.

The **network access layer** is concerned with the exchange of data between an end system (server, workstation, etc.) and the network to which it is attached. The sending computer must provide the network with the address of the destination computer, so that the network may route the data to the appropriate destination. The sending computer may wish to invoke certain services, such as priority, that might be provided by the network. The specific software used at this layer depends on the type of network to be used; different standards have been developed for circuit switching, packet switching (e.g., frame relay), LANs (e.g., Ethernet), and others. Thus it makes sense to separate those functions having to do with network access into a separate layer. By doing this, the remainder of the communications software, above the network access layer, need not be concerned about the specifics of the network to be used. The same higher-layer software should function properly regardless of the particular network to which the computer is attached.

The network access layer is concerned with access to and routing data across a network for two end systems attached to the same network. In those cases where two devices are attached to different networks, procedures are needed to allow data to traverse multiple interconnected networks. This is the function of the internet layer. The **Internet Protocol (IP)** is used at this layer to provide the routing function across multiple networks. This protocol is implemented not only in the end systems but also in routers. A **router** is a processor that connects two networks and whose primary function is to relay data from one network to the other on a route from the source to the destination end system.

Regardless of the nature of the applications that are exchanging data, there is usually a requirement that data be exchanged reliably. That is, we would like to be assured that all the data arrive at the destination application and that the data arrive in the same order in which they were sent. As we shall see, the mechanisms for providing reliability are essentially independent of the nature of the applications. Thus, it makes sense to collect those mechanisms in a common layer shared by all applications; this is referred to as the host-to-host layer, or **transport layer**. The Transmission Control Protocol (TCP) is the most commonly used protocol to provide this functionality.

Finally, the **application layer** contains the logic needed to support the various user applications. For each different type of application, such as file transfer, a separate module is needed that is peculiar to that application.

TCP and UDP For most applications running as part of the TCP/IP protocol architecture, the transport layer protocol is TCP. TCP provides a reliable connection for the transfer of data between applications. A connection is simply a temporary logical association between two entities in different systems. For the duration of the connection each entity keeps track of segments coming and going to the other entity, in order to regulate the flow of segments and to recover from lost or damaged segments.

Figure 2.19 shows the header format for TCP, which is a minimum of 20 octets, or 160 bits. The Source Port and Destination Port fields identify the applications at the source and destination systems that are using this connection. The Sequence Number, Acknowledgment Number, and Window fields provide flow control and error control. The checksum is a 16-bit code based on the contents of the segment used to detect errors in the TCP segment.

In addition to TCP, there is one other transport-level protocol that is in common use as part of the TCP/IP protocol suite: the User Datagram Protocol (UDP). UDP does not guarantee delivery, preservation of sequence, or protection against duplication. UDP enables a process to send messages to other processes with a minimum of protocol mechanism. Some transaction oriented applications make use of UDP; one example is SNMP (Simple Network Management Protocol), the standard network management protocol for TCP/IP networks. Because it is connectionless, UDP has very little to do. Essentially, it adds a port addressing capability to IP. This is best seen by examining the UDP header, shown in Figure 2.20.

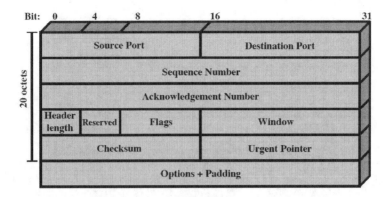

Figure 2.19: TCP header.

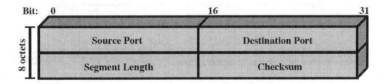

Figure 2.20: UDP header.

Operation of TCP/IP Figure 2.21 indicates how these protocols are configured for communications. Some sort of network access protocol, such as the Ethernet logic, is used to connect a computer to a network. This protocol enables the host to send data across the network to another host or, in the case of a host on another network, to a router. IP is implemented in all end systems and routers. It acts as a relay to move a block of data from one host, through one or more routers, to another host. TCP is implemented only in the end systems; it keeps track of the blocks of data being transferred to assure that all are delivered reliably to the appropriate application.

For successful communication, every entity in the overall system must have a unique address. In fact, two levels of addressing are needed. Each host on a network must have a unique global Internet address; this allows the data to be delivered to the proper host. This address is used by IP for routing and delivery. Each application within a host must have an address that is unique within the host; this allows the host-to-host protocol (TCP) to deliver data to the proper process. These latter addresses are known as ports.

Let us trace a simple operation. Suppose that a process, associated with port 3 at host A, wishes to send a message to another process, associated with port 2 at host B. The process at A hands the message down to TCP with instructions

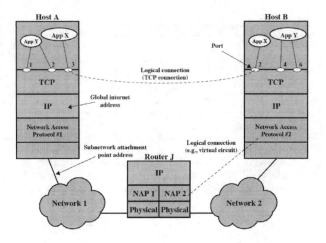

Figure 2.21: TCP/IP concept.

to send it to host B, port 2. TCP hands the message down to IP with instructions to send it to host B. Note that IP need not be told the identity of the destination port. All it needs to know is that the data are intended for host B. Next, IP hands the message down to the network access layer (e.g., Ethernet logic) with instructions to send it to router J (the first hop on the way to B).

To control this operation, control information as well as user data must be transmitted, as suggested in Figure 2.22. Let us say that the sending process generates a block of data and passes this to TCP. TCP may break this block into smaller pieces to make it more manageable. To each of these pieces, TCP appends control information known as the TCP header as shown in Figure 2.19, forming a **TCP segment**. The control information is to be used by the peer TCP protocol entity at host B. Examples of items in this header include

■ Destination port: When the TCP entity at B receives the segment, it must know to whom the data are to be delivered.

■ Sequence number: TCP numbers the segments that it sends to a particular destination port sequentially, so that if they arrive out of order, the TCP entity at B can reorder them.

■ Checksum: The sending TCP includes a code that is a function of the contents of the remainder of the segment. The receiving TCP performs the same calculation and compares the result with the incoming code. A discrepancy results if there has been some error in transmission.

Next, TCP hands each segment over to IP, with instructions to transmit it to B. These segments must be transmitted across one or more networks and relayed

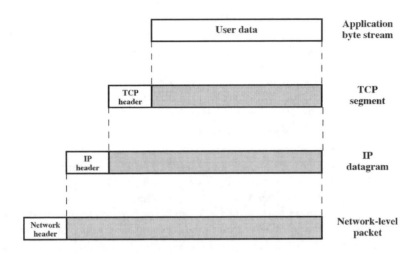

Figure 2.22: Protocol Data Unit in TCP/IP.

through one or more intermediate routers. This operation, too, requires the use of control information. Thus, IP appends a header of control information to each segment to form an **IP datagram** please refer to Chapter 4 for more details).

Finally, each IP datagram is presented to the network access layer for transmission across the first network in its journey to the destination. The network access layer appends its own header, creating a packet, or frame. The packet is transmitted across the network to router J. The packet header contains the information that the network needs in order to transfer the data across the network. Examples of items that may be contained in this header include:

■ Destination network address: The network must know to which attached device the packet is to be delivered, in this case router J.

■ Facilities requests: The network access protocol might request the use of certain network facilities, such as priority.

At router J, the packet header is stripped off and the IP header examined. On the basis of the destination address information in the IP header, the IP module in the router directs the datagram out across network 2 to B. To do this, the datagram is again augmented with a network access header.

When the data are received at B, the reverse process occurs. At each layer, the corresponding header is removed, and the remainder is passed on to the next higher layer, until the original user data are delivered to the destination process.

TCP/IP Applications A number of applications have been standardized to operate on top of TCP. We mention three of the most common here.

The **Simple Mail Transfer Protocol** (SMTP) provides a basic electronic mail facility. It provides a mechanism for transferring messages among separate hosts. Features of SMTP include mailing lists, return receipts, and forwarding. The SMTP protocol does not specify the way in which messages are to be created; some local editing or native electronic mail facility is required. Once a message is created, SMTP accepts the message and makes use of TCP to send it to an SMTP module on another host. The target SMTP module will make use of a local electronic mail package to store the incoming message in a user's mailbox.

The **File Transfer Protocol** (FTP) is used to send files from one system to another under user command. Both text and binary files are accommodated, and the protocol provides features for controlling user access. When a user wishes to engage in file transfer, FTP sets up a TCP connection to the target system for the exchange of control messages. This connection allows user ID and password to be transmitted and allows the user to specify the file and file actions desired. Once a file transfer is approved, a second TCP connection is set up for the data transfer. The file is transferred over the data connection, without the overhead of any headers or control information at the application level. When the transfer is complete, the control connection is used to signal the completion and to accept new file transfer commands.

TELNET provides a remote logon capability, which enables a user at a terminal or personal computer to logon to a remote computer and function as if directly connected to that computer. The protocol was designed to work with simple scroll-mode terminals. TELNET is actually implemented in two modules: User TELNET interacts with the terminal I/O module to communicate with a local terminal. It converts the characteristics of real terminals to the network standard and vice versa. Server TELNET interacts with an application, acting as a surrogate terminal handler so that remote terminals appear as local to the application. Terminal traffic between User and Server TELNET is carried on a TCP connection.

ANA Compartments and Layer Comparison

Network compartments can operate at various layers of the OSI model. That is, communication among compartment members can take place, for example, at the link layer, the network layer and/or the transport layer. A compartment can also combine the functionality of several layers (e.g., link layer and network layer) in one compartment. Compartments that operate at different layers or different scopes (e.g., local vs. global) can be layered on top of one another. For example, a compartment that offers end-to-end communication services across heterogeneous network domains can be overlaid on top of the compartments providing the functionality in each of the underlying network domains.

Unlike layers in the OSI model which rely on strict layering of layer X on top of layer X-1, compartments can be combined in much more flexible ways. Figure 2.23 illustrates the compartments semantics and functions of more than one layer (indicated by the blue rectangle), or it can provide only the functionality of a single layer (indicated by the red rectangle) or even just some aspects of a conventional OSI layer (e.g., just a control plane or management plane function). As such, compartments have much more fluid semantics (depending on the mission and the number of planes they span) and are less opaque than layers are in the OSI model. It is even possible that a single compartment implements a whole communication stack.

Another difference between layers and compartment is that compartments do not necessarily operate end-to-end, while OSI layers above layer 2 are all end-to-end. In other words, compartments cannot only interface with other compartments in a vertical manner, but also in a horizontal way in order to provide end-to-end communication. For example, a compartment can be composed of different types of network layers (e.g., an IPv4 and an IPv6 compartment).

Finally, compartments also extend the OSI layer model by supporting administrative policies, which enable flexible and fine-grained control of the operation of compartments and the entities that can participate, whereas layers implicitly involve all the entities that implement the (static) functionality provided by the layer.

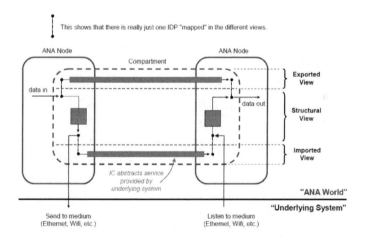

Figure 2.23: Structured, Imported and Exported view of ANA Compartments.

Layering Compartments The ability of layering compartments on top of one another depends on functionality (i.e., semantics) the upper compartment expects from an underlay compartment and the lower compartment can offer to an overlay compartment. In order to support layering of compartment X over compartment Y, one requires either that compartment X supports the particular compartment interface of compartment Y, which then simply "encapsulates" the data and opaquely passes them through the underlay compartment, or that an appropriate "interworking function exists between compartment X and Y (e.g., an appropriate FB) that can translate between different protocols and/or addressing schemes, or proxy communications of compartment members in the other compartment.

The overlay compartment (Compartment N) directly supports the syntax and semantics of the compartment interface exposed by the underlay compartment (Compartment L1). This implies that the output interface of the source FB on the overlay compartment (left top corner) is compatible with the input interface expected by the FB of the underlay compartment (left bottom corner) and vice versa for the receiving in the intermediate node.

The Interworking Functional Blocks (IFBs) are FBs that are conceptually part of both compartments. They must support the functionality required for communication in both compartments and be able to perform the necessary protocol and/or identifier translations. The latter approach (with the interworking functions) is advantageous in case a particular compartment can serve as the overlay compartment for many heterogeneous underlay compartments. In this case, the different IFBs can be used to translate between the overlay compartment and the various underlay compartments. Hence in that scenario, there is no need that all compartments must support exactly the same interface. The IFBs can hide the syntactical and semantical differences of the interface supported by the overlay compartment and the interface exposed by the underlay compartment.

It consists of Inter and Intra Compartments which are as follows:

Intra-Compartment Communication One common characteristic of ANA compartments is that all members agree on some common set of operational and policy rules. This recipe includes the communication principles, protocol(s) and policies to be used for intra-compartment communication. It defines for example:

- How communication elements are identified (i.e., naming and addressing).
- How identifiers are resolved (i.e. name lookup or address resolution).
- How to route information inside the compartment (i.e., routing).
- How to send/forward information (i.e., forwarding).
- What protocol is to be used to communicate between peer elements.

All nodes that want to be part of the compartment must provide the compartment stack (indicated by the blue boxes) - i.e., every node has to support the necessary functionality (i.e., functional block) to join the compartment and communicate according to the compartments communication scheme. Nodes that provide the required functionality are able to operate according to the compartment rules, and hence can participate in the compartment (indicated by the blue circle).

How communication inside the compartment is handled is entirely up to the compartment. Depending on the type and purpose of the compartment, different communication schemes can be applied. For example, a compartment that intends to provide the communication context for a Wireless Sensor Network, where the main goal is to aggregate sensor information on low-power devices, can implement a completely different communication scheme (i.e., addressing, routing, etc.) and protocol than a compartment that targets end-to-end communication among user terminals, such as for voice communication. While the former can use a very simple addressing and routing scheme that is able to aggregate the sensor information, the latter requires a naming or addressing scheme that supports end-to-end communication and a routing scheme that minimises end-to-end delay and jitter.

Since compartments have full autonomy on how to handle intra-compartment communication, there are no global invariants that have to be implemented by all compartments or all communication elements.

Inter-Compartment Communication The principles for this communication are as follows:

There is a need for a common compartment among communicating peers. Since compartments define the syntax and semantics for communication within a certain context, peers that want to communicate with each other must be part of a common compartment. Otherwise, they are not able to process (understand) the format and actual information carried in the exchanged data. *It is advantageous to have a common "interworking" or overlay compartment.* The use of a common interworking compartment that provides a uniform context for the communication among its members, allows hiding of potential heterogeneity at lower layers (e.g., different underlay compartments). As indicated in the conclusion above, a common overlay compartment that includes the gateway entities of the various underlay compartments also allows for efficient end-to-end routing at the underlay level. The fact that ANA support flexible and dynamic composition of communication stacks facilitates the introduction of such interworking "shims as the need arises. *There is a need for "interworking functionality between adjacent compartments.* As indicated in the analysis above, inter-compartment communication among directly adjacent or layered compartments that are of different nature require appropriate interworking functionality, which allows "translation between the different communication syntax and semantics of the compartments. Since the required interworking functionality depends entirely on the compartments that need to interwork with each other, there is no need for a common interworking function between all compartments along the end-to-end path –i.e., different interworking functions (depending on the compartments involved) can be provided.

Chapter 3

Security in Future Internet Architecture

3.1 Introduction

We discuss about the problems of the present Internet architecture and a way toward the development of various network architectures in the previous chapter. Any information passing over a network is vulnerable to various attacks like eavesdropping, masquarade, fabrication, etc. These attacks can cause loss to the data which may be sensitive. Precautions are to be considered to protect the services from illegal access. We present various threats for a networking environment as well as some threats that are specific to networks based on IP, such as spoofing, sniffing etc. Security requirements are different for different systems. Some require all six security services and others require less or more than those that are present in the current Internet architecture. We conclude by discussing various security services along with the mechanisms required for the Future Internet architecture.

3.2 Security

Security of the Internet is one of the important computer related issues. The main problems of today are information warfare and network security which raised it's importance with it's own reasons [100]. The issue of security was raised back in 1930 when an attack occurred on the enigma machine with Alan Turing who has broken the encrypted code that was developed in 1918 [64]. Securing the services over the network was started in the early 1960's when computers existed as huge mainframes with multiple networked terminals. The development of the Internet was brought forth by DARPA in 1969 with the involvement of four computer institutions namely the University of California at Santa Barbara, UCLA, The University of Utah and SRI collaboration named the network as ARPANET [39] [40]. Many other defense related companies, academic institutes, government organizations were joined later on by this network. For the purpose of stable communication TCP and IP was developed [12]. At the time of this development the security issues were limited, therefore security was considered as non-functional requirement and concentrated on creation of Internet infrastructure rather than its devastations [82]. For the improvement of system performance and decrease the complexity or cost of the systems security was discarded, as the performance of the system contributes the direct benefits to the user while the security provides indirect benefits to the user. Again at the end of 1960's and early 1970's the world had seen evidences toward the need of security [100] [120]. There was a boom in the mid-80's for personal computers and minicomputer industries which made the computers inexpensive. This forced the business people to club with Internet for the increase of their business by providing the Internet facility to its users for the first time which raised the use of the Internet exponentially. This resulted in threats as the users started sharing both unimportant and very important information over the net. Day by day the growth of the Internet is increasing which is exceeding the creator's imagination. Not only these many evidences made the security to evolve, security protocols were developed and incorporated into the Internet architecture.

The great success of today's Internet is due to the emergence of low cost broadband for business, institutes, homes, etc. It has increased the foul players who started hacking the information which made the security a major issue. Some aspects fall short for both current Internet like the reliable communication and future demands that are to be included on a network. The huge gap that existed in the past between the security technologists and network developers raised the security threats. The attributes which lack critically are related to security, trustworthy environment and high resilient, dependable availability for the communication between the systems in a network [58]. It is estimated approximately by now 950 million people use the Internet, incidences are also increasing toward the breaches [64] [120].

Many attacks are taking place day by day as the whole world is depending on the Internet by its usage. Security is required for the protection of information and the networks itself. It can be referred with hardware, software characteristics, operational procedures, access controls, feature accountability measures and the required policies for providing the level of protection for the services.

3.3   Pillars of Security

Threats are very common on the network. Network security is a field which deals with the protection of resources by providing reliability, integrity and safety to the communication over the network. Security is protecting something from unauthorized users in the network and it is a continuous process. It involves people, policies and technology. These are the main important considerations for the protection of the information over the network as shown in (Figure 3.1).

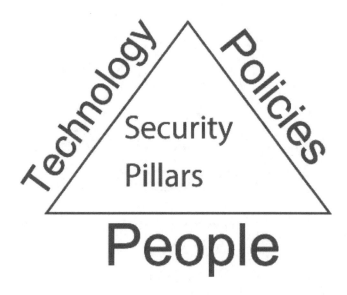

Figure 3.1: Pillars of security.

People: As the use of Internet increased by its users, they raised the need for security. People are prone to attacks knowingly or unknowingly while using Internet for various purposes. They act as strong pillar oneside and the otherside some are weak in using the same due to the lack of awareness. So make the people to access the websites and the links unknowingly and know about the importance of security in general to the applications. The security policies, mechanisms, services are developed of the people, by the people and for the people as shown in the (Figure 3.2).

Policies: Policies are very essential and without them the information security will be incomplete. They provide the guidance to everyone to access the services. Some of the policies are communication security policy, cryptographic controls, access control policies. Along with policies, procedures and processes are also required as these describe how to implement them. Procedures are the step by step process to implement the policies for which they are intended.

Technology: Technology plays a major role in protecting the information, resources over the network system. There are very good technologies which can seamlessly integrate with both business and security requirements. Some of the

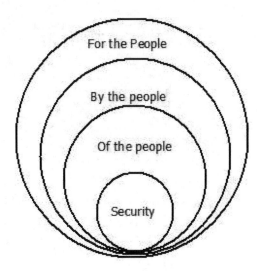

Figure 3.2: People's Security

technologies are automatic which detects and recover, prevent the damage, provide alerts etc,. some examples are anti-virus softwares, firewalls.

3.4 Basic Concepts of Security

With the discussion of Confidentiality, Integrity and Availability, we begin the discussion of various security issues and its principles to overcome those issues. These three are considered as the primary concepts of security which are compromised to various threats. This gives an outlook for discussing the basic concepts of security which pertains to data.

Confidentiality: Confidentiality is defined as information made unavailable to the unauthorized entities/users in the network. It is similar to privacy and the concept may be implemented to the level of processsess. The best example we can consider is the patient records that should not be disclosed to unauthorized entities.

Integrity: Integrity is defined as the prevention of changes to our protected data in any unauthorized manner by ensuring non-repudiation and authenticity. No changes to our data or any portion of data, deletion, modification, etc., protecting the resources completeness and accuracy. This can be provided to the users using proper authentication, proving application security, correct routing of the packets in the network.

Availability: Availability is ensuring the reliable and timely access to the information. The information is stored in databases, systems, and recently started storing in cloud. The availability of the important information always is necessary to perform the actions to take decisions else oppurtunities are lost in no time. If the network is made busy continuously for the resources, the network will be unable to respond to other request to the availability of resources which is commonly referred to as Denial of Service (DoS) attack.

The basic services like confidentiality, integrity and availability came from NIST and in the following sections we are going to discuss the various attacks and the services along with the mechanisms which are required for the various Internet architectures.

3.5   Attacks

In order to understand attacks we must know about the basic terms that affect us and they are threats, vulnerabilities and the risks which are associated with them.

3.5.1   Threat

Threat is a harm posed by something or someone to an asset or to an information. These are upto a specific environment. They can be posed from inside within the organization or from outside. They are categorised on the basis of the origin of the threat whether internally or externally.

Internal Threats: The internal threats occur with the hackers who are present within the organization. The entities of the organization who have the access to the resources, network infrastructure and understand the security loopholes can cause the internal threats to an organization. The entity within the organization can create the attacks by hiding its identity and already knows enough information. The internal threats are due to the weak security tools or the policies applied which includes unclassified information, no proper authentication or authorization or sharing the confidential information with others, lack of ownership or the responsibilities, segregation of duties and lack of hierarchy of the roles played by the employees of the company.

External Threats: The external threats are performed from outside the organization. They don't have authorized access for the network resources but still gain the access. The access to the resource is with an intention of damaging those resources or for their own profit. These threats are *structured* where the hackers are technically competent who highly motivate the individuals. These highly motivated individuals develop vulnerable tools and enter into the system without knowing anyone in the network. A group of hackers may be involved in major crimes. *Unstructured* hackers are the inexperienced but motivated individuals testing their skills using tools in public domains, which can do damage to the assets of a company. These threats may be physical, socio-economic specific to a nation or a country, network security threats, communication threats, legal threats like cybercrimes, which may effect partially or completely an organization, etc,.

3.5.2   Vulnerabilities

Vulnerabilities are the holes or the weaknesses that can be harmed by the threats. It is a specific application we can run from our office building and harm these systems in the network using various threats.

3.5.3   Risk

In order to have risk, the system needs both threat and a vulnerability so that a threat can be spread and vulnerability generates a loophole of weakness over the system. Let's consider fire as a threat and wood as a vulerability, the risk is more when they both come into contact. If the vulnerability is brick and the threat is the same i.e., wood, the risk is not so important. The sufficient heat can cause some damage but that event is less likely to happen. Similarly in the network evironment, the threat and vulnerability is estimated and precautions are to be considered based on the risk percentage.

3.6   IP Security Threats

The threats directly effect the fundamental principles like confidentiality, integrity availability of security. There are four categories of attacks which we might face are Interception, Interruption, Modification and fabrication attack. Each attack can effect one or more principles of security.

Interruption attack: This attack causes our assets unavailable temporarily or on a permanent basis. Loss of Availability of the services and the attacks on integrity are possible, due to the loss or corruption of data or a combination of the two.

Interception attack: This attack is observing the pattern of messages in the network like viewing or copying, eavesdropping on the data. Loss of confidentiality causes the interception attack as in (Figure 3.3). These attacks are very difficult to detect in the network.

Modification attack: This attack involves tampering of data. The unauthorized entity can access the authorized data and perform modification like alter the data, delete some of the contents, etc,. as in (Figure 3.4). This violates the security principles like availability, Integrity and confidentiality.

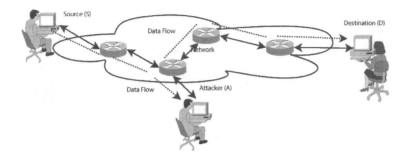

Figure 3.3: Interception Attack.

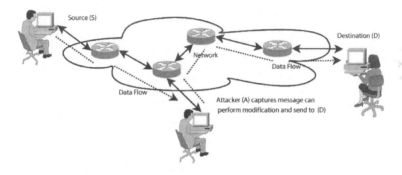

Figure 3.4: Modification Attack.

Fabrication attack: This kind of attack involves processing the generated data, similar activities with a system. Security principles like availability and Integrity are affected with this kind of attack as in (Figure 3.5). If an information is generated spuriously, it is a fabrication attack. Generating additional processes, web traffic or anything that consumes resources and makes unavailable to legal users of the system.

In the network environment, the IP packets routing are vulnerable to a range of security risks. If we want to be sure of our communication, we must ensure with whom we are communicating, there is no eavasdroping in your communication and finally no changes in the information passed through the communication channel. Network security threat is an event which tries to harm the resources of the network using impersonation attacks, modification attacks, interruption attacks, interception attacks, etc.. These threats can be classified as passive threats and active threats along with subtypes of attacks as shown in (Figure 3.6)

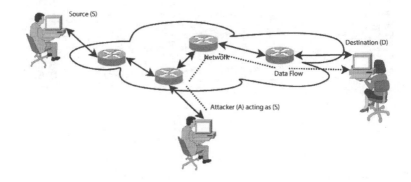

Figure 3.5: Fabrication Attack.

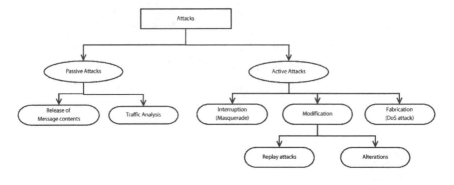

Figure 3.6: Classification of Attacks.

3.6.1 Passive Attacks

Passive threats don't do any harm to the system, but they observe the information being transferred over the network. These type of threats are very difficult to detect. Eavesdropping, traffic analysis and release of message content are some of the passive attacks where the attacker get the information by monitoring or through observation. Even though the information contents are masked with encryption techniques, the attackers can still trace the pattern of the message.

Eavesdropping

Eavesdropping on the data over the communication network is easier to obtain it rather than obtaining a telephonic conversation. The information in the network whether sensitive or precautions are not considered, it may be eavesdropped. Once the password or any sensitive data is obtained, then the access may be possible for the attacker. If the eavesdropper gains the information and tries to access the resources, then the attacker will be treated as an active attacker. If the information is sent via network without encryption, there is a possibility of the message being intercepted and read by others. The increasing use of Internet is providing some security features like SSH without addition of any extra hardware. TELNET and FTP protocols provide security to the password and data, transfer files without encrypting them for the first time.

3.6.2 Active Attacks

The active threats give the access to the resources to an unauthorized person. This even includes penetrating into one's system and deploying the threats into the system by any means. Detail information of the active attacks are as follows.

Masquerade attack: An entity (person or system) pretends to be a different one from what he really is. This is the most common way of penetrating a security barrier. When an entity act as another entity and accesses the resources and performs various operations on the information and this is known as a masquerade attack. It is not so easy to discover from where the packet has originated. This technique makes a packet coming from one machine to appear from some other machine by changing the IP address. The attacker from outside pretends to be an insider and spoofs the addresses by gaining access to the resources. This attack can also cause high network traffic over the transmitted channel. If the attacker ables to alter the routing table, the response from the resource may reach the spoofed address. It includes one of the active attacks like an authentication sequence can be captured and sent back after some valid authentication sequence has occured. This helps in activating some authorized entity to obtain extra privileges by impersonating an entity that has those privileges.

ARP spoofing and DNS spoofing attack: Address Resolution Protocol (ARP) attack tries to confuse the system and makes the system map to the wrong address which is present in the ARP table. Domain Name service (DNS) is to change the mapping of the DNS to a cache. Spoofing is gaining access to an unauthorized systems from an authorized host using a forgery process to obtain the source IP. To perform this attack, hackers use a various techniques to obtain the IP of a trusted system. After obtaining the trusted IP, the attacker modifies the packet addresses that are present in the IP header. Usage of new routers and firewalls may offer protection from these kind of attacks up to a certain level.

Session Hijacking: Starting a session with a person after authenticating themselves doesn't mean that they are actually in the transit until the completion of the session. Some methods are used for session fixing and session prediction. A valid session is taken over by the attacker. Weak configuration in a router gives a new point for vulnerability. We require a scheme to authenticate the source data throughout the communication, as someone can take over one's place and communicate with the opposite person.

Sniffing attack: It is a technique for collecting each packet in the network. It is a Network Interface Card (NIC) that listens to the packets and responds to the specified packets addressed to. It means it can collect all the packets flowing on that particular line. A tool called sniffer can take this as an advantage and record all the traffic passing through. This tool is helpful for the network technicians, but can help the attackers to eavesdrop on the messages.

The Man-in-the-middle attack: The best way to overcome with IP threats is to use the encipherment and authenticate the data passed in the packets. For the encryption of data, the keys are to be exchanged between the parties. Exchange of keys in an unprotected way could cause interception attack. The man-in-middle can trace the keys over the network and work on it and plant his own key for the exchange of information. The actual user believes that he is communicating with the party but he is actually communicating with the man-in-middle. This kind of attack in communication is called man-in-middle attack or TCP hijacking. This allows the attacker to perform both the operations like an eavesdropper as well as to divert, alter, change, reroute, etc., the data.

Denial-of-Service (DoS) and Distributed Denial-of-Service (DDoS) attack: The system becomes unavailable for the normal functions as the attacker makes the target system busy by sending continuous request. With lots of requests the system becomes overloaded and will be unable to respond to the legitimate user. With this, the system may crash or unable to fulfill the ordinary requests. DDoS attack occurs as a stream of requests which are launched from many locations at a time to a target system. Any system which is connected to TCP/IP network based services are vulnerable to DoS and DDoS attacks. These attacks can be launched on a system, router or the network servers if they use TCP services. DDoS attack is launched using a preparation phase where the thousands of zombie systems are developed, activated remotely by the attacker. These attacks are more difficult to defend, as there are no controlling of these attacks that any organization can apply. However, there are some organizations that defend DDoS attacks among a group of service providers. DDoS is considered as a weapon for mass destruction on the Internet.

Brute Force attack: Brute force attack can sometimes be called as password attack as it tries to obtain every possible combination of password for accessing commonly used network resources. To avoid this kind of attack, the manufacturers default names and passwords are changed. The attacks are rarely successful if the users adopt the manufacturer's security practices. Controls that limit the unsuccessful attempts, elapsed time per unit are effective methods againt this attack.

Dictionary attack: This attack is a variation of brute force attack which selects the target account and their commonly used passwords as in a dictionary instead of random combinations. The organizations can use these passwords to disallow them during the reset process, not allowing the guessing attacks. Usage of special characters, numbers, etc,. in the password help to reduce this kind of attack.

The passive attacks are difficult to detect whereas it is very difficult to prevent active attacks. The goal is to discover the active attacks in the network and try to recover or avoid their success using some encipher techniques, or some recovery tools etc. The security attacks discussed are common and faced in the current Internet architecture. There is a possibility of these attacks or advancements of these attacks in Future Internet architectures. So, to overcome them we require some service and mechanisms to deploy at the design level instead of adding it as an ingredient after the development of the architecture.

3.7   Security Services and Mechanisms

Security is protecting the information, resources and the services from unwanted attacks in the network environment. These valuable information passing in the network are to be protected as they are accidentally or intentionally accessed by unauthorized entities, who may alter or destroy the message, etc., causing interruption in the communication. The activities of these users, who violate the policies of security in the network are called the threats and if the threats are performed intentionally, they are called attacks. The motivation of the security attack may be political, revenge, publicity or anything that harms the organization. The rapid growth of Internet which has connected the world together has increased the threats in the network. The network resources, information has to be protected and this protection of the network from various attacks is called network security. The main principle of security in the networking environment is to protect the information from security attacks and threats using various security services and mechanisms through policy enforcement.

3.7.1   Security Services

Security service is defined as protocols communicating with the open systems in a secure fashion having adequate security mechanisms. RFC 2828 defines security as a service provided by a system to protect the resources from attacks by implementing security policies and thus implementing mechanisms of security accordingly. The security services which are required for any network architecture or any organization are as follows

3.7.1.1   Authentication Service

An entity identifing itself to a network or a system with the help of some identification is an authenticated service. The identified entity gets authenticated by providing proof to the system as to whom it claims to be, by what it has such as unique ID. For an ongoing interaction, at the time of connection intialization the two level entity verification is performed. Next it verifies the connection is not under any masquarade attack. Various authentication protocols can be used for ensuring the communication is authentic. Authentication can be performed in two ways, i.e., *unidirectional* or *mutual authentication*. In *unidirectional* only the entity gets authenticated with the

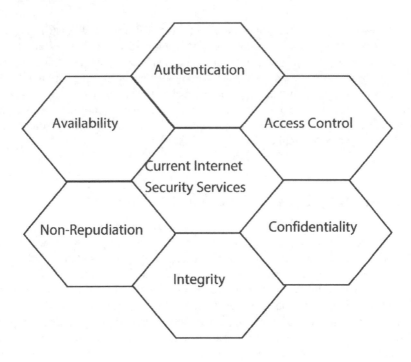

Figure 3.7: Principles of security.

server for example email, etc,. In *mutual authentication* where both the entities are authenticated with each other with the help of a third party, i.e., with the help of a Certification Authority (CA) which acts as a trusted party using asymmetric key cryptosystem.

The services provided by authentication are *peer entity authentication* which is combined with a logical connection to provide confidence that the identity of the entities are the same as they have stored in the database. It tries to protect from masquarade as well as replay attacks from an unauthorized connection. The best example for this is Biometric authentication where the information about the entity is fed in advance and authenticated whenever required like fingerprint, etc,. *Data origin authentication* best suits for the applications where there are no prior interactions between the parties. The examples for this are password for an email, etc., and is not protected from duplication or modification of the data.

3.7.1.2   *Access Control*

Access control in the network is to limit the operations of the users. This is enforced after the users are identified and authenticated. The access rights, explains the user right to access the resources, and how these entities can be accessed and at what conditions. The permissions of the entities are changed by an administrator. Some of the privileges are creation, content addition or modification, reading, exporting or importing of some information services. The resources, network elements and the confidential, secret information can be accessed at different security levels. It is basically related to two areas: *Role Management* and *Rule management*. *Role Mangament* deals with the user side, i.e., a user can do what kind of actions where as *Rule management* deals with what kind of resources can be assesed and at what kind of situations. Based on this, a matrix is prepared which gives a detailed list of users against the list of resources they can access. Access control list may be used even for protection of individual resources. The owner of the resources can allow or deny the access of the resources of a single entity or a group of entities.

3.7.1.3   Confidentiality

Confidentiality is the characteristic of security which ensures that the information is being shared among authorized entities in an authorized manner. This can also be called privacy or secrecy and refers to the protection of information from attackers in the network. Usually this can be achieved using encryption mechanisms available in the present infrastructure. Many experts considered authentication, authorization and confidentiality, as a separate security goal [129] [169] but Ruth Brue and Michal Hafner described authentication and authorization under the concept of confidentiality [85] which can be achieved by the enforcement of access control mechanism. Each entity must secure the information that is exchanged between them along with the address of the location. The services can be sent over the unsecured channel after applying the encryption techniques to the application [28]. Privacy is to prevent identity leakage to any other entities in the network while confidentiality is maintaining the secret of the exchanged information from those who are not allowed to access it. In current or future Internet architecture, transmission of the information to the intended entity of the network passes through several routers where there is a possibility of eavesdropping, misdelivery of the messages, exposure of the data in the medium, etc. For solving such problems, authentication of the entities are not enough. Some encryption techniques along with authentication will be helpful in solving such type of attacks. If encryption is not applied on the packets, the transmission of data lacks privacy in the network. Encryption of services is not compulsory for authentication purposes. All that is required is some type of assurance that the information passed over the network is correct and not modified in the transit. Confidentiality can be achieved by encrypting messages by using various algorithms such as message digest algorithm, message encryption, digital signature, key management, etc. Hamza Aldabbas *et al.* proposed in their work that confidentiality can be achieved by using the access control mechanisms for the services based on their sensitivity [11] [107] such as a bank transaction when performed, the security provided by authentication is not sufficient. Though sometimes data/service authentication does not allow modification of information, it allows an attacker to read the information that was transmitted over the network. To avoid these, confidentiality techniques are to be used along with authentication and access control for the services to perform secure communication.

It ensures the protection of both in terms of storing the information in the database which is known as *content confidentiality* as well as the transmitted information in the network known to be *message flow confidentiality*. Without authorization no one should be able to access the information stored in the database as well as no one should intercept the communication between the other network entities. The confidentiality service protects the whole communication flow between the two users for a period of time, i.e., *Traffic flow confidentiality* which may be lost by observing the patterns of information in the network. The *message flow confidentiality* uses the encipherment mechanisms along with an enveloper technique to conceal the message from the originator to avoid deriving messages from observation. This helps in protecting the information from the traffic analysis threat. The other aspects of confidentiality are *connection confidentiality* which provides the protection for the data over a connection oriented network. *Connectionless confidentiality* protects the user data on a connectionless network. *Selective Field confidentiality* provides the confidentiality to the selected fields in a data block both in connection oriented and connectionless network.

3.7.1.4 Integrity

Integrity ensures that the message was not modified in the communication transit. This allows only authorized entities for altering a message in an authorized way [86] [210]. The corruption of the message may occur due to the malicious entities present in the network or other reasons like noise, etc. Integrity is the assurance of accuracy, authentication and completeness of the received application or data. Integrity acts as a primary indicator of security in information systems [8]. It is enforced using a set of rules or constraints which are the integral part of the system. This refers to the validation of data, entity control which should not be changed, for a change which can lead to service interruptions and results in breach [107]. It provides the security for the content as well as message sequence. The content security ensures that the content of network resources are not inserted or modified whereas the message sequence preserves the ordering of the messages transmitted over the network. To avoid the message sequencing attacks, this service is provided to each recepient in the network. This service can be provided along with the various security mechanisms such as digital signature, message authentication code, etc.

The various types of services provided by integrity are *Connection Integrity with Recovery* which provides the integrity for the user data that is communicated on a connection, it detects any replay or modification in any data sequence then a recovery mechanism is applied. *Connection Integrity without Recovery* provides Integrity to the data on a connection, without any recovery even if any replay or modification in the message is detected. *Selective Field connection Integrity* provides integrity to the selected fields within the data block transmitted over a connection oriented network and does not allow any kind of modifications in the selected fields of data block. *Connectionless Integrity* provides Integrity to single data block in a connectionless network and even takes care of detecting any modifications in that particular block. *Selective Field connectionless Integrity* provides Integrity for the selected fields in a connectionless network and is responsible for detecting any modification or reply attacks.

3.7.1.5 Nonrepudiation

Nonrepudiation is a security service where the entities cannot deny their participation in a communication. It is treated as the proof of origin and proof of delivery of the services to the entities involved in the communication. It is considered as one of the essential security services in networks which is applied in message handling systems and electronic commerce [222]. It is the protection of the parties involved in the exchange of services against the other user denying of accepting the resources. These are required to establish the accountability of parties involved in the communication for the requesting and receiving of the services. When the entities misbehave, the disputes are investigated to find the hackers in the network [11] [207].

The types of services it provides are the *Nonrepudiation, Origin* which provides a proof that the party has sent the information to the network to reach the destination. *Nonrepudiation, Destination* provides the proof that the party has received the information. *Nonrepudiation, Submission* creates a proof of information related to submission and provides the proof when required. And finally, *Nonrepudiation, transport* creates and stores the proof of transported information over the network. These four types protects the information denying by sender or the receiver in the network. To provide this service, digital signatures are used which are created by the senders only and verified by others.

3.7.1.6 Availability

Availability is the assurance that the required data, applications/services is available for the proper functioning of the system. Availability is also an assurance that relevant information provided to the entity on a timely basis [86]. There are specifically designed systems available today with computing resources whose architectures are toward improving availability. Depending on a specific design, these may result in power outages, network outages, upgrades, and hardware failures [107]. This assures the stability of the system even at the time of attack such as DOS attack [11]. The applications in the network need to be made available when requested, even in the presence of faults. Resources are made unavailable intentionally to the authorized entities is attack on availability. Some of the attacks can be recovered by countermeasures which are automated such as encipherment techniques, some require a physical action for the recovery of availability of the services. It totally depends on the control of system services that depends on the access control permissions and other services of security. Availability of resources will be in danger due to interruption attack.

3.7.2 Security Mechanisms

There are two categories of mechnisms specific and pervasive. The basic three mechanisms like encipherment, digital signature and access Control which are essential for smooth functioning of the system. Other than these, the mechanisms which are required for the smooth communication are authentication exchange, data integrity, routing control, traffic padding, notarization. Some of the mechanisms which are known as pervasive which are generally required for any service and at any layer which are related to ISO7498-2 are trusted functionality, event detection, security audit trial and security recovery.

Encipherment and Data Confidentiality: It translates the data into some unreadeable form. The main purpose of this is to ensure privacy by hiding the information from the unintended persons even if they trap the data, only the encrypted data will be seen. Encyption is performed on plaintext to produce encrypted data which can be otherwise called ciphertext. Reverse operation of encryption is decryption which is performed to obtain the plaintext. These techniques may use symmetric or asymmetric keys. For encryption or for decryption we require the same secret key information known as symmetric key encryption. In asymmetric key technique, we use public and private keys where public keys are shared and private keys are not shared with anyone. If a private key gets compromised the system is no longer secure. Encipherment provides confidentiality for data or for the traffic flow information. There are many mechanisms available for encipherment which are provided for the authenticated principles in the network.

Digital Signature: Digital signature involves the communicating parties with an assumption that the source public key is known to the destination. It can be formed by ecnciphering the text using the private key of the sender or by using the hashcode with the private key of the sender. This involves two units namely signing a data unit and verifing the signed data. The procedure involves the signers private key to produce encrypted message or a cryptographic value produced from the data. It uses the public key of the sender to verify whether the signature was produced by the senders private key or not.

Access Control: It enforces the entity's access rights using authenticated identity of the user, information gathered about the user and the capabilities. Access controls are the set of controls that restrict the access to some of the resources. Entity must be authenticated and permissions are to be granted to access the system and its applications. Upon successful authentication, the user will be granted permission to access one or more applications. For each user profile, the permissions are associated and stored in the form of a matrix in the database. The database will control the access to the records or part of the records. The database has to make a decision on each and every individual access attempt. The decision depends not only on the identity of the user but also on the specific portions of the data being accessed. The matrix in the database consists of the *subject* which is capable of accessing the objects. Users are the subjects and *object* is anything like files or portions of files or programs, etc., to which the permissions are granted. Objects may be in the form of groups, individual records or even the entire database. *Access grant* is the permission given to the subject to access an object. In the matrix, one axis indicates the identified subjects and the other axis indicates the objects that can be accessed by that subject. If the authorized user tries to access an unauthorized object then the access right of that user will be rejected. Resource Access Control Facility (RACF) of IBM provides a set of access control mechanisms like user security, resource control, etc,. For the purpose of user security, RACF first verifies the user identity and based on the permissions and the security levels, the resources or the services are issued to get accessed.

Authentication Exchange: It deals with identifying the entities of the network. It uses authenticated information, some encipherment techniques, etc. The exchange can be done using the handshaking protocols along with timestamping. It is a mechanism that identifies the intended user with the exchange of information.

Data Integrity: It deals with integrity of single data units, selective fields of data units or stream of data fields. There are two processes to verify the integrity of a data unit. In the first process, a value can be produced at the source side and append it to the data unit. The value might be a cryptographic value or some code which will be recieved at the destination side. In the second process, it generates a corresponding value from the data received at the destination and compares with the received value or code for the detection of any modification that might have occured in the transmission. If the transmission is connection oriented, then cryptographic chaining, time stamp, etc., can be used and if the mode is connectionless, the protection of the data units against the replay attack is very limited using timestamping. As this deals with active attacks, we take care of detection rather than prevention. If some voilation is detected, it is reported so that some human intervention or the software is used to recover that violation. Automated recovery mechanisms are more useful in the network.

Routing Control: It takes care of the route from source to destination and controls the manipulation attacks in the route. It is better to opt the pre-established routes rather than the dynamic routes for the delivery of messages.

Traffic Padding: This mechanism provides security at various levels against the traffic analysis. This can be effective if combined with confidentiality service.

Notarization: It provides the assurance of the property communicated over the network from source to destination. This is generally an agreement provided by a third party in the form of notary. Whenever a communication occurs, this helps in protecting the information using encipherment, digital signature, or the mechanisms they are agreed upon.

Trusted Functionality: This mechanism is used to extend the trust on any security mechanism. It provides the protection on the above layer associated at which the protection is applied. The security mechanisms provided to the entities should be trustworthy.

security labels: This is used to know the sensitivity level of a particular mechanism. These labels are implicit within the data like the source address or the route they have to adopt to reach the destination. These labels must be securely bound with the data which are clearly identifiable and appropriately checked.

Event Detection: This includes the detection of the security violations and the normal event detection for the successful transmission from source to destination. This triggers with local reporting of the event, logging of the event, and recovery action taken if any in the transmission.

Security Audit Trial: The main purpose is to ensure the adequacy of the system control, operational procedures, aid in damage assessment, recommend any changes in the controls or policies or the procedures. It records the security relevant information and analyzes the information in the audit trial.

Security Recovery: It takes the action from the mechanism available to fulfill the request in event handling or management functions. These actions may be temporary, immediate or long term in nature.

3.8   IP Security —Layerwise

There are various security protocols designed for each layer in the network. How it is applied depends on the requirements of the application and it is up to the user interest to decide where to implement the security. The network implements the basic services irrespective of the user requirements like authorization, key management, integrity and confidentiality. These services are provided to the layers in the combination of one or more together. A detail list of the services provided by each layer in the stack is as follows.

3.8.1   Application Layer

The security in this layer is implemented at the end systems. Providing security to this layer allows easy access to the private keys, non-repudiation service. Applications are executed without depending on the operating system for these services. Applications are capable of understanding the information and provide appropriate security. Generally, PGP and SSL are the protocols which provide security to the application layer. The disadvantage in this layer is for each application security mechanism has to be designed seperately. Security mechanism for email is PGP and these clients are extented to look at the public keys in the local database of that particular user, the mechanisms such as nonrepudiation, authentication are provided to access the services. If the security need is specific and cannot be provided by the lower layers then the provider has to design new protocols based on the requirements.

3.8.2   Transport Layer

Providing security for the transport layer is easy as there is no need for designing new protocols based on the requirements as in the application layer. Like application layer security, the security on the transport layer is implemented on the end systems. The Transport Layer Security (TLS) protocol provides the security services like authentication, Integrity and confidentiality on top of TCP. If the security services are implemented at network layer then the service of the transport layer, i.e., TLS is replaced. The applications still need to be modified to fetch the services from the transport layer. Key management service may be duplicated for each transport protocol.

3.8.3   Network Layer

Security implementation at the security layer will decrease the overheads of key negotiations. This is due to sharing of key infrastructure provided by the network layer for protecting the resources, information, etc., over the communication. Security has to be provided for higher layers, with its own security mechanisms. It becomes very difficult to handle the issues of nonrepudiation in the communication. The mechanisms are being used on per user basis on the end systems. There is no problem on the network layer as there is no user in the context of routers present in the network layer.

3.8.4   Data Link Layer

If the information over the network is encrypted and sent through a dedicated line, it will increase the speed for delivering the data. The use of Automatic Teller machines (ATMs) for connecting the devices through dedicated lines to the main server will serve the purpose. If the lines are not dedicated and connected to an IP network, the DLL security will not be sufficient and it might be moved one layer up for the implementation of security.

3.9   Security Approaches for Future Internet

The problems that are raised from the architectural perspective with the current Internet state the requirement of a new process [58]. Many researchers and industries are working to counter them, yet they are facing difficulties for significant gains. In this regard, many discussions were held among the researchers and a conclusion was derived for developing the new architectures with three alternative approaches. The main idea is that the emerging infrastructures are required to inculcate and support at least the same level of security as of the present architecture to avoid some of the security problems of the current Internet architecture in the emerging architectures. The approaches described for the architectural development [81] [217] can be viewed with respect to security and they are

1. Re-engineering of today's Internet protocols may help us in solving several limitations that are based on Internet protocols but extensions will become a burden and make the architecture lose its identity.

2. Apply an evolutionary approach to existing architecture. Evolutionary change is caused by modification of the process definition affecting all new process instances [179]. It helps in finding immediate solutions to the problems by including them in the form of patches. If this addition of patches increases the burden on the Internet, it may not sustain long. It is a step by step and time consuming process as wel asl increases the burden on the overall architecture. The Internet has a built on evolution approach that will conceptualize the practical problems and find feasible solutions for commercial rollout [156]. This approach contains several drawbacks when solving the issues efficiently. Most of the issues which require solutions are derived from the TCP/IP architectural principles [174]. Some of the architectures that emerged using this approach are Recursive Network Architecture (RNA) [195] [197].

3. Start from scratch, i.e., clean state approach to solve all the problems and fulfill future needs. To envision the future Internet which may be vastly different from the current Internet it is better to avoid the trap of considering the layering concept of the current Internet, i.e., consider the features of this approach for the development of the future Internet. The evaluation of the new architecture is a bigger challenge in this approach. The architectures that have emerged or emerging using this type of concept are Role Based Architecture (RBA) [33], Autonomic Network Architecture (ANA) [30] [95], Service Integration, controL, and Optimisation (SILO) [72], Content Centric Networks (CCN) [67], Next Generation Networks (NGN) [27], SOA [122] [158], SONATE [141] [167], etc.

Almost both evolutionary and clean state approaches target the same vision, i.e., synchronized on phased agendas. Evolutionary or clean state approaches are the mix of those that can be equally considered in the view of security [192]. The basic feature of all these three approaches is to support the future needs. Clean state architectures are being developed in a flexible and extendable manner in order to avoid the problems that raised due to the ossified and fragile nature of the current Internet.

In the clean state approach, the existing features may be considered as a base for the development of new architecture. The challenge of developing a new architecture is not a change for the sake of change but to make an informed speculation about future requirements to propose a creative research and networking concepts to meet those requirements and represent a defendable architecture. Then a question arises, how to measure the success of the new architecture? The answer is to deploy it in wholesale in the place of the existing one. But it is not as easy as the current is carrying its baggage from the past three decades of evolution. Even then it couldn't be able to meet the requirements which are expected in the future. Another goal of these emerging architectures is a long-term vision for where the Internet should go. The research community has to set a vision of where the Internet should be after 10 years and provide a feasible solution for the success of the Internet [58].

Organizations like ICT, SOA4ALL, Next Generation Network (NGN) , Future Network Design (FIND), 4WARD, Service Oriented Network Architecture (SONATE) from G-Lab etc are working for the development of the future Internet (Please refer to Section2.6). Not only these many other organizations are concentrating on developing a flexible and extendable architecture that can support the future requirements in a secure manner. When a comparison is done between different architectural characteristics, security often becomes an important factor to consider. It is very difficult to decide which architecture provides more security than others or we can even say it is very difficult to deduce how secure an architecture is. Compared with other architectures, it is easy to compare the characteristics like overall performance, speed, congestion, etc., but it is difficult to measure security. It is difficult to decide which architecture is more secure among available different architectures. Sometimes it is easy to state that one system is more robust against attacks but it is hard to know how much it is as a whole [89]. For example, when service of a user is considered as an important parameter, then the design must able to manage all the services and able to encapsulate those services. These all are to be protected from attacks by using security measures. Even in a talk which was delivered by Darleen Fishers noted that security is nothing but a new problem and has been finding solutions to the attacks which have been occurring for over 15 years. David Clark in a talk noted about clean state approach and suggested the security community to be a part during the design phase but not after the architecture is complete. He insisted that future Internet must focus on security instead of concentrating on data delivery [27]. It makes clear that security has to be incorporated as a first tier objective in the architectures rather than adding after complete development of the architecture.

3.9.1 Security Establishment Proposal

There is a need of an effective plan to be built based on a thorough understanding of the security issues consisting of potential attackers, level of security required, and the factors that make a network vulnerable toward an attack. The minimum level of understanding these issues helps in defining the levels of security that are appropriate. Before developing a security strategy, potential hackers are to be identified, i.e., is it a person who is looking for a fun, or for fame or a well-defined financial organization [71]. Find whether one user is targeted in a group of the target class or more. It is difficult to discourage attackers if the target is only one out of many of a target class. A security technique is enough to avoid the attack which consists of a class of targets by diverting the attacker to other systems.

3.9.2 Risk Level Determination

There is a need to find out the threshold of an attack that a user can tolerate. Threshold represents how much a user can tolerate an attack that happens on a service. The developer should know the variety of services provided by the provider and the services that are to be protected out of many, determine the limitations and the levels of security to be provided to protect the services from the attacks. There is a say-ing that "When you have nothing, you have nothing to lose" which is impossible in a network [71]. The connecting world consists of a vast network infrastructure connecting with organizations of business; military information which requires confidentiality on government systems, personal computers within homes, etc. Not only this, there are many more contributions which lead to an attack. An attack makes a user/customer to lose confidence on the use of a secure Internet. Users may not wish to share sensitive information via the Internet when an attack occurs. With this, it is clearly understood that there is much to lose if security is not provided. The minimum security modules are to be included in the developing stage of architecture. Security methods, strategies help in decreasing the attacks which are caused by attackers. It is not possible to ensure absolute security of any architecture [62] [156].

Security has to be provided for the Future Internet to provide protection against existing and emerging threats. The massive Internet infrastructure which was constructed has no built-in security mechanisms to protect itself from attacks [100][161]. The people who developed the Internet were Government employees and scholars who were concerned with the discovery of Internet rather than finding its devastations [184]. They considered security as a non-functional requirement, but when attacks were found security protocols were developed and included in the architecture. The addition of several new protocols including security protocols resulted in patches which made the architecture lose its identity. To avoid some of these problems in the future Internet,"Network security should be initiated at the beginning of a network design and development process and to be managed throughout the lifecycle" [109] [184].

3.9.3   Future Internet- Objectives of Security

The architecture has to enforce the security properties of components and relationships among them. It should able to specify the security policies and level of security for closer enforcement of mechanisms that can transfer service in a secure way [75] [109]. It is stated by Schiller that the security for architecture must be easy to use and easy to deploy. The goals that are required for the purpose of secure communication over the Internet are

1. Security modules should be flexible and extendable and able to recover from possible attacks.

2. Communication that takes place across the network must be free from attacks like eavesdropping, modification, DOS, etc.

3. The architecture that is flexible and loosely coupled should be robust from attacks.

4. Architecture must able to recover from possible attacks.

5. Different architectures follow different security policies that are to be supported by the architecture.

6. The basic services like authentication, confidentiality, trust, integrity, etc, are to be made available.

7. According to the requirements of the user different levels of security has to be provided .

In addition to this, some other important goals are

Availability: If the users wish to communicate and both are authenticated and well behaved then they are to be allowed to communicate using policies for accessing the services they wish to exchange or communicate. But it is not an easy goal as it first requires a clarification of well behaved and connectivity involves economics and the services for which payment is required or not and whether the services requested by the user are within the permissions, etc. Availability implies changing request to identify any barriers related to it, ranging from stability of routing to handling of DOS attacks. This should be given priority in the flexible network architecture.

End-to-end security: One of the most bothering issues of today is protecting the services from attacks, i.e., end-to- end security and even it is important to consider the end host security. If good security is posed, then it promises to provide good security. It is also to be considered as another issue and to be given to a small group to solve these problems. Providing solutions for end-to-end attacks in a network, allow the users to utilize the network for secure communication and it indirectly helps to gain the confidence of the user. Part of this has to be considered and propose a consistent division of responsibility between the network and end-host systems. In spite of this, an approach has to be followed to build secure Internet architecture.

Flexibility: The architecture of the Internet should be flexible and loosely coupled, scalable and economic, easy to maintain, extendable and robust in nature, secure and support for innovations. The current architecture has been proven as rigid, difficult to modify, less capable to handle the large-scale changes. The future secure Internet should learn from past lessons and be designed as flexible, easy to modify, handle the changes, etc. Security mechanisms must be robust and different levels of security are to be provided according to the requirements of the user, able to extend these mechanisms, able to replace the outdated one with a new one, etc. Flexibility of the security modules should be given highest priority in the future Internet.

3.9.4 Security Requirements

The emerging flexible architectures are opened to be self-organized, flexible, and loosely coupled. The usage of the concept of SOA in the development of flexible network architectures helps in development of architecture in a flexible and loosely coupled manner and it's services also. One of the architectures among many is SONATE [56] [141] [167] which is flexible, loosely coupled, self manageable, maintainable, scalable, robust, etc. The model allows shift to P2P, end-to end, overlay, broadcasting, multicasting, etc., on distributed environment. These features create a great influence on security which has to be incorporated into the architecture. The design retirement, a part of security lifecycle [100] helps in attaining a concrete method for the design and development of network security. Considering these characteristics, the flexible architectures allow a variety of services, network heterogeneity, and a variety of security services to protect the services from some attacks. Of the above the general security requirements are as follows:

- Confidentiality: ensure the transmission of services over the network is hidden.

- Integrity: assurance of providing untampered information.

- Privacy: information of brokers and users request of services must be kept secret.

- Nonrepudiation: evidence of party is indeed the sender/receiver of certain service

- ID management: the brokers ids are to be managed in the network for the communication with other brokers in the network. These brokers communicate for the request/delivery of services from one to the other in the network.

- Access control: authorized users are facilitated with a communication network to communicate to and fro i.e the resources to be used, software, network connections, etc.

- Authentication: whether the origin of communication is authentic or not has to be ensured, i.e., the user, broker whom they claim to be.

- Detection: alleviates for detecting attacks related to security, generating warning/indications etc.

- Recovery: recovery the network after the attack has occurred.

- Security management: coordinating service requirements, mechanism implementation and operations throughput across Inter-network. It has to follow some security policies by which trust is gained. There are several trust models for communication and representations of the systems to gain trust and security management even takes care of trust management which indeed deals with trust relationship and risk assessment.

3.10 Security Requirements—SONATE

The security aspects that are applicable to all three components, User, Broker, Provider are necessary for the correct service Provisioning (Figure 3.8). The service consumer requires authentication, authorization and confidentiality mechanisms. The authenticated users should only be authorized to avail the services. The broker should be limited to the services authorized for by the mechanism of authentication and it should not suffer from attacks such as denial of service. Finally for correct service provisioning, providers must ensure the integrity of the services and also the availability of the services.

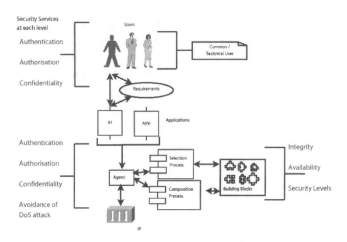

Figure 3.8: SONATE —Security Aspects.

Access to a service can be restricted in many ways. The services are to be granted to the requested users once their authentication and authorizations are proved. Authentication and access control are well-known techniques for the software architectures to limit the access of various entities of the network. In the context of SONATE, both approaches are used for the prevention of attacks as well as limiting the damages. However, authentication helps in securing the services but does not make the architecture secure but authentication along with access control mechanisms helps in securing and avoiding many security threats. New threats emerge constantly, the architecture must be able to handle them using continuous practices and solve them. Most of the solutions mentioned are close to the existing mechanisms but there is a need to develop a fine-grained module that suites the architecture. Security in SONATE is not just about messaging or end-to-end but is a process as a whole.

3.11   Summary

In this chapter, a detailed explanation of the security attacks with respect to current and future Internet architecture has been discussed. The incorporation of security requirements is of significance as it not only makes the system more secure, but also helps to determine whether it can be improved further or not in future. The security provided by the architecture should not effect the users who follow the rules for secure communication. The security measures include the authentication, authorization, confidentiality, integrity, availability of the services and these are correlated with informational tasks such as message security, transport security, application security for the development of secure architecture of Future Internet. Security capabilities can be used to empower these informational tasks by training, education, awareness, etc. The future Internet architectures may use one or more security services to provide a secure communication over the network. The architecture AKARI uses AAA security, SONATE uses authentication, authorization, availability, integrity but not nonrepudiation and so on with other architectures. The addressed security issues are not just for the early stage but these are required even the deployment of the architecture as a whole for the protection of the system itself.

Appendix—3A

Introduction to the OSI Seven Layer Model

Networking is a prime concern for information security. The ubiquitous nature of network connectivity may let us access the world from our computer, but it also lets that same world gain access back to us in ways we may not desire. No matter how well we secure our own hosts, we are still vulnerable if the parts of the infrastructure between our distant destinations and ourselves fall victim to intentional exploitation or unwitting mishap. Information security and data networking are inextricably linked topics. Todays network engineer has no choice but to be security-conscious, and the security engineer has no choice but to understand the network he is tasked to secure.

A great deal of formalized study has been devoted to the science and methodology of designing and maintaining networks. One formal system that network engineers discuss and apply frequently is the OSI Seven Layer Model for Networking, developed by the ISO (International Standards Organization) to define a standardized method for designing networks and the functions that support them. This model describes seven layers of interaction for an information system communicating over a network, presenting a stack of layers representing major function areas that are generally required or useful for data communication between nodes in a distributed environment. Starting from a high-level application perspective, data is sent down the stack layer by layer, each layer adding information around the originally presented data until that original data plus its layers of added content are represented at the bottommost layer as a physical medium such as bursts of colored light or voltage across a wire in order for that data to physically travel from one point to the other in the real world.

Once the data takes this real-world journey, the true power of the model comes into play, as the protocols at each layer are mandated by the design model to strip cleanly away the information and formatting added by their corresponding layer at the sending end of the conversation as the data rises back up through the seven layers at the receiving side, acting on the transmitted content at their layer and pushing back up the stack what was originally pushed down at the other end. What was presented to layer three at the sending side should be exactly what layer three on the receiving side passes back up to the layer above. This can be described as the layers "communicating" between one another on the sending and receiving side, all the way up to the application layer at the top, where pure data is sent from one side and received intact and unchanged on the other. There are exceptions to this concept such as application-aware NAT, where lower layer protocols may alter the data passed to them from above, but this is an exceptional case and a technical violation of the model. The isolation of layers also allows abstraction such that lower layers are not dependant on upper layers beyond what is needed to exchange data between the layers. This is especially important at the lower levels where the same data may have to travel across different media or link-layer protocols to get where it is going. This delivers a key goal of the model—interchangeability of layers such that different environments can use the stack to standardize communications and interconnect on a common basis.

Like many ISO standards, much of its formal theory does not make it into the real world of actual implementation, but the powerful concepts that the OSI model present are a key element in most modern network system designs. Anyone who has worked with data networking or security has likely heard the terms "layer three" or "layer two" or "application layer". This terminology stems directly from the ISO model and how it is applied to practical solutions. The model concepts are conventionally used to design and troubleshoot networks, and the seven-layer model is standard fare on any network engineering certification exam or interview. Careful study of the model can show us support for concepts we have learned from more conventional forms of information security theory, and understanding and applying the model to information security scenarios can also help us assess and address information security threats in a network environment, allowing us to organize efforts to make security assessments and perform forensic analysis of compromised systems and threats presented in theory and found in the wild.

Using the model as an objective measure for security is closely related to this concept of defense-in-depth, and by way of deconstructing the layers and then examining how they interact, we can see supporting evidence and clear rationale for the need of that blended, defense-in-depth approach in securing networks, systems, applications, and data. The following sections will take each layer and examine them on the basis of their formal definition and their practical place in the network, show example security threats, and present possible controls of those risks that apply to the layer in question.

LAYER ONE —PHYSICAL LAYER

The physical layer is responsible for the physical communication between end stations. It is concerned with the actual encoding and transmission of data in electromechanical terms of voltage and wavelength. For purposes of information security we can widen this definition to apply to all physical world factors, such as physical media and input device access, power supply, and any other issue bounded by physical terms. As already mentioned, the physical layer is critical to data communications. It is also the most vulnerable and changeable, not depending upon the logic and organization of the electronic world, but on the vagaries of physics. Denial of Service is a mere circuit breaker or lead pipe away when dealing with the physical layer. Something as simple as unplugging the power or removing a network cable can cause untraceable havoc on a network. It should be noted that this is the most likely realm for accidental violation —who hasn't heard the classic story of a cleaning crew or intern pulling the power cord from a critical piece of production hardware? The physical realm is also the hardest to maintain an audit log or monitor. No level of logical or programmatic controls can easily detect that a host has been detached from its normal network connection and is now connecting through an Ethernet tap, which may be silently duplicating any inbound or outbound communications for eavesdropping purposes. As far as eavesdropping is concerned, physical contact may not even be necessary. In what is regarded as a seminal paper on non-intrusive electronic eavesdropping published in 1985, Wim Van Eck states the following - (emphasis added):

"It is possible in some cases to obtain information on the signals used inside the equipment when the radiation is picked up and the received signals are decoded. Especially in the case of digital equipment this possibility constitutes a problem, because remote reconstruction of signals inside the equipment may enable reconstruction of the data the equipment is processing."

What was groundbreaking about Van Eck's paper was not the possibility of such eavesdropping, as he states that this possibility has been well known for decades but dismissed as demanding a high degree of sophistication, specialization, and expensive resources. The noteworthy part was instead that techniques had been identified by him to allow such eavesdropping that were inexpensive, used common materials, and only required a moderate level of technical sophistication. Based on this paper, the term Van Eck Phreaking was coined to describe remote eavesdropping on the signals in a CRT or VDT display. This term is referenced in the U.S. Government's classified Tempest project, which many believe was used to develop application for use of electromagnetic eavesdropping as well as protections against such intrusions.

Fortunately, physical security for information technology can benefit from the more general discipline of physical security in the general world. As the somatic components of information technology are subject to the same threats as other "real assets, they are also able to benefit from the same protections that the more mundane security disciplines have implemented from the beginning of modern civilization. This means that critical assets must be behind strong locks, with strict controls on who may pass those locks, and constant monitoring, logging, and review of that access. Such monitoring may include video surveillance, card-lock logging of entry and exit with PIN-based passwords, and even biometric validation to augment password and hardware based credentials to validate actual physical identity. On the information technology side, data storage cryptography is an additional security control at the physical layer, allowing control of access to data even when the physical media or resource may be wholly in the control of unauthorized elements. The aforementioned Tempest project developed standards for electromagnetic shielding to prevent monitoring of highly sensitive systems such as PKI Certificate Authorities. Techniques have also been developed to modify screen fonts in ways that attenuate the signal emanated by a CRT displaying them, reducing the RF emitted in the critical ranges that Van Eck phreaking devices use to pick up their information.

Physical Layer Vulnerabilities

Loss of Power, Loss of Environmental Control, Physical Theft of Data and Hardware, Physical Damage or Destruction of Data And Hardware, Unauthorized changes to the functional environment (data connections, removable media, adding/removing resources), Disconnection of Physical Data Links, Undetectable Interception of Data, Keystroke and Other Input Logging

Physical Layer Controls

Locked perimeters and enclosures, Electronic lock mechanisms for logging and detailed authorization, Video and Audio Surveillance, PIN and password secured locks, Biometric authentication systems, Data Storage Cryptography, Electromagnetic Shielding

LAYER TWO —DATA LINK LAYER

The Data Link Layer (DLL) is concerned with the logical elements of transmissions between two directly connected stations. It deals with issues of local topology where many stations may share a common local media. This is the layer where data packets are prepared for transmission by the physical layer. The data link layer is the realm of MAC addresses and VLANs as well as WAN protocols such as Frame Relay and ATM. Switch issues such as broadcast and collision domains are a layer two concern. It is also the realm of wireless protocols such as the various flavors of 802.11 wireless networking. For discussion purposes we will consider layer two to pertain to any direct data transmission issue, including modems, wireless and WAN circuits. The data link layer has been a long-neglected area of study for information security, lost between the physical issues of layer one and the dominating realm of the firewall in layers three and four. This lack of attention made it an area ripe for exploitation, and some of the hottest new issues in information security have heavy involvement in layer two. Wardriving, the act of traveling around public areas and randomly accessing 802.11 wireless access points with lax or default security settings, is a prime example of a vulnerability with both layer one and two elements. The wireless hardware solution may have an initial goal of ease of deployment and use, but this goal is used as a weakness to exploit the solution for unanticipated purposes on the basis of the solution exceeding its anticipated physical boundaries. The wireless signal extends from the wireless access points inside location out to the outside public street. And lacking sufficient use of control at layer two by letting anyone with a signal at layer one to freely connect. Due to its interaction with a variety of media and flavors of hardware, this layer is critical to network compatibility and as such is heavily dependant on rigid protocol standards for interoperability. This dependency can allow poorly designed standards to impede security, and make the correction of issues a ponderous and drawn-out process. In the aforementioned 802.11 scenario, there are tools available to secure the layer two issues, using encryption protocols to authenticate valid users and protect their traffic from unauthorized access. Unfortunately, weaknesses were found in this encryption scheme that have to date only been partially addressed.

Weaknesses have also been found in the much-touted Ethernet switch. Originally thought to be the answer to the problem of promiscuous mode sniffing of network traffic because of their learning and selective forwarding, switches have fallen victim to the efforts of creative hackers, who have been hard at work finding the means to circumvent this protection. Some of the key issues lie in the ARP protocol. This protocol establishes the relationship between local stations that can communicate over the layer two channel, and their corresponding layer three IP addressing. The ARP process is very basic, and has no means for authentication or validation. Any station in the local layer two environment can claim any IP address. ARP typically operates on a broadcast basis, but attacks against ARP have been developed using unicast transmissions to specific targets. Known as ARP spoofing, these attacks create an artificial view of what the layer two environment looks like to specific targets, and allows man-in-the-middle attacks where an attacking machine intercepts the data communication between two hosts by intercepting their traffic and forcing it to bypass through the attacking machine.

Layer two switches are also vulnerable to attacks on their virtual separation of segments known as VLANs. Recent vulnerabilities have been found in Ciscos automatic configuration of VLAN trunks, allowing hosts that can send 802.1Q trunking protocol signaling (an ability that is becoming more and more common in modern operating systems and NIC drivers) to negotiate access to multiple VLANs. Cisco provides configurations to disable this behavior, but the default behavior is to allow automatic VLAN configuration. As a newly emergent battleground, the threats tend to outweigh the controls on the link-layer, with the only strong tools being manual MAC filtering to enforce an explicit layer two policy, and strong network design to minimize exposure from the outset. The inherent design of most layer two communication imposes a layer of involuntary trust.

Link Layer Vulnerability Examples

MAC Address Spoofing (station claims the identity of another), VLAN circumvention (station may force direct communication with other stations, bypassing logical controls such as subnets and firewalls.), Spanning Tree errors may be accidentally or purposefully introduced, causing the layer two environment to transmit packets in infinite loops. In wireless media situations, layer two protocols may allow free connection to the network by unauthorized entities, or weak authentication and encryption may allow a false sense of security. Switches may be forced to flood traffic to all VLAN ports rather than selectively forwarding to the appropriate ports, allowing interception of data by any device connected to a VLAN.

Link Layer Controls

MAC Address Filtering –Identifying stations by address and cross-referencing, physical port or logical access, do not use VLANs to enforce secure designs. Layers of trust should be physically isolated from one another, with policy engines such as firewalls between. Wireless applications must be carefully evaluated for unauthorized access exposure. Built-in encryption, authentication, and MAC filtering may be applied to secure networks.

LAYER THREE —NETWORK LAYER

The Network layer is concerned with the global topology of the internetwork–it is used to determine what path a packet would need to take to reach a final destination over multiple possible data links and paths over numerous intermediate hosts. This layer typically uses constructs such as IP addresses to identify nodes, and routing tables to identify overall paths through the network and the more immediate next-hop that a packet may be forwarded to. Protocols such as ARP facilitate that process, giving layer two mapping to layer three addresses, and telling layer three what link-layer path should be taken to follow its routing tables indication of the appropriate path. In the opposite direction, protocols such as IP will identify their higher-level layer four transmission protocol such as TCP or UDP in order to direct layer four as to how the incoming data should be handled.

Layer three is the last layer that has a rough physical correspondence to the real world. A given host will typically have a single layer three address or single layer three address per interface. This tends to make layer three addressing critical not only to network topology but also to node identity. In a traditional firewall, the layer three address is the primary qualifying value in a filtering rule, with some rules using them as a sole identifier (examples –denying common RFC1918 "private addresses or other address ranges designated as invalid. Denying inbound packets from the outside that claim a source address from an inside network - so called "packet spoofing) layer three addressing is also used by applications to identify resources, using DNS resolution to map a hostname to an address or group of addresses. Layer three protocols often have mechanisms for broadcast or multicast of data to multiple machines in finite or arbitrary scopes.

In filling these many roles, a variety of means for attack at layer three become exposed. In the realm of routing, especially public routing situations such as over the Internet, most routing protocols have only an elementary level of security. Two peers may exchange routing information securely, but they have no means to validate routes that may have propagated from untrusted parts of the network. Attackers can steal entire network ranges with the right resources, allowing further attacks at layer three and above. Identity is always a classic vector for attack –most layer three protocols have no built-in means to authenticate source addresses or other protocol data which may be used to attempt to establish identity, so when we rely upon what a packet claims to be a source address, we have little reason to actually expect that address to be correct. Resource identification falls victim to the same lack of authentication –DNS servers can be forced to present incorrect addresses, or by routing or the earlier ARP spoofing techniques, an illicit host can take a given address and claim to be the resource which is located therein. Techniques have also been developed to abuse broadcast mechanisms, amplifying data into crushing streams of packets that can paralyze a host, often using untraceable spoofed addressing against unsecured third-party machines which are turned into unwitting tools for abuse.

The ubiquitous control for layer three is the firewall –when correctly configured it will let only the necessary traffic pass through its boundaries. However, well-thought out policies that take into consideration the problems of identity must be part of the firewall deployment. Encryption and authentication technologies such as IPSEC can be used to more reliably identify the source of IP communications. Routers must have strict policies regarding their exchange of routes, and use reliable means of authentication and communication with their peers. Route filters should be applied to prevent the accidental or intentional introduction of spurious network routes. On the Internet, Route Registries and the Routing Arbiter Database (RADB) offer the means to register route announcements. The RADB also provides filter information that allows building of local policies to validate foreign route announcement.

Network Layer Vulnerabilities

Route spoofing - propagation of false network topology, IP Address Spoofing-false source addressing on malicious packets Identity and Resource ID Vulnerability - Reliance on addressing to identify resources and peers can be brittle and vulnerable.

Network Layer Controls

Route policy controls - Use strict anti-spoofing and route filters at network edges, Firewalls with strong filter and anti-spoof policy, ARP/Broadcast monitoring software, Implementations that minimize the ability to abuse protocol features such as broadcast.

LAYER FOUR —TRANSPORT LAYER

The Transport Layer is concerned with the transmission of data streams into the lower layers of the model, taking data streams from above and packaging them for transport, and with the reassembly and passing of incoming data packets back into a coherent stream for the upper layers of the model. Transport protocols may be designed for high reliability and use mechanisms to ensure data arrives complete at its destination, such as the TCP protocol, or protocols may choose to reduce overhead and simply depend upon the best efforts of the lower layers to deliver the data, and the protocols of the upper layers to ensure success to the levels they require, such as with the UDP protocol. Transport protocols may implement flow control, quality of service, and other data stream controls to meet their transmission needs.

The Transport Layer is the first purely logical layer in the model. It is the primary point where multiple data conversations from or to a single host are multiplexed. Some transport protocols such as TCP and UDP use the concept of port numbers to allow multiple simultaneous conversations between numerous destinations to individual local protocols or applications. Other protocols such as ICMP might rely on higher-layer data to sort out multiplexing. Because the transport layer is where data conversations to a given host are multiplexed and sorted, it is often used as the primary means of service identification within a given host, much as how layer three addresses are used to identify service locations within the context of the entire network.

Some of the key vulnerabilities found at the transport layer come from poor handling of undefined conditions. Many transport protocols seem to have been implemented under the belief that they would be dealing with well-behaved communication from both the upper and lower levels –a false assumption in the hostile world of the global public Internet. This means that protocols are subjected to unexpected or deliberately perverse input or handling exploiting the more obscure protocol details and so-called impossible conditions, and as a result often have unexpected behavior. Attacks such as Winnuke used an obscure and out-of-specification TCP flag when connecting to an open TCP port on a Windows machine, and the result was an operating system crash. The behavior of a given host when presented with TCP and UDP packets with varying arbitrary contents can be used to "fingerprint an OS and select more focused attacks due to differences in response between different operating systems and network stacks.

Another vulnerability lies in the use and re-use of ports for multiple functions. This is found quite often in the Windows arena, where differing functions such as file and print sharing, remote administration, LAN messaging, RPC functions, and a myriad of other applications all use a handful of UDP and TCP ports. This overuse of ports makes restriction of access at layer four by a firewall difficult. If any of the functions are needed, then the firewall ports are opened and in theory most if not all functions that use those ports could flow through unchecked. Imagine the surprise of a firewall administrator to open a port on a perimeter firewall supposedly for the purpose of authentication or drive sharing, only to have messenger-based spam advertising or remote vulnerabilities let in by the same rule. This overloading limits the effectiveness of network-based controls such as firewalls, and forces reliance on individual host level security controls, which are often not a practical proposition in large enterprise environments with a large amount of machines operated in many different administrative environments and functional roles.

Most transmission protocols were built with an emphasis on utility and performance. As such, they usually do not implement strong controls to validate the source of a transmission, or that a packet is a legitimate part of a data conversation. This leads to the ability to forge packets that can interrupt or redirect the flow of a transmission. Some protocols such as UDP can be trivially spoofed and fooled due to a complete lack of sequencing or state at layer four. Other protocols such as TCP are more difficult due to their more extensive flow control and integrity checking. However, with most such protocols, integrity pertains more to the accidental loss of data due to errors or packet loss rather than the deliberate attempt to attack the protocol. Thus, such protocols can also fall to more sophisticated attack. The practice of TCP session hijacking is one such sophisticated attack, where the attacker must guess factors such as initial and TCP sequence numbers, and then inject fake packets to manipulate the data flow by interrupting then falsifying the flow of higher-level data. Such an attack is one-way-control may be gained but information does not return to the attacker unless he uses the control channel to open additional covert channels of attack.

Conventional firewalls are the most common control at layer four as well as layer three. Firewall rules should be written to be as strict as possible regarding transport layer identity. This means that transport layer protocols should be specified individually in rules where possible rather than permitting any communication between two layer three nodes. In terms of TCP/IP communication, this means that rules should be written applying matches for layer four protocols such as UDP/TCP/ICMP as well as subprotocol details such as UDP/TCP port numbers or ICMP types. Modern firewall technology allows for "stateful inspection", which allows firewalls to inspect the layer four details of a packet and determine the state of a transmission at the transport layer. This allows the firewall to determine if a packet is likely to be in response to an existing flow of data rather than a random packet trying to "sneak by" based on all aspects that govern flow in a given protocol, rather than a more arbitrary packet filter that may only check port number or simple flags which may be easily determined and set in an arbitrarily assembled packet.

Stronger mechanisms are possible in layer four implementations to make session hijacking more difficult as well. Recent improvements in TCP sequence number assignment based on random number generation rather than arbitrary and predictable sequences have made the blind takeover of TCP sessions much more difficult. The Cisco PIX firewall provides a randomized TCP sequence number to traffic it passes as part of its NAT-based Adaptive Security Algorithm (ASA), fixing the problem for TCP implementations which are still non-random and predictable.

Transport Layer Vulnerabilities Mishandling of undefined, poorly defined, or "illegal" conditions, Differences in transport protocol implementation allow "fingerprinting" and other enumeration of host information. Overloading of transport-layer mechanisms such as port numbers limit the ability to effectively filter and qualify traffic. Transmission mechanisms can be subject to spoofing and attack based on crafted packets and the educated guessing of flow and transmission values, allowing the disruption or seizure of control of communications.

Transport Layer Controls

Strict firewall rules limiting access to specific transmission protocols and subprotocol information such as TCP/UDP port number or ICMP type Stateful inspection at firewall layer, preventing out-of-state packets, illegal flags, and other phony packet profiles from entering the perimeter Stronger transmission and layer session identification mechanisms to prevent the attack and takeover of communications.

LAYER FIVE —SESSION LAYER

The Session Layer is concerned with the organization of data communications into logical flows. It takes the higher layer requests to send data and organizes the initiation and cessation of communication with the far end host. The session layer then presents its data flows to the transport layer below where actual transmission begins. Session protocols will often deal with issues of access and accessibility, allowing local applications to identify and connect to remote services, and advertising services to remote clients and dealing with subsequent requests to connect. The session layer also deals with higher-order flow control from an application perspective; just as the transport layer may control transmission from a network-oriented perspective and limit the flow to match the available network capacity, the session layer may control the flow up through to the application layer and limit the rate that data enters or leaves that realm based on arbitrary or dynamic limits.

The Session Layer in networking is a more obscure topic because it is fairly neglected in the TCP/IP communications model that dominates modern data communications. The Department of Defense model for TCP/IP essentially compresses the

ISO Session (layer five), Presentation (layer six), and Application (layer seven) layers into a process/application layer. As both models are frameworks for design rather than unbendable standards, in implementation many TCP/IP based protocols break out into what can be classified as Session Layer behavior. Common examples include network utility protocols such as RPC, Microsofts .NET system, and CORBA, which create frameworks for higher-level applications to sort out the availability and use of resources distributed over a network. Secure authentication protocols such as SSL and Kerberos have specific function in the session area, negotiating and controlling the flow of information for higher-level applications. On the other hand, many applications encapsulate the session functions in their application protocols. Basic network tools such as FTP and Telnet negotiate sessions within their own protocol boundaries. Also included in the Session Layer are multimedia protocols such as H.323, VoiceOverIP protocols such as SIP, and other media-streaming and communication protocols. These protocols often are required to negotiate both session creation and session-path parameters such as quality-of-service and bandwidth.

As the Session Layer deals with the creation and control of access to the higher-level applications, the issue of authorization and access is a natural weakness in this layer. Similar to problems we've seen already in lower-layer protocols, multiplexing services such as RPC, .NET and CORBA which provide a wide range of services through a single channel narrow the ability of lower layers of the network to control access to resources. If these protocols themselves do not provide robust security internally they become a prime target for abuse. Even if they meet this challenge at best they still remain a single layer of protection. Many session layer protocols lack strong protection for their authorization facilities. Protocols such as standard telnet and FTP pass usernames and passwords in the clear, allowing any layer beneath them to intercept their credentials. Protocols with "stronger" protection of passwords such as the Microsoft implementation of CIFS (Common Internet File System, used by MS for file and printer sharing) often fall prey to cryptographic or implementation weaknesses in the handling of passwords and authentication.

Even assuming perfect protection of a user's credentials in transit over the network, it is all too common that the passwords themselves are weak and subject to attack. The session layer can exacerbate this problem by poor or non-existent logging of failed access attempts, allowing an attacker unlimited and undetected attempts to guess likely passwords, or use an even cruder technique of brute-force exhaustion of all possible or probable password strings. Mechanisms within the session layer can also be used to enumerate possible usernames to pair with such guessing and brute-force attacks. On traditional Unix-based systems there were often services such as finger or who enabled to show logged-in users and associated information such as where a remote user may be logged in from or how long a user may have been idle. On Windows machines it is common for the Messenger network service to be activated as a default option. This service is intended to receive "net send USER MESSAGE" messages sent remotely to the local users. In order to make message services available, this service advertises a logged-in user name to any node status request for service names on the machine, allowing the use of such queries to enumerate user names remotely.

Some services such as SIP and other Voice-over-IP protocols share similar problems to those discussed at layer four with the identification of valid traffic within a session. Mostly based on UDP for performance and overhead purposes, these protocols often still must implement transport session identification such as packet sequence in layers five and above. These sequencing and flow identifiers are just as subject to guessing and attack, in many instances more so due to the open nature of UDP and the emphasis on low overhead and functionality common for real-time protocols.

As discussion has shown so far, identity is an issue with all layers in the model, with the attributes of each layer often applied as a standard for identification and authorization. In the Session Layer, identity is the key factor, and the main controls at this layer focus on the establishment of identity. Secure channels of user and session authentication are essential to private communications. Cryptography technology allows for both the reliable identification of remote parties and the means for protecting the exchange of data from prying eyes. Passwords and other user credentials should be passed and stored in encrypted form to prevent interception or theft. User accounts should have expiration dates based on both usage and fixed time, requiring the update of credentials and reauthorization of access. Session identification may need to be based on a cryptography technology in order to protect sensitive communications in real-time environments.

To prevent brute-force or focused guessing of session credentials, failed attempts can be properly logged and limited to a fixed amount of failures before an account or service is locked out. This approach is a two-edged sword in that legitimate users may be locked out by illicit access attempts either inadvertently or as the basis for a denial-of-service attack. A safer possible approach is to limit connection attempts on a time basis such as only once every 30 seconds, or temporary lockout on failure with a brief enough duration that legitimate user access will recover in a practical amount of time, but a brute force attack would be rendered impractical.

Session Layer Vulnerabilities

Weak or non-existent authentication mechanisms, Passing of session credentials such as user ID and password in the clear, allowing intercept and unauthorized use Session identification may be subject to spoofing and hijack. Leakage of information based on failed authentication attempts, Unlimited failed sessions allow brute-force attacks on access credentials.

Session Layer Controls

Encrypted password exchange and storage, Accounts have specific expirations for credentials and authorization, Protect session identification information via random/cryptographic means Limit failed session attempts via timing mechanism, not lockout.

LAYER SIX —PRESENTATION LAYER

The Presentation Layer deals with the organization of data passed from the application layer into the network. This layer allows for the standardization of data and the communication of data between dissimilar hosts, such as platforms with different binary number representation schemes or character sets (ASCII vs. UNICODE, for example.) Presentation Layer protocols typically rely upon a standardized data format for use on the network, and various conversion schemes to convert from the standardized format into and out of specific local formats. The Presentation Layer can also control network-layer enhancements such as compression or encryption.

The Presentation Layer is another obscure layer, usually hidden deep in the implementation of applications and operating systems. End users may need to be passingly familiar with the outermost details such as JPEG picture formats or SSL encryption, but leave the details to their applications to sort out. For discussion purposes the Presentation Layer can be considered to be all interfaces implemented by or called from an application to prepare and present data to the network for transmission, such as program library functions that take data and re-order into "network-byte" order. Taken more broadly for an information security viewpoint, we can evaluate at this level any system or library functions that take data input and process it into standard formatting or condition for all purposes. Many applications make use of SSL and TLS libraries to secure communications, where secure in this context means the use of strong authentication, data encryption, and other assurance functions based on cryptography. These features are nearly always presented to the application layer as an API into a standard library of functions. Some presentation services may use separate channels to control passage as well as directly pass data, allowing control at from higher levels of the presentation of the data stream.

Vulnerabilities at this layer often originate from weaknesses or shortcomings in the implementation of the presentation layer functions. Continuing on the theme of taking advantage of the original atmosphere of implicit trust and simple functionality that systems were (and continue to be) built in, attackers feed unexpected or illegal input into presentation-layer facilities, gaining results that are undesired or contrary to what the original designers intended. Buffer overflows, where program execution can be redirected into completely unintended areas, can be classified at this level as a problem with the presentation of data by an application into the execution environment of the machine. When the presentation from the application exceeds or mismatches the required convention at the presentation layer, unexpected events can happen.

A recently recognized weakness known as format string vulnerability can also be classified in the Presentation Layer. Format string vulnerabilities take advantage of applications that use user-supplied information for the basis of input into I/O libraries in such a way that the user-supplied data stream could control how that data is transmitted, formatted, or stored in the process of transmission. This occurs due to either the direct or indirect use of the user input in the format portion of routines used to process the data. Many routines allow this type of use for unformatted, simple output.

The assumption is that the user input is passed unformatted and verbatim through the routine. The actual result however, is that the user has access to pass control information through his data channel, and can use this access to crash the program, control its execution, or display arbitrary information on the other end of the output stream.

Cryptographic presentation services can fall prey to weaknesses in their implementation or fundamental design. Many secure web servers using SSL have had subtle bugs in the underlying cryptography of the SSL implementation turn into either theoretical or practical security exploits.

Controls at the Presentation Layer will typically take the form of cautious and untrusting coding practices when using routines and facilities for network and other inter-process communications. Checking and rechecking input from both the network and the user/application for proper form, and not relying upon lower/upper layers to present properly formed data is a must in an environment thick with arbitrary and deliberately perverse manipulations of communications. Assumptions that ease implementation or time-to-market for systems that shortcut this process may end up being disastrous from a security perspective. User and peer input should always be highly suspect, whether the input is received from a remote station or a local user. Careful specification is needed to determine what is expected from input, and code that carefully checks that input is needed to enforce that specification.

Cryptography is a fast-moving target, and technology and hardware capabilities advance constantly. The cryptographic strength of data protection services in the presentation layer should be selected carefully and reviewed periodically. Many cryptography protocols have been found to have subtle flaws well after being declared secure, so a process of periodic re-evaluation of crypto solutions is also vital.

Presentation Layer Vulnerabilities

Poor handling of unexpected input can lead to application crashes or surrender of control to execute arbitrary instructions. Unintentional or ill-advised use of externally supplied input in control contexts may allow remote manipulation or information leakage. Cryptographic flaws may be exploited to circumvent privacy protections.

Presentation Layer Controls

Careful specification and checking of received input incoming into applications or library functions. Separation of user input and program control functions- input should be sanitized and sanity checked before being passed into functions that use the input to control operation, Careful and continuous review of cryptography solutions to ensure current security versus known and emerging threats.

LAYER SEVEN —APPLICATION LAYER

The Application Layer deals with the high-level functions of programs that may utilize the network. User interface and primary function live at this layer. All functions not pertaining directly to network operation occur at this layer. Occupying the top-end of the stack, the Application Layer is the most open ended of all of the layers, and can be considered the catchall for any issues not addressed within the other six layers. Taking a more narrow view from a protocol perspective, user-oriented protocols such as naming (DNS, WINS), file-transfer (HTTP, FTP), messaging (SMTP, TOC/OSCAR [used by AIM]), and access (Telnet, RDP) all fall within the Application Layer in a more strict interpretation that views even higher level functions as outside the model completely. For the purposes of information security, the Application Layer can be considered the realm where user interaction is obtained and high-level functions operate above the network layer. These high level functions access the network from either a client or server perspective, with peer-based systems filling both functions simultaneously.

Similar to the physical-layer, the open-ended nature of the Application Layer groups many threats together at its end of the stack. One of the prime threats at the Application Layer is poor or nonexistent security design of the basic function of an application. Some applications may insecurely handle sensitive information by placing it in publicly accessible files or encoding it in "hidden" areas which are trivially displayed, such as in the HTML code of a web form. Programs may have well-known backdoors or shortcuts that bypass otherwise secure controls and provide unauthorized access. Applications with weak or no authentication are prime targets for unauthorized use and abuse over the network. The TFTP protocol is extensively used for booting of diskless workstations and network device management, but does not require any sort of username or password authentication to use its file access ability, giving an intruder possible access to configuration and access information without challenge other than the need to guess filenames. (This could equally be considered a session-layer vulnerability, or the failure to use session-layer controls.) Applications may rely upon untrustworthy channels to establish identity or set privilege. The Unix rlogin, rsh, and other "r-functions" typically use the implied trust of a local list of trusted remote hosts and remote users without a strong means of verifying the identity this trust is based upon. DNS names can be spoofed or DNS servers can be compromised, and compromised or maliciously controlled remote hosts can report whatever user identity is desired. Even worse, universal trust could be established to any user from any machine by placing the string "+ +" or "+" in specific system configuration files. This "trust the world" profile was shipped as the default on some commercial Unix systems.

Applications often grant excessive access to resources, allowing unprivileged users excessive access or imposing inadequate control to prevent the corruption or loss of data. The lack of detailed controls lead many data systems to have access granted on an "all or nothing" basis, forcing administrators to either give unlimited access or none at all. Overly complex access controls may seem to protect access but fail to prevent unauthorized activity due to poorly understood or written access rules.

From the higher levels outside of the model, user input is a significant threat from both deliberate and accidental standpoints. Users may provide unexpected input into the application environment, which if not handled properly could lead to crashes or other unexpected behavior. The unsuspecting hapless user may cause his application to crash or otherwise fail. A malicious user may be able to use bugs and program flaws to attack and gain access to resources or data.

Some of the most prevalent controls at the application layer relate to strong design practices in application design and implementation. Applications should make use of the secure facilities available to them in the lower network layers, carefully check incoming and outgoing data, and assume that communications can and will be subject to attack, requiring the use of strong authentication and encryption to validate and protect data as it travels across the network. Applications should also implement their own security controls, allowing for fine-grained control of privilege to access resources and data, ideally using a mechanism that is straightforward and strikes a balance between usability and effectiveness. Detailed logging and audit capability should be a standard feature of any application that handles sensitive or valuable data.

Testing and review is also critical as a control for the application layer. Given the wide variety of both problems and solutions, standards and practices will not be able to capture all possible twists and turns in the application environment. Developers will often have conflicting motivations and agendas regarding their applications, and in a structured programming environment, mandated code security review and application security testing are critical parts of a secure Software Development Life Cycle (SDLC).

On the hardware front, Intrusion Detection Systems (IDS) can observe data traffic for known profiles of network activity that can indicate probes for vulnerable applications or an imminent or ongoing attack, as well as detecting the presence of undesirable application traffic.

Many current host-based firewall systems also include the means to control the access of applications to the network. This control is useful in preventing the unauthorized or covert use of network resources by local programs, as well as providing the conventional layer three and four control functions of a firewall. Many also include basic IDS functionality as well.

Application Layer Vulnerabilities

Open design issues allow free use of application resources by unintended parties Backdoors and application design flaws bypass standard security controls . Inadequate security controls force "all-or-nothing" approach, resulting in either excessive or insufficient access. Overly complex application security controls tend to be bypassed or poorly understood and implemented. Program logic flaws may be accidentally or purposely used to crash programs or cause undesired behavior.

Application Layer Controls

Application level access controls to define and enforce access to application resources. Controls must be detailed and flexible, but also straightforward to prevent complexity issues from masking policy and implementation weakness Standards, testing, and review of application code and functionality-A baseline is used to measure application implementation and recommend improvements. IDS systems to monitor application inquiries and activity. Some host-based firewall systems can regulate traffic by application, preventing unauthorized or covert use of the network.

Interlayer Communication and Extensions to the Model for Information Security

The presentation of the layer-by-layer issues has focused on elements within each layer. However, the purpose of the seven-layer model is communication, and communication between layers is where many key issues lie. Understanding the layers individually now gives us a framework to examine how they communicate between one another, between matching layers on remote hosts, and how they contribute to the communication of data over the network.

An alternate way of organizing the seven-layer model is by concentrating on the borders of the layers rather than by examining what each layer encompasses. This approach focuses on the communication between the layer above and the layer below. Even the formal definitions presented earlier for each layer sometimes touch on these issues, and the actual implementations of network protocols are rarely as clean as the theoretical model. An example of such an issue is the process of ARP where a layer three protocol (IP) communicates into layer two to associate a remote MAC address with an IP address the local host is seeking to transmit to. There is a definite communication between the two layers to negotiate the issues required to match up a MAC address to its corresponding IP address and transmit the outbound data. The IP layer maintains a MAC to IP table based on this gathered information, essentially tracking and following layer two details at layer three.

To draw a parallel in the information security realm, multiple hosts secured behind firewalls on a single subnet present some interesting layer two versus layer three problems. The firewall may be able to prevent outside subnets from communicating into the local subnet, but will not be able to prevent communication between the hosts on the local subnet. The hosts will be able to use ARP and discover one another, and packets will be forwarded across the layer two environment directly between hosts. One solution to this problem is to segregate hosts on to their own dedicated subnets. This approach is highly secure but is inefficient in that it wastes IP address space; each subnet requires reserved addresses for broadcast and network identity, as well as an address on each subnet for the firewall itself. This approach would also waste physical interfaces on the firewall and switch environment. The option to use VLAN trunking is sometimes available, but is a poor choice in a secure environment based on potential vulnerabilities such as those mentioned in the layer two analyses.

There are options to secure the hosts on the shared subnet. Static ARP entries can prevent traffic interception, and many Ethernet switches offer options to secure their ports in order to limit traffic or MAC addresses to pass only into authorized ports. These solutions must be carefully deployed, however, as the layer two environments may unexpectedly pass traffic or create unobvious relationships. Take as an example a scenario the author has encountered in an active production network; An Internet-facing DMZ is secured via the private VLAN function provided by switches made by a particular hardware vendor. This feature allows the designation of a port as "secure". This designation prevents communication from any other port also designated as "secure". At least it did in theory. In practice, it was found that "secured" hosts were still communicating in some instances. The problem was found in the fact that multiple switches were deployed in the environment to support redundancy and reduce the risk of outage should a single switch fail. The trunk between the switches could not be designated as private in either direction as the high-availability firewall pair serving as a gateway onto the DMZ subnet had a firewall attached one each to both switches, and hosts on one switch may need to traverse the connection between the switches to reach the firewall attached to the adjacent switch should that particular firewall be primary in the HA pair at that moment. Of course, once the packet passed through the switch trunk, it was no longer on a private port, and it was eligible to be forwarded to any port, "secure" or not. In essence, this can be considered a physical layer issue in that the policy control of a specific ports privilege does not extend past the boundaries of a single switch. A more robust control perhaps would account for the fact that multiple switches may require a uniform access policy across their shared environment.

Network Address Translation (NAT) is a special case in the seven-layer model, and is an excellent way to introduce how a clean theoretical model starts to get messy in actual implementation. On its surface, it is a straightforward function. NAT devices divide the network into two areas: those on the "outside" and those on the "inside". When packets enter a NAT-enabled device, rules are applied based on source and destination IP addresses of the packets as well as direction of traffic (heading "outside" vs. heading "inside"). Rules may dictate that individual given addresses appearing as either sources or destinations translate to different addresses on a one-to-one basis. This is often referred to as static NAT, and is often used to reference servers or other resources that must be consistently accessed by a consistent IP address. Another option is for NAT rules to define ranges or conditions (such as "all inside traffic") and apply a pool or single address to all traffic that matches the rule. This is referred to as dynamic NAT, and is usually used to translate traffic that does not require a consistent address or where details of individual hosts in the range are not relevant or should not be divulged.

Static NAT is a simple matter of finding data packets that match the rule, and rewriting the packet to the parameters of the NAT rule. This typically means replacing the layer three address with a translated one. Dynamic NAT is trickier in that multiple inside hosts may have the same outside address. The NAT device must have some way to identify traffic, and so must maintain a table of layer three source and destination addresses along with layer four information, such as UDP/TCP source and destination port numbers. The layer four information is critical for sorting out the condition where two or more inside hosts connect to the same destination address/port with the same ephemeral source port. This means on the outside area of the NAT translation where the two inside hosts appear as one source address, there may be two identical connections sent to a single destination. The server side would not be able to multiplex these connections properly, and the NAT device would not have a deterministic way to separate return traffic for one host versus another when ephemeral ports. Thus, with dynamic NAT, layer four ports must also be tracked and occasionally translated in order to avoid collisions.

In addition to the logistical issues at layers three and four, there is often a challenge presented to NAT at layer seven. Some applications may embed information pertaining to network issues in the application layer of the network conversation. This is usually used functionally to identify remote hosts or set up additional communications. The problem arises when such an application attempts connection through a path subject to NAT translation. If the NAT implementation simply rewrites the layer three and four information, there will now be a divergence between the layer three and four information in the packet which are critical to get correct for proper return communications, and the layer seven data which reflects the applications viewpoint of an untranslated inside address. The classic example of this behavior is the FTP protocol. In simple terms, FTP uses two channels of communication to conduct business - A control channel which is opened by the client to initiate a session and issue instructions such as requests to send files or list directories, and one or more data channels which are opened and closed at the point where files or other bulk data need to be passed across the network. The control channel will open the data channel by specifying an address and port the FTP server is to initiate the data connection to. If this transaction were to be attempted through a NAT translation, the control channel would likely specify an unreachable or otherwise invalid IP address for the FTP server to connect to, and the data transfer would likely never occur. Applications such as the example FTP, SNMP, IRC, SIP, and others, as well as quasi-applications such as IPSEC and DNS all have issues with NAT. These issues typically require intelligence to be written into the NAT implementation to inspect and translate the application-layer data to be in sync with the layer three and four translations occurring elsewhere.

The examination of NAT shows a network issue that extends over multiple model layers in both its problem set and the possible solutions examined. Information security problems and solutions often can be taken in this same multi-layer approach. In the layer description sections, many vulnerabilities and controls were covered that address single issues in a single layer. As was shown with NAT, the network often must be considered in its entirety to root out potential problems. Controls that impose policy at the lower layers may be ineffective against higher-layer problems due to the intrinsic transparency of the network layers. A firewall may operate at layers three and four when imposing a policy that says only connections to port 80 may go to a certain IP address, giving us a solid control for these layers, but if unpatched or poorly written software lurks at the other end of that connection, or if session controls depend upon a weak password, our packet-filter firewall will be helpless to impose further control on the security vulnerabilities that occur at higher levels. Stateful inspection engines and so called intrusion prevention devices can possibly mitigate some of the risk posed by these higher-layer threats, but only to a certain extent. Meantime, other risks dwell on the bottom-end of the model. A firewall is effectively useless if network or other types of connections physically bypass it. A common network design flaw is to traverse a firewall on administrative or utility networks, or to implement the different areas of trust divided by the firewall on the same physical switch using VLANs. Those VLANs may be subject to attack and circumvention. On full examination of the multi-level threats, the IT managers common assertion that "our network is secure, we have a firewall" is beginning to sound a little suspect. A thorough security review must always consider the whole situation, and the derived security solution must address those concerns.

Another area of interest for examination of multi-layer issues is the world of wireless networking. Removing the physical barrier of cabling and connection has created an environment that seriously tests some of the assumptions that traditional networking has been built upon. There was never a concern prior to wireless that some nerd with a laptop that cost more than his car would park said laptop and car outside your house and use your Internet connection as he pleased. With the advent of 802.11b, once the problem of getting a wireless network card to easily function at distance with a minimum of configuration for the user was solved, a new problem developed; how do we keep everyone else's wireless network cards from also working so easily? The radio signals from wireless devices easily travel, especially when boosted by specialized antennas, making layer one physical separation very impractical to enforce. The layer two identities of various stations on the wireless network could be easily learned and emulated, making any sort of pure layer two control marginally effective at best. In the wired world, measures such as MAC filters often depend in part upon the mapping of physical attributes such as physical port number to the layer two attributes used as the basis for the control. There are no such physical attributes to match to in the wireless realm. The 802.11 basic standards have some controls for associating such as a Service Set Identifier (SSID), but ease of configuration concern has mostly removed this as a barrier. Concern for these security issues prompted the inclusion of encryption technology for authorization and privacy at layer two, but numerous problems have been found in the encryption technology chosen for the standard and as a result there remains no solid layer two security control. Even if there were, wireless manufacturers want to make their customers happy, and the average customer would rather a wireless device work right out of the box than be secure. Thus, almost all wireless devices ship with the modest protection they have disabled. Thus, wireless users seeking security have been forced to look elsewhere for their security solutions. Wireless networks are defined as untrusted and connected behind firewalls, and solutions such as layer three IPSEC VPNs or layer six/seven application encryption such as SSL/TLS are used to provide more secure authentication and privacy to valid wireless user sessions.

Chapter 4

Significance of Authentication —Future Internet Architecture

4.1   Introduction

The previous chapter provided a brief overview of the importance of security establishment, objectives, requirements, security mechanisms required for Future Internet architecture. The following chapter explains the significance of authentication along with the authentication mechanisms required for the architectures. The main goal of this chapter is to discuss an authentication mechanism for Future Internet architectures, a case study of an architecture is considered to compare the performance analysis with TCP/IP in the distributed environment.

4.2   What is Authentication?

Authentication is a process of verifying the identity of someone or something who it states to be. The best example of it can be the online applications like banking, shopping, etc. The common form is using the passwords for authentication. Once the identity is claimed, authorization states what a user can do and can see in the application and accounting keeps track of all the actions done by the user. This is like a chain process where if one principle fails automatically the others fall apart. This states the importance of authentication [35] [132].

4.3 Challenges in Secure Authentication

When a high level of secure authentication is provided in the form of tokens, phrases, etc, instead of passwords, it will lower the usability of the users. The increase of users/entities to use Internet raised the development of new architectures and simultaneously raised threats which require a secure authentication mechanism that suites the Future Internet.

4.4 Authentication Protocols

An authentication protocol is a defined sequence of messages between a claimant and a verifier that enables the verifier to verify that the claimant has control of a valid token to establish his or her identity. An exchange of messages between a claimant and a verifier that results in the authentication (or authentication failure) of the claimant is a protocol run.

4.4.1 Authentication Threats

Threats involve attacks against the authentication protocols itself, and the attacks that reveal tokens or any sensitive information. These tokens can be used to identify the subscriber are worse than the compromising on some sensitive information.

4.4.1.1 Protocol Threats

The trustworthy parties like CSPs, Certification Authorities (CA's), verifiers are also vulnerable and can be malicious to an attack. To avoid these attacks even the trustworthy parties should not expose to long-term authentication secrets. It is very important to protect the data as well as to protect the identity on the Internet itself, or else it leads to identity spoofing. An attacker can impersonate and access the confidential data. IP addresses are being used to identify the users by the security systems which are being fooled by the attackers. The threats even include eavesdroppers observing the protocol and how it runs and analyze it later. After analysis, the attacker intercept between CSP and the verifier, rather than the user and the verifier. Once the attacker obtains the token, the attacker claims to be an original user and proceeds with the communication. The attackers may pose as the subscribers to the verifier to test the tokens which are guessed by the attacker or can be used to obtain the information of a specific subscriber. The attackers can act as verifier to a genuine user and obtain the tokens that can be used to impersonate. Attackers can hijack a session which is already authenticated, pose as a user to the third party and learn about the information which is sensitive or send an invalid information. The other attacks that are possible are replay attacks, password guessing attacks, impersonation attacks, man in middle attack, etc,. Although we use the TLS protocol to avoid such attacks the results are not satisfactory. Other threats include the malicious code that is compromised to obtain the authentication tokens, intrusion attacks that can obtain the tokens by penetrating the system, tokens lost by social engineering or by shoulder-surfing, intentional repudiation by the users who compromise on their own tokens.

In order to obtain the user's token of authentication, a malicious code is introduced into the user's system. The code can be introduced into the system by any means of the threats included above. There are measures that can be considered and to avoid the code to enter into the system. It is a good practice to mitigate the threats using hardware tokens like a secret token from a hardware token. Shared keys are to be protected by CSPs and CSPs will not issue the long-term keys to users. The verifiers will be given a challenge response information one time independently, if the response is a password then the mechanisms applied are vulnerable to threats. Some insider threats can be avoided using firewalls, intrusion detection, etc,. Hardware tokens and cryptographic methods provide the keys and password protection against some of the attacks. Public key cryptosystems are less vulnerable to the attacks, encryption of the long-term shared secret keys reduces the risk of attacks.

4.4.1.2 Encryption Technique Problems

The information is made unreadable by using these techniques. So the third parties, or the server administrators or any other mechanism is not required to access the plaintext but still the problems exists. In **symmetric encryption**, we use a single key for both encryption and decryption. It is quite fast but has an inherent weakness of sharing the keys between the communication parties. This requires a high level of trust, if an attacker gains the key for that transaction he can decrypt all the messages for that particular transaction. The trust problem is being solved by **asymmetric methods** where it uses two keys, public key for encryption and private key for decryption. The public key is freely available and private key is with the owner. These two keys have a mathematical relationship, calculation of a private key is impossible even though we know the public key. To generate a digital signature, we can use private keys, later can be verified by public key. This method take a long processing time compared to symmetric algorithm. In order to overcome the problem, a combination of symmetric and asymmetric method can be used where symmetric for encryption of message and asymmetric for the exchange of symmetric keys [17] [211].

4.4.1.3 Resistance to Threats

☞ Eavesdropping resistance protocol does not allow the attacker to perform any offline attacks when the authentication protocol runs between the user and the verifier. This makes the attacker learn about the password, secret key or the private key is impossible.

☞ Password guessing resistance will disable the attacker to guess the passwords with many authentication attempts without any prior knowledge. This protocol makes the targeted password guessing impractical by using the high entropy passwords and limiting the number of unsuccessful attempts. To resist this attack, the verifier may control the actions with the help of network security controls.

☞ Replay resistance is possible if the attacker is not successful although the message in the communication is recorded and replayed

☞ Hijacking resistance is possible if the adversary is unable to takeover a session after a successful authentication. If the per session secret is generated for the authentication process between the verifier and the user, then the resistance for the hijacking attack is possible.

☞ Impersonation resistance is possible if the impersonator is unable to learn about the tokens when acting as the verifier. Sometimes, the secure protocols are bypassed by the attackers which is due to the usage of another protocol or overriding of the controls.

☞ Man-in-the-middle resistance is possible when both the parties are authenticated without allowing a third party to detect the information within the channel. Sometimes the attacker will be able to attain the information by bypassing the controls of security.

4.4.2 *Authentication Mechanisms*

Authentication was acceptably described in the literature as a reliable means of identity verification [35] [116] [127] [146]. There are various ranges of mechanisms available from simple to complex. The security provided varies upon the technique and how it has been deployed. The common form of it is simply using a password along with a username. But this also leads to various threats. The popular authentication one involves knowledge that the user knows like password, possession the user has like smartcard or the token and the attribute that the user itself is like biometrics. Based on these three factors, i.e., knowledge, possession and the attributes, authentication schemes are divided into two and they are Single factor and the multi factor authentication. *Single factor* is based on one factor such as something the user knows like password etc.. *Multifactor* is based on more than one factor like certificates, biometrics, one time passwords, tokens, etc. This multifactor authentication provides various levels of security which imposes some level of difficulty to the user. The best example we can take for this is the ATM card, something which we have and something we knows to access it. This provides the user a simple way to verify that they are connected to the intended site. The usage of digital certificates in the encrypted communications is treated as strong authentication like Secure Socket Layer (SSL), use of digital images is another technique.

4.4.2.1 *Shared Secrets (Passwords)*

The information shared by both users and the authenticating authority using passwords are the primary means of authentication and the weakest means of authentication. The tools are available to protect passwords, these efforts are of no use as the hackers try to hack, crack, trap and find the secure passwords. In general, the passwords are very easy to reveal by the attackers as the users try to choose an easy password to remember like the date of birth, name, etc. The Infosecurity Europe in 2004 revealed that the users volunteered their passwords without any bribe. Some attacks directly attack the core operating systems, in order to protect them, a layer identity strategy can be applied.

4.4.2.2   One Time Passwords (OTP)

These change on every usage. These are generated randomly and kept by the user and the system. These can be generated on demand by means like *scratch cards* which contain randomly generated numbers or the letters arranged in a row and column and are cheap. If it is misplaced or lost, the replacement is easy and less cost. It is used in Multifactor authentication where first username and password is entered, then the system asks to enter the characters on the card as the second authentication. The difficulty with this method is if the card is compromised, it can be used for future access by others. The acceptance of this method depends on the clients. *Time-based* uses RSA SecureID3 which is another type of password in which the password changes every minute. The algorithm is known to the system and the user's authentication device only. This is a small card or a liquid crystal display. It is very easy to use and the password is created based on the current time. The token once expired, the internal clock creates a new password within the time range using key and the current time as input. The basic challenge with this is the time synchronization. The server has to cope with the internal clock computing many passwords within the couple of seconds. This allows multiple passwords to be accepted as correct. Another difficulty is the key which is preinitialized by the manufacturer. For this, the manufacturer has to save the copy of passwords and these passwords are valid for 24 to 60 months and after they are expired, it has to be replaced. This increases the cost as the licenses to get these passwords in the form of tokens are expensive. *Challenge Response Based* is used when the system generates random challenges once the user logins. The token is unlocked when a user login with its password, i.e., PIN, starts the task. This calculates the response and displays the response. The user sends this response as a challenge to the system. It is similar to a time-based system, as the time is replaced by the challenge. A server generated challenge is used instead of time. This is treated as a bit more secure compared to time based system as the challenge is maintained by a third party and the password for unlocking a token. *Out of band Transmission* uses a different channel from the user who is trying to initiate a communication. This provides an additional security, as the attacker has to intercept the two channels. This is basically used for second authentication like OTP and it can be an email or a call or fax. Once the server receives the request, a one-time password is sent to the mobile to confirm the transaction.

4.4.2.3   Soft Tokens or Certificates

Soft tokens or the certificates are sent to mobile or a laptop. This can be used as additional authentication along with what the user has. These are less expensive and are flexible rather than the hardware solutions. These are the most used SSL certificates. This not only authenticates the client but also authenticates the web server.

This authenticates during the handshake, i.e., at the transport layer using these certificates. The mutual authentication provided by this protects from phishing attacks along with various similar attacks. These certificates are used to authenticate based on what the users have like a certificate and a private key and what the users know like the phrase of the private key. Whenever the client browses to the server it requests a pass phrase of the certificate. This provides a strong two factor authentication, convenient to merge the certificates onto the device, and support a wide range of platforms. Disadvantage of this is used only on the host where the software resides and is vulnerable to malware, keylogger as well as visual spoofing attacks.

4.4.2.4 Hardware Tokens

These are physical devices that the user has and it is a part of multifactor authentication. Some of the tokens are USB token and smart card. These store the digital certificates which are used in Public Key Infrastructure (PKI) to perform cryptographic operations. The USB tokens are directly plugged into USB computer port and require no installation of any hardware. Once the token is recognized, it asks the users to enter the password to gain access to the system. The password acts as second authentication. Smart card contains a microprocessor which enables it to process the data and store the same and the size is of a credit card. The recognition of the smart card by the system is the first authentication and prompting for password is the second level to complete the process of authentication. These are hard to create duplicates and tamper, they are relatively secure for storing the data which is sensitive. These are easy to carry and easy to use. The difficulty that we face with these are the installation of the hardware reader and the drivers associated with it. Smart cards are divided based on the card components, interface and the OS used. The cards can be a memory card or the chip cards which are of less cost. The card can be accessed after a code is provided. The card becomes expensive when they contain CPU, RAM which carries various instructions along with EEPROM and ROM. These are ideal for credit and financial cards as they are capable of executing the instruction of encryption and decryption. The protocols such as SSL/TLS can be used to provide strong authentication [132].

4.4.2.5 Lightweight Directory Access Protocol (LDAP) Authentication

As the customers access, the enterprise applications have increased the need to know about the user from the security point of view. The strength of the authentication derives the user access for an application along with what kind of authorization rights have been issued to that particular user. As the frequency has increased for authenticating the users, the need for LADP has increased as it performs a quick read for identifying a user than a traditional databases. These are of low cost and some of them are available for free. These also provide virtual LADP's which allows a fast link between multiple databases and directories. These directories perform rapid LADP authentication against any digitized authentication. It enables quick interaction between the enterprises and allows the exchange of information with universal protocol.

In order to improve the performance and network load, the directories are partitioned and placed near the user.

4.4.2.6 Biometric Authentication

Nowadays, the usage of biometrics is in fashion by many industries. Some of the applications are the U.S. government for personal identification in their visas, passports, etc., and some others for identifying and accessing the banking machines, door access, etc. Authentication is a process of determining a user who they claim to be whereas biometric authentication is a process of recognizing the person using a digitized biological piece of the human. Some of the famous biological pieces which are used for recognition are voice recognition, fingerprints, iris scan, skin texture, etc.. Biometrics along with some mechanisms can play a major role in verifying the identity.

4.4.2.7 Public Key Infrastructure (PKI)

This contains hardware, software, policies and procedures which are required to manage, store and generate keys and cryptographic key distribution and the certificates. The services are implemented by using the encryption concepts using asymmetric algorithms. This system is used to identity authentication using a third party called as a Certificate Authority (CA) who performs attestation along with public and private keys of cryptography [124]. CA can authenticate the user using digital certificates, email or sometimes by name and background check. If the user trusts CA certificate, they can trust all the certificates issued by the CA. The trustworthiness depends on the server attestation instead of certificate attestation. For attestation, the upper level CA's charge the lower level CA's like a hierarchical tree. The authority of CA's is distributed to share the task of authentication within the network. Sometimes the CA gains the reputation in the network by the trust and the recommendation. The authors proposed a concept of local and cross authentication protocol for P2P network for the purpose of identity-based public key cryptography (ID-PKC). In this scheme a public key can be any string like IP address, etc., which removes the concept of a public key certificate. In ID-PKC, needs a third party to generate aprivate key. Therefore, ID-PKC can be used only for small networks. The other technique which can be used is one way cumulative function to authenticate the P2P nodes in a network. They allow the users to authenticate with each other directly. In the traditional PKI system, authentication is performed using Identity Authentication Code Distribution Center (IAC) for unique identification code. But if IAC is under attack, single point failure occurs. Certificate management is a main issue due to the inherent property of PKI and ID-PKC [54]. So it is necessary to implement identity authentication based on PKI in the peer to peer network. The usage of certificates provides confidentiality, integrity of the message and authentication without exchanging the secrets in advance [216].

Encryption Techniques: The protocols which exist in the current Internet architecture are based on conventional and public key encryptions. In **conventional**

techniques a secret key is shared between both parties like SHA, HMACs, DES, AES, MD5 [200], etc. The **public key based techniques** involve sharing of two keys where the public key is shared in a network and private key is for decryption of the message. This involves a third-party interference for the exchange of the keys. Some public key based protocols like Diffie Hellman key exchange algorithm [166], Needham and Schroeder authentication protocols, Kerberos [114], RSA [108] and so on. These protocols were developed from many years for solving different problems that were raised at the application level authentication and digital signature [2] [191]. Most of the distributed systems rely on authentication for the prevention of some basic attacks like masquerade attack, spoofing attacks, brute force and so on. As the development of the attack is out of control, research organizations are growing their attention toward's the direction of development of security mechanisms to deal with the attacks of the present day world and the attacks that may arise in the future of the Internet [83]. There are different types of protocols available in current Internet architecture that can be used in an effective manner because of their long run in current Internet architecture. Authentication of the principals is found as an important issue in SONATE for the performance of secure communication in the distributed environment. Not only in SONATE, RBA, AKARI, etc., uses Authentication for secure communication over the network. Many protocols were developed and many are in progress in the field of flexible network architecture.

Key Management: The management of keys raises the main issue as the attacker targets the management level rather than the algorithm itself. Once the key is generated and transferred in the network it must remain secret until the communication between the two parties is over. This deals with generation of keys, storage of keys, and the distribution of the keys between the parties. The user will obtain the keys securely based on the security need and the efficiency of the communication. If the private key is lost, they must intimate others not to use those keys or not to accept the message signed with the lost keys. Private keys must be kept secret, but it must be made accessible by the legitimate users. Keys are to be made valid for a limited period, the date can be extended and publicize it in an authenticated channel.

4.4.2.8   CASCADED Authentication

Cascaded authentication is the solution to a set of problems that have arisen from confederations of autonomous systems. The problems occur when disparate computer systems are being called upon to cooperate in the absence of complete trust of each other. Futhermore, the systems are utilized in a cascaded fashion, where one invokes a second, which invokes a third, and so on, until the final service is invoked.

4.5   Future Internet —Authentication Objectives

The objective of the authentication service is to provide the functionality of request and validate the information about an authenticating user against a specific authentication mechanism and create a session for validating the application participating, upon a successful authentication. The main focus of this is to enable the modules of authentication plugins for different purposes after successful validation of the entitie's credentials. The services of the authentication can be accessed by the users once they get authenticated using an authentication mechanism. After authentication, the user is allowed to access the services based on the requested credentials. The authentication services provided by Future Internet should perform the following:

☞   Identify the requestor's requirements.

☞   Generate dynamic agent connection as per the required authentication module.

☞   Maintenance of state information.

☞   Activation of sessions after successful authentication.

☞   Population of all user-authenticated properties into valid session.

☞   Support pluggable authentication modules.

☞   Create session identifiers.

☞   Generate different time-dependent alerts and session expiration.

☞   Provide remote authentication between users and agents present in the network.

4.5.1   *Authentication Mechanism in SONATE —Case Study*

Authentication is the process of identifying the principals of the network associated with accessing the applications. This serves as proof of identification that the principals/entities are the same as they claim to be. Once the principals are authenticated, they are believed to be communicated among themselves but not with the malicious agents of the network. Authentication can be used for different purposes depending on the application types. The main goal of authentication is to allow a principal to communicate with, to and fro fetching the services of the network which assures the following:

1. The verification of the identity of the principal from where the service was requested or sent, i.e., user and broker authentication (principals authentication).

2. The service was not modified in transit over the network, i.e., service authentication.

In a distributed network, the principals who meet the above criteria need not be constrained but ironically many attacks are possible through the principals. This is one of the reason, to make the principals get authenticated and those who got authenticated does not mean access to all types of services or request any type of service from other principals of the network.

1. Principal authentication: In this, it must prove that the principal of the service sent is the one who is expected to be. when a request for a service is sent then the broker requests for a selection process to know its availability in its repository. If it is not available, then a request is sent to another broker via routers of the network. The routers will accept the packets based on the authentication list available with it. It may accept the packet or simply reject and forward to the next router (Figure 4.1). And with this, avoidance of the masquerade attack is possible.

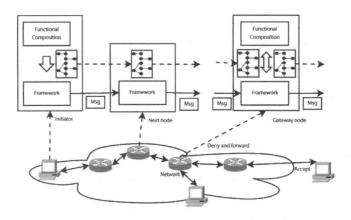

Figure 4.1: Router involvement for packet accept/deny.

2. Service authentication: The second issue is the tranmission of the information to the intented principal of the network which passes through several routers where there is a possibility of a snooping attack, sniffing attack, man in the middle attack, etc. When a service is transferred, it may get hacked by the hacker. Attacker may modify the data then sent to intended system. For solving this type of situations only authentication of the principals is not enough. To avoid such modification on the data, the message must be encrypted. As without encryption the transmission of data lacks privacy in the network. Encryption of services is not compulsorily required for only authentication purposes. All that is required is some type of confidence that the information passed over the network is correct and not modified in the transit. This can be achieved by using various algorithms such as message digest algorithm without encrypt-

ing the service. Some confidential services such as the bank transactions when performed, the security provided by authentication is not sufficient. Sometimes data/service authentication does not allow modification of information but allows an attacker to read the information that was transmitted over the network; to avoid this, service must be authenticated.

The authentication mechanism used for the purpose of secure communication in SONATE is based on PKI which provides a foundation for the security services like confidentiality, nonrepudiation, integrity and authentication. Its primary function is to allow the distribution of the keys, maintain the certificates with security. It consists of the security policies, security services and the protocols which support the use of public key cryptography for the management of the keys and the certificates. The certificates are issued by the CA via broker in SONATE.

In order to provide security services to the entities in SONATE *authentication* is used as an initial process to identify it using its secret credentials. The credentials include sourceID, certificates, signature, public key for verification. The verification is performed using the CA via a broker of the system. With this, the information security and service integrity is maintained using encryption and service authentication. Therefore, authentication is directly related to architectural security in terms of entities, information and integrity of the data.

4.5.2   SONATE —Public Key Infrastructure (PKI)

A PKI- based architecture [59] is an effective solution to cope with the emerging threats. It allows

- Entities authentication in more secure fashion

- Encrytion of sensitive information

- Documents are electronically signed

It is usually defined as a set of policies, practices and technologies involved in several processes like management, storage, reveocation of public key certificates when asymmetric key is used. The aim is to develop "Chain of Trust" for securing the data and authenticating the entities. The PKI concept has been modified in many ways for the management of public keys, certificates of various entities of the network. A single system level authentication process is shown in (Figure 4.2). At the network level, where many systems exist, the brokers contact with the AS to get authenticated by themselves and allow users to get authenticated via brokers of the system. For the development of secure architecture, authentication plays a vital role in the verification of the identification of the entities. It is important to verify the request sent from an authenticated user but not from a hacker. The identification and verification process along with the management of the keys is explained in the following sections.

The feasibility of a PKI is discussed which is adopted for the upcoming emerging architectures. A herierachical process was followed for the certification of the entities

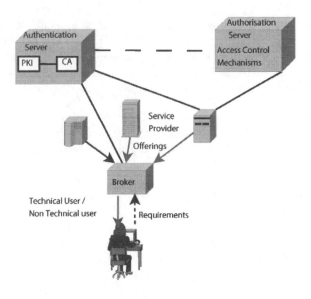

Figure 4.2: System level Authentication.

and key management was also discussed. Online Certificate Status Protocol (OCSP) [142] and Certificate Revocation Lists (CRL's) [59] were used for the decrease of network and computational overheads.

4.5.2.1 PKI Cryptographic Resources

The components which are used for smooth and secure communication are as follows:

- Public and private keys: Each and every entity of the system holds two keys: one for encryption and the other for decryption. The private key is kept secret whereas the public key is made available publicly. These are the one-way functions, which are difficult to decrypt if the message is encrypted with one of the keys. RSA [168] is used as it is a well-known asymmetric algorithm based on the keys.

- Digital certificates: X.509 certificates are used as it is widely used for Internet applications [59]. These certificates are the central elements for the asymmetric key pair technique. The certificates are used for binding the entities with a public key in an authentic way. The certificate delivers the information like Source_ID, certificate number which is unique, the algorithm used for the generation of the signature, public key and the validation period. Other fields like type and purpose of the certificate can be included.

- Hashing: Hash function is used as it is one-way, collision free and produces fixed output. SHA-1 [48] is used for the computation of the 160-bit length hashes. In the PKI of SONATE, hashes are used to produce the digital signature. A hybrid model which is a combination of MAC and CBC-MAC was used as it is a double hashing technique and there is no need to add any type of paddings.

■ Digital signature: It is used for certifying the entities signature and integrity of the data. For the verification of the digital signature, the first condition is to validate the signer's digital certificate which is not revoked or expired. To obtain the hash value of the user, the broker decrypts the signature using the public key of the user. The broker computes the hash data and compares the two obtained hashes. If both are the same, then it is assumed that the integrity of data is maintained.

4.5.2.2   Components of PKI

The components that are required in PKI with respect to SONATE architecture are as follows:

■ Certificate Authority (CA): The core component that can issue the public key certificates is CA. These are responsible CRL's to the issuer. It manages, stores, generates, revocate and the certificates whenever required. It functions as a third party that provides key management services. It certifies the identity of the end entities, accomplished by providing sufficient proof of the entities. X.509 public key certificates [59] are used for the exchange certificates between the entities and the CA. The functions of CA are to generate the certificates, and revoke the certificates.

■ Broker: This verifies the user's identity and forwards the request to CA for the issue of digital certificate, forwards the user request to the provider for the fulfillment of the services.

■ End Entities: A user or the device is used to denote as entity that requires a digital certificate. In the context of SONATE, the principals/entities of the architecture are the Consumer/user, Broker and the Provider which are required to get authenticated before accessing the services.

■ Repository: It is a storage device for the storage of the certificates and CRL's for easy retrieval whenever required.

4.5.3   Architecture for the Identity Management of the Entities

The identity of the entities is important for the exchange of the services over the network and for the protection of the services from the attackers. The users can only interact with the service brokers for requesting the services by sending the application/service request. Identification of the entities can be performed by using the IP address as sourceID or the userID. In both cases, the entity's have to get authenticated with the authentication server via the broker of the system.

4.5.3.1 Service Consumer Identity

Each entity involved in a transaction must be authenticated as the first step by using its ID. If the entity is already authenticated and requesting a service then the request is fulfilled by forwarding the request to the service provider after the verification of the identity of the entity (Figure 4.3). At present IP address, MAC address is considered a UniqueID for the identification of the user which is stored in Valid-IP table of the system.

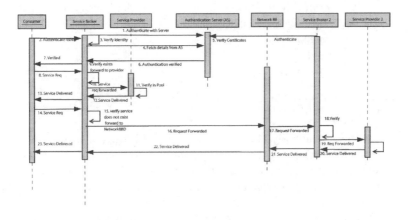

Figure 4.3: Sequence Diagram of Authentication Mechanism in SONATE.

Valid-IP Table

For maintaining the validity of packets along with its entity identity it is required to store the valid hop count and MAC address and the IP address of the system. The source IP address is obtained from the packet and if it is valid it considers the packet or else drops the packet. Frequency count has been stored along with Hop count, MAC address, IP address for future use (for more details please refer to Chapter 6). The mapping of the IP address to hop count and MAC address is required when a packet is captured and its IP address and hop count are compared with the stored hop count against the corresponding IP address. Since hop count is not constant and may vary as every packet is free to follow any existing path to reach the destination, compulsory measures are to be considered for updating the hop count value. The hop count value is obtained using the IP address and TTL field value from the packet and subtracting the TTL value from the initial value of TTL which can be obtained by the if-else ladder (Algorithm 4.1). The most modern OS use only selected initial TTL values and they are 30, 32, 60, 64, 128 and 255 [205]. This valid IP table is also used to store a frequency count for updating the hop count information.

Algorithm 4.1
If ladder

1. *If(ttl <=32)*

2. *Hop=32 - ttl;*

3. *If(ttl <= 64 && ttl >32)*

4. *Hop=64 ttl;*

5. *If(ttl<= 128 && ttl >64)*

6. *Hop=128-ttl;*

4.5.3.2   Service Broker's Identity

The broker communicates with the consumers/users at the front end to accept the service request and the provider at the backend to fetch the services. The broker has to fetch the services from other brokers of the network if the service is not available within the registered provider of the system. The brokers are identified with the broker's ID which is authenticated within the network.

4.5.3.3   Service Provider's Identity

For the identity of the service provider's of the system, the service providers get registered with the brokers of the network along with the list of services they provide before offering the services to the user via a broker.

4.5.4   SONATE: Generation of the Keys

The major issues for the transaction of the services over the network of SONATE are i) how can the entities verify each others identity, ii) exchange of encrypted services, iii) creation and verification of the signatures. PKI is a well-established approach for addressing these issues [59]. Technically, PKI is referred to as a technique to enable the public key encryption or digital signature over the distributed networks. The function of PKI is to distribute the keys to those who want to encrypt the services. This process involves the issue of digital certificates by the CA to the users via brokers and the brokers who get registered with that CA. For the issuance of the certificates to the entities, it requests authentication, usually by the broker of the system. It can extend its functions to renewal of the certificates for the entities of the architecture of SONATE. The main functions of PKI are

➢ To generate the key pairs (public and private keys)

➢ To store the certificates in the authentication server and

➢ Generation and verification of the signatures that are produced digitally.

4.5.4.1   PKI Consumer Functionalities

The user sends a request for the requirements of an application along with its sourceID, i.e., UserID or IP address of the system, if already registered with the broker of the system. If the user is not registered then the functionalities to get registered with the provider for accessing the services are as follows:

1. User sends a request to get authenticated by sending a request of invoking *Generate_Key pair( )* function along with its sourceID for the generation of public and private key pair.

2. Whenever a user sends a request that requires a digital signature, the user invokes digital signing function which helps in creating a hash of the message and generates the digital signature.

3. Verification of the certificate signature can be performed using the public key of the sender.

4.5.4.2   Key Establishment Process

The user/broker generates its private key and sends it to the broker in the encrypted format using the system's public key. Hashing technique is used for the transmission of the keys over the network. For the computation of the certificate services, MD5 or MAC services are utilized. The private key is established with the help of the authentication server's authority and the public key which consists of two session keys one for each direction. Once the session is established, all the traffic over the network is encrypted over both directions. The private key can be used for multiple sessions for fetching the services, ultimately reducing the overhead of the private key operations. For the development of the session keys, MD5 can be used. The certificate of the user can be stored within the authentication server and can be used for future purposes.

4.5.5   Certificate Management Service —SONATE

The purpose of use of the PKI in SONATE is for the management of the certificates. The functions provided by the Certification Authority (CA), PKI via authentication server are certificate request, certificate revocation and the certificate verification service.

4.5.5.1   SONATE –Certificate Request Process

The functions of the certificate request are as follows (Figure 4.4):

1. The service consumers/users use PKI to generate the asymmetric key pair and send *Certificate_Request* message to the communication broker of the system. The broker forwards it to the authentication server. The message contains information like the sourceID and it is signed with the user's private key as attachment.

2. The CA of the authentication server verifies the entities digital signature with the public key. If it is successful, a randomly generated *authentication code* is sent to the broker as specified in the *Certificate_Request*. This code is used to identify the certificate request.

3. When the broker receives the message from PKI via AS, it stores the details in its repository and forwards the authentication code to the user of the system. The user sends its code along with its sourceID to the broker as in step 1. The broker verifies the user with the received code from the authentication server(AS). If it is correct then it sends a verification signed by the broker's private key to PKI of AS.

4. CA verifies the user's signature which is received via the broker and checks the random codes for the identification of the specific certificate request. If the verification is successful, it invokes a *Certificate_Request*. The service request contains PKCS#10 [149] certificate message request.

5. The CA issues the certificate based on the identity of the user by sending a response message PKCS#7 [110] to the broker as service response which is forwarded to the user. This message contains X.509 certificate details signed by the service provider of the CA of the authentication server.

6. The CA of the PKI verifies the user's signature with users certificate which was loaded during the initialization phase. If the signatures are same then the CA of PKI stores the X.509 certificate along with the public key, permissions of the services to be accessed. The same is also stored with the broker of the systems for the verification of the user for the next time. The key is stored with the service provider for the issue of services in an encrypted form to the user via a broker.

4.5.5.2   SONATE –Certificate Revocation Process

The revocation process is useful when the key is lost or compromised. There exists two approaches for the revocation and verification of the certificates namely: CRL which provides a list of revoked certificates that are received less frequently and OCSP which provides a real time revocation process about the certificates for the issuing authority (Figure 4.5). OCSP method has been adopted in this architecture where the broker acts as a responder and the process is as follows:

1. User sends a *Revocation_Certificate_Request* which includes the sourceID and the reason for the revocation to the broker.

2. The Service Broker sends the user's certificate request to the CA after verifying its identity in its repository. Once the verification is successful at the broker, it forwards it to the CA by creating a *Revocation_Certificate* message signed by its private key.

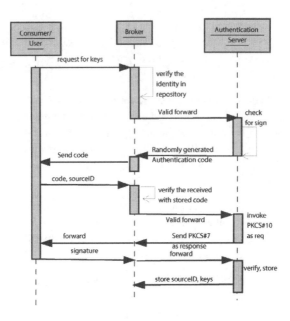

Figure 4.4: Certificate request process

3. CA verifies the broker signature. If user is valid, then the broker checks for the request to get fulfilled by revoking the certificate. It sends the *Revocation _Response* to the requested broker which is forwarded to the user.

4. Once the broker receives the authority signature, it verifies the signature and removes the certificates that were revocated from its list. Then the broker sends a response to the user as *Revocation_Certificate_Response* signed by the brokers private key as acknowledgement.

4.5.5.3 SONATE –Certificate Verification Process

Once the user gets the certificate by the above process (refer request process) the user can use it for authentication before fetching the services from the provider of the system/other broker of the network via a broker. OCSP process is used for checking the status of the certificates. The authentication protocol provides a strong authentication as specified in FIPS 196. Mutual authentication is performed between the brokers and the providers of the network based on the digital signature and exchange of certificates and one way authentication with the exchange of the keys and signing of the certificates is performed between service user and service broker of the system (Figure 4.6). The process is as follows:

1. The service consumer/user sends a service request message to the broker. The

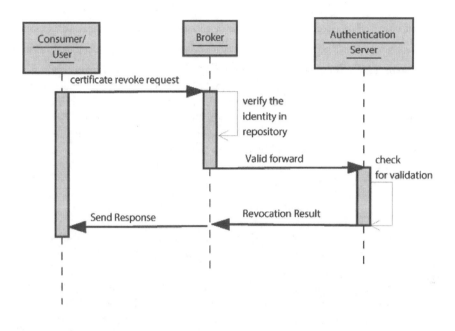

Figure 4.5: Certificate revocation process.

message contains the sessionID, sourceID and an indicator which identify the message as an authenticated request.

2. The service broker verifies in its repository and decides to terminate or initiate the session of the authentication process. If it decides to authenticate the user, the broker generates a random number challenge $R_{[b]}$ and sends it with a sessionID to the user of the system.

3. The consumer/user generates a random number challenge, $R_{[user]}$ and sends it to the broker with the inclusion of the following data: $R_{[b]}$, sessionID, sourceID and $S_{[user]}(R_{[user]}, R_{[b]})$ where S is a service request and $S_{[x]}(M)$ describes the signed message with "X's" private key.

4. After receiving the service message, the broker verifies the entity's certificate by sending the *verification_Certificate_Request* which contains the users X.509 certificate to the AS. The CA of AS searches for the certificate based on X.509 and verifies the status using OCSP protocol. The CA sends an OCSP based response after verification to the broker. CA of the PKI verifies the broker's signature using the public key of the broker which was pre-loaded at the initialisation phase. The verification result is returned to the broker in a signed format as *Verification_ Certificate_Response* along with the public key. CA of AS verifies the public key of the broker using the public key which is loaded at initial phase. It verifies $R_{[b]}$, as it was retained in step 2. If all verification is successful, it means the broker has authenticated the user successfully or else

a failure notification is sent to the user. Finally, the broker returns a message along with the authentication result and it is $R_{[b]}, R_{[user]}$, and $S_{[user]}(R_{[b]}, R_{[user]})$.

5. The broker verifies the provider who gets registered with the broker of the system for offering the services using step 4 of the process. The user verifies the broker by sending the request along with the public key. If all the verifications are successful, it means the user is authenticated and using steps 3 and 4 the brokers of the network get authenticated with each other for the exchange of keys along with certificates.The brokers of the network of the proposed architecture of SONATE are mutually authenticated using the concept of hierarchical certification process with the integrated PKI concept.

6. After a successful authentication process between the entities of the architecture they agree on and the keys are established for the encryption of the messages. The entities generate a message that consists of a session key and the algorithm ID (RSA-1, MD5-2 etc.) sign and encrypt with the entities public key and sends it to the broker of the system. After receiving this message, the entity decrypts it with its private key and verifies the signature using the public key of the sent entity. Once the verification and establishment of the session are done, the provider entities encrypt all the services using the algorithm and the key specified and forward it to the broker of the system, and these are forwarded to the users by the brokers of the system.

4.5.6   Secure Communication Model for SONATE

Service Oriented Network Architecture (SONATE), the user will request for any services. For this particular service broker or agent will generate workflow by using service selection and composition process. The specific service requires the integration of BBs according to the sequence of BBs generated by workflow. In selecting any services which are available in the form of BBs, the broker or agent will choose the best possible services in the form of BBs. Now the next step is searching for BBs will perform in the local repository. If BBs are not available on the local system, then the request will be sent to another remote system for particular BBs. After getting the requested BBs the local repository will be updated (Figure 4.7). For the successful completion of the request, the broker first checks the consumer/user's authentication using the above- mentioned process.

4.5.7   Functional Overview

The operation of the service broker communication works in accordance with the workflow of the information generated by the service consumers. A user requests a service by sending a required information *(Msg1)* (Figure 4.7). The service broker analyzes the request after checking its authentication and makes a list of BBs required for fulfilling the workflow. Then it checks for local availability. An XML list

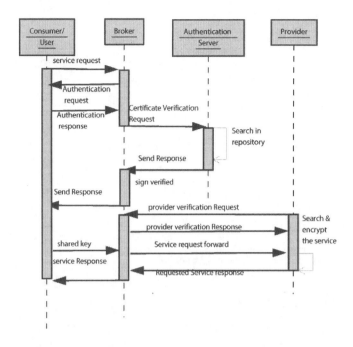

Figure 4.6: Certificate verification process.

of nonexisting BB's on the local system is sent to *Application BB (Msg2)*. The *Application BB* frames the file name and the file data in bytes, corresponding to a type in *MessageList object (Msg3) along with the key and its ID*. *Network BB* receives the message *(Msg3)* and sends it to the other systems.The other system receives the message *(Msg3)* from *Network BB* and transfers to the *Application BB*. The *Application BB* extracts data and frames it to *MessageList* object *(Msg4)*. This message is sent to service broker for to check its availability on that system. If the requested service is not available then the same message is passed to the next node and this process continues until the request is successfully identified. After successfully locating the availability, the system will send the list of services that it can serve to the Service Consumer system via the intermediate nodes from where it was queried. The response will be in XML format *(Msg5)*. The *Application BB* prepares the *MessageList* object and sends a message in encrypted form *(Msg6)* to *Network BB* via authentication BB. This message is sent to the succeeding node. The received message is sent to *Application BB* in this way all the required messages are collected in encrypted form and checked for the possibility of completion of the user's request. If it fulfills then that service is executed successfully. The request is fulfilled when the broker proves its identity or else the request is dropped by sending a negative acknowledgement.

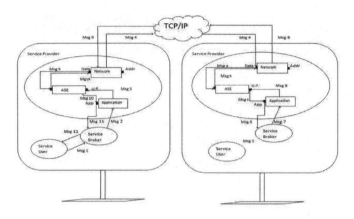

Figure 4.7: Message Communication Process.

4.5.7.1   SONATE Packet Format

For the enhancement of Flexible Network architecture different level of phases are identified and to make these phases compatible with each other the packet formats required to be modified (Please refer to Chapter 2 for more details). To provide compatibility with existing networks as well as upcoming technological changes, different phases are identified. Three different types of header formats are identified for this purpose (Figure 4.8). In the initial phase of research work TCP/IP protocol is used for networking to establish a communication link, and in the rest of the phases TLV (Type, Length and Value) or a combination of TLV format is used in accordance with the Phase need.

Type 1:   It is the presently existing Internet packet format used in network communication.

Type 2:   This type of packet format is used to provide compatibility between application level and network level. It is used during Phase2 to 6 for the communication link establishment.

Type 3:   This type of header format is used for Phase7 type of connection where establishment of a communication link is formed with the help of TLV packet format. In this Phase, SONATE framework acts as a middleware and supports for establishing a network connectivity among all SONATE framework equipped systems. This middleware has the capability to modify the packet formats according to the need.

During Phase8, the above-mentioned types of packet formats are used for a smooth information exchange among all interconnected systems and also provide a backward compatibility with the legacy systems.

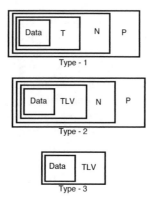

Figure 4.8: SONATE packet formats.

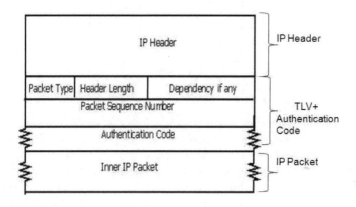

Figure 4.9: Authentication Packet of SONATE.

The packet format for the proposed architecture is different. At the initiative level Type1 packet format is used, i.e., the current Internet packet format. Type2 packet format is used to provide compatibility at application level and the network level for connection establishment. Type3 format is used where establishment for communication is done with the help of TLV packet format (Figure 4.8). In this level, SONATE framework acts as a middleware and supports for SONATE equipped systems to make network connectivity. This middleware has the capability to change the packet format according to the need. Once the deployment of SONATE is done in the communication path as well as in the systems the above mentioned formats are used to provide backward compatibility with legacy systems which requires security for the protection of services from breach.

A network contains a large number of principals who communicate and may not have authoritative descriptions, and the purpose of the services for which they are being requested. For secure communication, principals are to be authenticated which can be performed using various cryptographic techniques. There are many authentication protocols available in the current Internet which are based on both the conventional and public key encryption methods. These protocols are to be developed in flexible and loosely coupled to suite the future Internet which makes it easy for modification of protocols and yield better results or replace the old one with new protocols with the emerging demands. Assigning numbers to the developed security protocols allow easy to find out the required protocols with the provider. An example for assigning numbers to the famous algorithms has been considered in (Table 4.1).

Table 4.1: Code Assigned Security Protocols

Security Protocols	Assigned No.	Code
DES	1	0000
AES	2	0001
MD5	3	0010
AES	4	0011
Digital Signature	5	0100
RSA	6	0101

To avoid the attacks in this framework, the flexible protocols are developed and a 4-bit binary code is assigned to the respective security protocols as the packet format use TLVs. And these TLVs use a binary format that makes the data smaller, easy generation of XML for the human inspection of the data, can be easily searched using the generalized parsing functions and these can be placed anywhere and in any order inside the payload. The TLVs that were received from the older device (session finish) will be ignored and the rest of the payload is considered [52]. SONATE uses TLV along with the IP packet (Figure 4.9) which includes an authentication header code where the authentication algorithm code is declared so that both the principals can have mutual understanding of the algorithm and communicate for the usage of authentication for encryption and decryption of the services with the help of the key. Let us consider a case where an agent uses RSA algorithm then the code is declared as 0101 at the place of authentication code along with packet type and packet sequence number if any as described in the packet. When layer concept becomes absolute then the consideration of packet headers does not yield good results, so SONATE sends its information using TLVs which are authenticated and encrypted with the key in the form of bits and bytes over the network.

The size of the headers used in different phases of SONATE are Transport header (T) = 20 bytes, Network header (N) = 20 bytes, and Maximum Transmission Unit (MTU) = 1500 bytes, Maximum Segment Size (MSS) = (1500 - 20 - 20) = 1460 bytes, TLV = (Type = 32 bits for IPv4 and 128 bits for IPv6, Length = 32 bits for IPv4 and 128 bits for IPv6, Value = It is variable of size). The allocation of binary code for authentication is performed using 6 bits where 4 bit binary code is used in the current scenario and 2 bits for future use. And in cases where a conflict occurs for the assignment of binary codes to the security protocols, a holistic approach is followed where their will be a tradeoffs between bit and the security protocols. The authentication protocol list is made available with all the brokers.

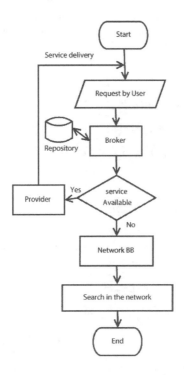

Figure 4.10: Flow of service.

The process of fulfilling a service request is shown in a generalized flowchart (Figure 4.10) where, the request from the user is accepted by the broker. After receiving the request the broker checks in its repository for the availability of the service, if the service is available in the list then it is forwarded to the provider to fetch it for the fulfillment of the request. And if the requested service does not reside in its repository then the request is forwarded to the network via network BB. The requested services can be transferred over the distributed network. A simple example of file transfer is explained (Algorithm 4.2) which is one of the basic services of the distributed system. There are various services which incorporate functionality of file transfer during the service, such as NFS; which is completely based on distributed sytem. Before transfering a file from one system to another, the broker of one system verifies the authentication of the system. Transferring a file in smaller chunks is easier than transferring a larger file over the network. Therefore, a larger file is made into chunks of smaller sized messages and sent over the network in encrypted form. At the destination side these encrypted chunks of messages are collected for decryption and reassembled to get the original message. The proposed framework supports this type of operation. For the avoidance of permanent connection establishment between two brokers of the network a session control mechanism is introduced. Using this mechanism the required authenication service can be made available for a definite period of time. As soon as the session completes the authentication BB becomes obsolete such as the bank transaction session ends after a certain amount of time.

Algorithm 4.2
Secure file transfer code of available services

1. *Get **service name** and its path*

2. *Send **request** to **Application BB***

3. *Pass file name to **Network BB***

4. *Provide authentication to broker*

5. *Get key for file authentication*

6.   *If authentication type matches*

7.   *Fragment the file with key*

8.   *While fragmentation number $\neq 0$*

9.   *Send selected data fragments to **network BB***

10.   *Send **file** to another system*

11.   *Repeat for all fragments*

12.   *Decrypt the received file*

13.   *Send acknowledgment of receiving*

14.   *else*

15.   *Get **authentication mechanism***

16. *Repeat steps 7 to 13 untill the session completes*

4.6   Evaluation

It is important to evaluate any designed secure system, which helps to evaluate, whether it can support the expected security services or not. This section deals with the evaluation of the security proposed for SONATE architecture on the basis of the threat model. A threat model was designed using the attacker based approach. Then verified whether the proposed protocols can prevent the consequences or not. Identity management system was analyzed from the attacker's point of view, and considered the following possible attacks: eavesdropping, replay attack, impersonation and data tampering. Then analyses were performed whether these security services are capable of solving these security issues. All messages are digitally signed using the sender's private key and encrypted with the receiver's public key which helps in preventing the interception and replay attack. Since a strong authentication method was applied before each session, it solves the problem of an impersonation attack. A simple file transfer can use simple cryptographic functions, such as hash that can prevent only tampering attack. For the prevention of interception, replay attack along with data tampering it is better to use the digital signature, which consists of the sender's private key and encrypted with the receiver's public key. Before each session, the entities who want to communicate perform a strong authentication in order to establish a secure session. Until and unless the entities prove their identity and authenticate themselves the exchange of the services are not allowed. In the certificate request phase, for each session, a sessionID is randomly generated which avoids a replay attack. Each service transaction is based on the challenge response mode and if an attack occurs, there is a possibility to cancel the transaction by the broker of the system or network and send an acknowledgement to the sender system. For the revocation process, the above-mentioned attacks can be prevented due to the above-mentioned reasons. In addition to this, use of certificates provides integrity and authentication for the services.

Table 4.2: Authentication Evaluation Results

	Replay Attack	Data Tampering	Impersonation	Eavesdropping
Identity Verification	Yes	Yes	Yes	Yes
Certificate Request	Yes	Yes	Yes	Yes
Certificate Revocation	Yes	Yes	Yes	Yes
Certificate Verification	Yes	Yes	Yes	Yes

4.6.1   Performance Analysis

Hierarchical certification model has been developed and tested on a case study of Future Internet architecture of SONATE. But a combination of hierarchical and cross-certification will be used in the future for the easy management of the cerificates. After the PKI establishment a set of files was sent using encryption and hashing techniques. The modules are developed on the concept on SOA to suite the architecture of SONATE such as CRC, AES-256, MD5, Service Authentication Code [28], digital signature, etc., were successfully incorporated in SONATE. The feasibility by both standalone and distributed environment for TCP and UDP cases are considered using a real time scenario and both sending and receiving data was performed successfully. The verification and validation of data is performed on the text file sent over the systems. The experimental results of throughput and execution time on standalone and distributed system is almost constant for both the cases of TCP and UDP. A series of 38 files was sent for the comparision of the execution time and throughput and the graphs obtained.

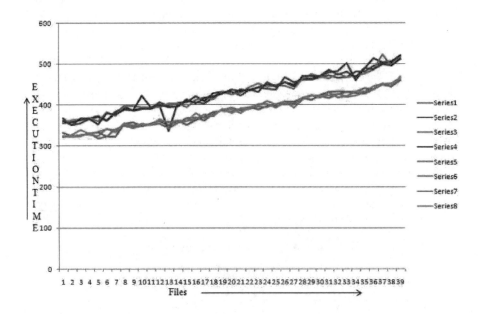

Figure 4.11: Comparison of execution time (milliseconds) of a secure file transfer in SONATE and TCP/IP interface.

The graph (Figure 4.11) obtained shows the 8 series where first four series (above series line) represent the execution time for SONATE and below series for TCP interface. The throughput for TCP interface is more compared with SONATE (Figure 4.12). The first 4 above series shows the throughput of TCP and below shows the SONATE interface output. We can conclude that the throughput is less and execution time is more for SONATE interface when compared with TCP interface. It is observed that the security payload decreases and the throughput of the file increases

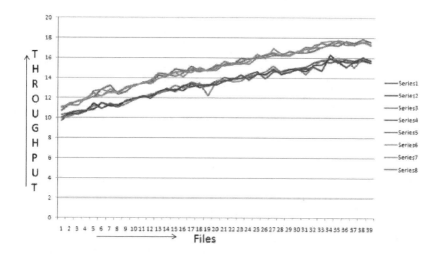

Figure 4.12: Comparison of throughput (bytes/milliseconds) of a secure file transfer in SONATE and TCP/IP interface.

which was tested by considering the 35 files of each 3568 bytes (Figure 4.13). The service files were sent through the distributed network and these are encrypted using various authentication techniques. The execution time was noted in (Table 4.3) and related comparison graph is obtained (Figure 4.14) for TCP/IP interface and SONATE interface. Similarly, four encrypted files are sent and its throughput is (Table 4.4) compared with TCP/IP and its related graph (Figure 4.15) is obtained in bytes per milliseconds. We can conclude that the execution time is more and throughput is less for SONATE. This is due to the selection and composition process for the selection of best services from the available service repository.

Table 4.3: Comparison of Execution Time

Services	TCP/IP Interface	SONATE Interface
File 1	0.7321345	0.8132145
File 2	0.6777896	0.7522234
File 3	0.6500121	0.7221345
File 4	0.1400125	0.1556789

Table 4.4: Comparison of Throughput Time

Services	TCP/IP Interface	SONATE Interface
File 1	4.8743211	4.3890111
File 2	5.270017	4.7455221
File 3	5.4899999	4.9422222
File 4	27.03023323	24.2722333

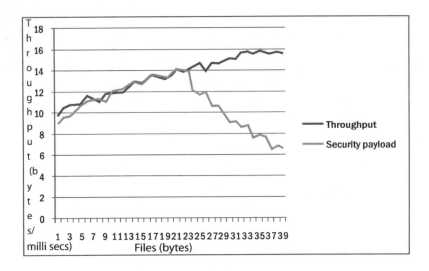

Figure 4.13: Security payload on SONATE.

4.7 Summary

Authentication of the entities is imperative for the satisfactory working of Future Internet architectures and for avoidance of security vulnerabilities. The entities of the architectures are independent, and require mutual authentication at the initiation of every service request cycle for the avoidance of attacks. Thus, authentication is the most important security measure. It allows smooth service provisioning without external threats like man in middle attack etc. In this a casestudy has been considered and examined, a mechanism based on PKI is proposed for SONATE environment due to the functional properties for the fulfillment of authentication in the networks. In addition, security, usability and interoperability of the PKI solution must be taken into account in the context of providing secure services. As the result, we a solution is proposed based on the concept of PKI and its trusted authorities. The proposed mechanism includes PKI server and CA Server and three services: certificate request service, certificate revocation service, and certificate verification service. This solution not only solves the authentication issues, but also provides flexibility and interoperability for its deployment. Finally, the evaluation of usability and security is also given. Based on the evaluation results, it is concluded that the proposed PKI solution is easy and secure to use. The performance analysis considered for both the scenarios of TCP and SONATE which uses UDP for transferring the messages over the network. It is observed that the execution time is more and throughput is less for UDP when compared to TCP due to the service orchestration process for the delivery of the best possible services by the architecture.

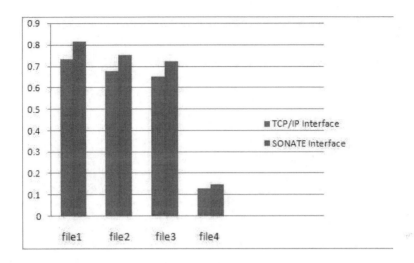

Figure 4.14: Comparison of Execution Time (secs).

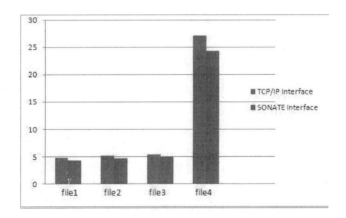

Figure 4.15: Comparison of Throughput (bytes/milliseconds).

Appendix —4A

Internet Protocol of Current Architecture

An internet protocol (IP) provides the functionality for interconnecting end systems across multiple networks. For this purpose, IP is implemented in each end system and in routers, which are devices that provide connection between networks. Higher-level data at a source end system are encapsulated in an IP protocol data unit (PDU) for transmission. This PDU is then passed through one or more networks and connecting routers to reach the destination end system. The router must be able to cope with a variety of differences among networks, including:

Addressing schemes: The networks may use different schemes for assigning addresses to devices. For example, an IEEE 802 LAN uses either 16-bit or 48-bit binary addresses for each attached device; an X.25 public packet-switching network uses 12-digit decimal addresses (encoded as 4 bits per digit for a 48-bit address). Some form of global network addressing must be provided, as well as a directory service.

Maximum packet sizes: Packets from one network may have to be broken into smaller pieces to be transmitted on another network, a process known as fragmentation. For example, Ethernet imposes a maximum packet size of 1500 bytes; a maximum packet size of 1000 bytes is common on X.25 networks. A packet that is transmitted on an Ethernet system and picked up by a router for retransmission on an X.25 network may have to fragment the incoming packet into two smaller ones. *Interfaces:* The hardware and software interfaces to various networks differ. The concept of a router must be independent of these differences.

Reliability: Various network services may provide anything from a reliable end-to-end virtual circuit to an unreliable service. The operation of the routers should not depend on an assumption of network reliability.

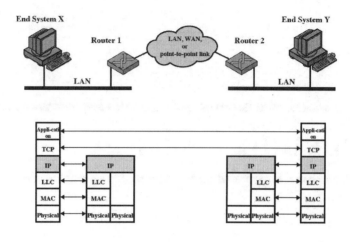

Figure 4.16: TCP/IP configuration example.

The operation of the router, as Figure 4.16 indicates, depends on an Internet protocol. In this example, the Internet Protocol (IP) of the TCP/IP protocol suite performs that function. IP must be implemented in all end systems on all networks as well as on the routers. In addition, each end system must have compatible protocols above IP to communicate successfully.

Consider the transfer of a block of data from end system X to end system Y in Figure 4.16. The IP layer at X receives blocks of data to be sent to Y from TCP in X. The IP layer attaches a header that specifies the global Internet address of Y. That address is in two parts: network identifier and end system identifier. Let us refer to this block as the IP packet. Next, IP recognizes that the destination (Y) is on another subnetwork. So the first step is to send the packet to a router, in this case router 1. To accomplish this, IP hands its data unit down to LLC with the appropriate addressing information. LLC creates an LLC PDU, which is handed down to the MAC layer. The MAC layer constructs a MAC packet whose header contains the address of router 1.

Next, the packet travels through LAN to router 1. The router removes the packet and LLC headers and trailers and analyzes the IP header to determine the ultimate destination of the data, in this case Y. The router must now make a routing decision. There are two possibilities:

1. The destination end system Y is connected directly to one of the subnetworks to which the router is attached.

2. To reach the destination, one or more additional routers must be traversed.

In this example, the packet must be routed through router 2 before reaching the destination. So router 1 passes the IP packet to router 2 via the intermediate network. For this purpose, the protocols of that network are used. For example, if the intermediate network is an X.25 network, the IP data unit is wrapped in an X.25 packet with appropriate addressing information to reach router 2. When this packet arrives at router 2, the packet header is stripped off. The router determines that this IP packet is destined for Y, which is connected directly to a subnetwork to which the router is attached. The router therefore creates a packet with a destination address of Y and sends it out onto the LAN. The data finally arrive at Y, where the packet, LLC, and internet headers and trailers can be stripped off.

This service offered by IP is an unreliable one. That is, IP does not guarantee that all data will be delivered or that the data that are delivered will arrive in the proper order. It is the responsibility of the next higher layer, in this case TCP, to recover from any errors that occur. This approach provides for a great deal of flexibility. Because delivery is not guaranteed, there is no particular reliability requirement on any of the subnetworks. Thus, the protocol will work with any combination of subnetwork types. Because the sequence of delivery is not guaranteed, successive packets can follow different paths through the Internet. This allows the protocol to react to congestion and failure in the Internet by changing routes.

IPv4

For decades, the keystone of the TCP/IP protocol architecture has been the Internet Protocol (IP) version 4. Figure 4.17 shows the IP header format, which is a minimum of 20 octets, or 160 bits. The fields are

■ Version (4 bits): Indicates version number, to allow evolution of the protocol; the value is 4.

■ Internet Header Length (IHL) (4 bits): Length of header in 32-bit words. The minimum value is five, for a minimum header length of 20 octets.

■ DS/ECN (8 bits): Prior to the introduction of differentiated services, this field was referred to as the **Type of Service** field and specified reliability, precedence, delay, and throughput parameters. This interpretation has now been superseded. The first 6 bits of the TOS field are now referred to as the DS (Differentiated Services) field. The remaining 2 bits are reserved for an ECN (Explicit Congestion Notification) field.

■ Total Length (16 bits): Total IP packet length, in octets.

■ Identification (16 bits): A sequence number that, together with the source address, destination address, and user protocol, is intended to identify a packet uniquely. Thus, this number should be unique for the packet's source address, destination address, and user protocol for the time during which the packet will remain in the Internet.

■ Flags (3 bits): Only two of the bits are currently defined. When a packet is fragmented, the more bit indicates whether this is the last fragment in the original packet. The don't fragment bit prohibits fragmentation when set.

This bit may be useful if it is known that the destination does not have the capability to reassemble fragments. However, if this bit is set, the packet will be discarded if it exceeds the maximum size of an en route subnetwork. Therefore, if the bit is set, it may be advisable to use source routing to avoid subnetworks with small maximum packet size.

■ Fragment Offset (13 bits): Indicates where in the original packet this fragment belongs, measured in 64-bit units. This implies that fragments other than the last fragment must contain a data field that is a multiple of 64 bits in length.

■ Time to Live (8 bits): Specifies how long, in seconds, a packet is allowed to remain in the Internet. Every router that processes a packet must decrease the TTL by at least one, so the TTL is somewhat similar to a hop count.

■ Protocol (8 bits): Indicates the next higher level protocol, which is to receive the data field at the destination; thus, this field identifies the type of the next header in the packet after the IP header.

■ Header Checksum (16 bits): An error-detecting code applied to the header only. Because some header fields may change during transit (e.g., time to live, segmentation-related fields), this is reverified and recomputed at each router. The checksum field is the 16-bit one's complement addition of all 16-bit words in the header. For purposes of computation, the checksum field is itself initialized to a value of zero.

■ Source Address (32 bits): Coded to allow a variable allocation of bits to specify the network and the end system attached to the specified network (7 and 24 bits, 14 and 16 bits, or 21 and 8 bits).

■ Destination Address (32 bits): Same characteristics as source address.

■ Options (variable): Encodes the options requested by the sending user; these may include security label, source routing, record routing, and timestamping.

■ Padding (variable): Used to ensure that the packet header is a multiple of 32 bits in length.

IPv6

In 1995, the Internet Engineering Task Force (IETF), which develops protocol standards for the Internet, issued a specification for a next-generation IP, known then as IPng. This specification was turned into a standard in 1996 known as IPv6. IPv6 provides a number of functional enhancements over the existing IP (known as IPv4), designed to accommodate the higher speeds of today's networks and the mix of data streams, including graphic and video, that are becoming more prevalent. But the

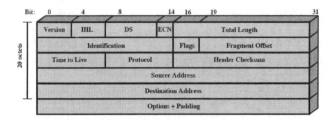

Figure 4.17: IPv4 header.

driving force behind the development of the new protocol was the need for more addresses. IPv4 uses a 32-bit address to specify a source or destination. With the explosive growth of the Internet and of private networks attached to the Internet, this address length became insufficient to accommodate all systems needing addresses. As Figure 4.18 shows, IPv6 includes 128-bit source and destination address fields. Ultimately, all installations using TCP/IP are expected to migrate from the current IP to IPv6, but this process will take many years, if not decades.

IPv6 Header The IPv6 header has a fixed length of 40 octets, consisting of the following fields Figure 4.18:

■ Version (4 bits): Internet Protocol version number; the value is 6.

■ DS/ECN (8 bits): Prior to the introduction of differentiated services, this field was referred to as the Traffic Class field and was reserved for use by originating nodes and/or forwarding routers to identify and distinguish between different classes or priorities of IPv6 packets. The first six bits of the traffic class field are now referred to as the DS (Differentiated Services) field. The remaining 2 bits are reserved for an ECN (Explicit Congestion Notification) field.

■ Flow Label (20 bits): May be used by a host to label those packets for which it is requesting special handling by routers within a network. Flow labeling may assist resource reservation and real-time traffic processing.

■ Payload Length (16 bits): Length of the remainder of the IPv6 packet following the header, in octets. In other words, this is the total length of all of the extension headers plus the transport-level PDU.

■ Next Header (8 bits): Identifies the type of header immediately following the IPv6 header; this will either be an IPv6 extension header or a higher-layer header, such as TCP or UDP.

■ Hop Limit (8 bits): The remaining number of allowable hops for this packet. The hop limit is set to some desired maximum value by the source and decremented by 1 by each node that forwards the packet. The packet is discarded if hop limit is decremented to zero.

■ Source Address (128 bits): The address of the originator of the packet.

■ Destination Address (128 bits): The address of the intended recipient of the packet. This may not in fact be the intended ultimate destination if a routing extension header is present, as explained later.

Although the IPv6 header is longer than the mandatory portion of the IPv4 header (40 octets vs. 20 octets), it contains fewer fields (8 vs. 12). Thus, routers have less processing to do per header, which should speed up routing.

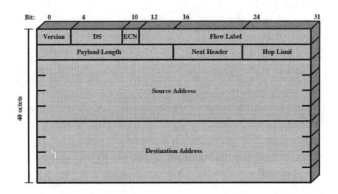

Figure 4.18: IPv6 header.

IPv6 Extension Header: An IPv6 packet includes the IPv6 header, just discussed, and zero or more extension headers. Outside of IPSec, the following extension headers have been defined:

■ Hop-by-Hop Options Header: Defines special options that require hop-by-hop processing

■ Routing Header: Provides extended routing, similar to IPv4 source routing

■ Fragment Header: Contains fragmentation and reassembly information

■ Authentication Header: Provides packet integrity and authentication

■ Encapsulating Security Payload Header: Provides privacy

■ Destination Options Header: Contains optional information to be examined by the destination node

The IPv6 standard recommends that, when multiple extension headers are used, the IPv6 headers appear in the following order:

1. IPv6 header: Mandatory, must always appear first

2. Hop-by-Hop Options header

3. Destination Options header: For options to be processed by the first destination that appears in the IPv6 Destination Address field plus subsequent destinations listed in the routing header

4. Routing header

5. Fragment header

6. Authentication header

7. Encapsulating Security Payload header

8. Destination Options header: For options to be processed only by the final destination of the packet

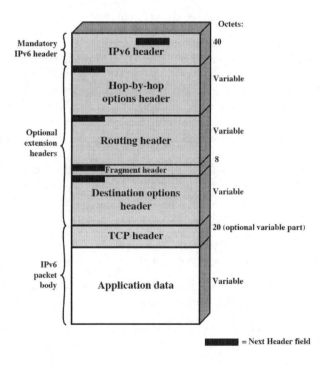

Figure 4.19: IPv6 Extension header.

Figure 4.19 shows an example of an IPv6 packet that includes an instance of each nonsecurity header. Note that the IPv6 header and each extension header include a next header field. This field identifies the type of the immediately following header. If the next header is an extension header, then this field contains the type identifier of that header. Otherwise, this field contains the protocol identifier of the upper-layer protocol using IPv6 (typically a transport-level protocol), using the same values as the IPv4 protocol field. In the figure, the upper-layer protocol is TCP, so the upper-layer data carried by the IPv6 packet consist of a TCP header followed by a block of application data.

The hop-by-hop Options header carries optional information that, if present, must be examined by every router along the path. The header consists of the following fields:

- Next Header (8 bits): Identifies the type of header immediately following this header.

- Header Extension Length (8 bits): Length of this header in 64-bit units, not including the first 64 bits.

- Options: Contains one or more options. Each option consists of three sub-fields: a tag, indicating the option type; a length, and a value.

Only one option has so far been defined: the jumbo payload option, used to send IPv6 packets with payloads longer than 2^{16} 1 = 65,535 octets. The option data field of this option is 32 bits long and gives the length of the packet in octets, excluding the IPv6 header. For such packets, the payload length field in the IPv6 header must be set to zero, and there must be no Fragment header. With this option, IPv6 supports packet sizes up to more than 4 billion octets. This facilitates the transmission of large video packets and enables IPv6 to make the best use of available capacity over any transmission medium.

The **Routing header** contains a list of one or more intermediate nodes to be visited on the way to a packet's destination. All routing headers start with a 32-bit block consisting of four 8-bit fields, followed by routing data specific to a given routing type. The four 8-bit fields are Next Header, Header Extension Length, and

- Routing Type: Identifies a particular Routing header variant. If a router does not recognize the Routing Type value, it must discard the packet.

- Segments Left: Number of explicitly listed intermediate nodes still to be visited before reaching the final destination.

In addition to this general header definition, the IPv6 specification defines the Type 0 Routing header. When using the Type 0 Routing header, the source node does not place the ultimate destination address in the IPv6 header. Instead, that address is the last address listed in the Routing header, and the IPv6 header contains the destination address of the first desired router on the path. The Routing header will not be examined until the packet reaches the node identified in the IPv6 header. At that point, the IPv6 and Routing header contents are updated and the packet is forwarded. The update consists of placing the next address to be visited in the IPv6 header and decrementing the Segments Left field in the Routing header.

IPv6 requires an IPv6 node to reverse routes in a packet it receives containing a Routing header, to return a packet to the sender.

The **Fragment header** is used by a source when fragmentation is required. In

IPv6, fragmentation may only be performed by source nodes, not by routers along a packet's delivery path. To take full advantage of the internetworking environment, a node must perform a path discovery algorithm that enables it to learn the smallest maximum transmission unit (MTU) supported by any subnetwork on the path. In other words, the path discovery algorithm enables a node to learn the MTU of the "bottleneck" subnetwork on the path. With this knowledge, the source node will fragment, as required, for each given destination address. Otherwise the source must limit all packets to 1280 octets, which is the minimum MTU that must be supported by each subnetwork. In addition to the Next Header field, the fragment header includes the following fields:

- Fragment Offset (13 bits): Indicates where in the original packet the payload of this fragment belongs. It is measured in 64-bit units. This implies that fragments (other than the last fragment) must contain a data field that is a multiple of 64 bits long.

- Res (2 bits): Reserved for future use.

- M Flag (1 bit): 1 = more fragments; 0 = last fragment.

- Identification (32 bits): Intended to identify uniquely the original packet. The identifier must be unique for the packet's source address and destination address for the time during which the packet will remain in the internet. All fragments with the same identifier, source address, and destination address are reassembled to form the original packet.

The **Destination Options header** carries optional information that, if present, is examined only by the packet's destination node. The format of this header is the same as that of the Hop-by-Hop Options header.

X.509 Authentication Service

ITU-T (International Telecommunication Union Telecommunication Standardization Sector) recommendation X.509 is a part of the X.500 series of recommendations that define a directory service. The directory is a server or distributed set of servers that maintains a database of information about users. The information includes a mapping from user name to network address, as well as other attributes and information about the users. X.509 defines a framework for the provision of authentication services by the X.500 directory to its users. The directory may serve as a repository of public-key certificates. Each certificate contains the public key of a user and is signed with the private key of a trusted certification authority. X.509 defines alternative authentication protocols based on the use of public-key certificates. X.509 is an important standard because the certificate structure and authentication protocols defined in X.509 are used in variety of contexts (SSL, SET, etc.). A third version of X.509 was issued in 1995 and revised in 2000.

Certificates The heart of X.509 scheme is the public-key certificate associated with each user. These user certificates are assumed to be created by some trusted certificate authority (CA) and placed in the directory by the CA or by the user. The directory itself is not responsible for the creation of public keys or for the certification function; it merely provides an easily accessible location for users to obtain certificates.

X.509 is based on the use of public-key cryptography and digital signatures. The standard does not dictate the use of a specific algorithm but recommends RSA. The digital signature scheme is assumed to require the use of a hash function. Again, the standard does not dictate a specific hash algorithm. The 1988 recommendation included the description of a recommended hash algorithm; this algorithm has since been shown to be insecure and was dropped from the 1993 recommendation. Figure 4.20 illustrates the generation of a public-key certificate.

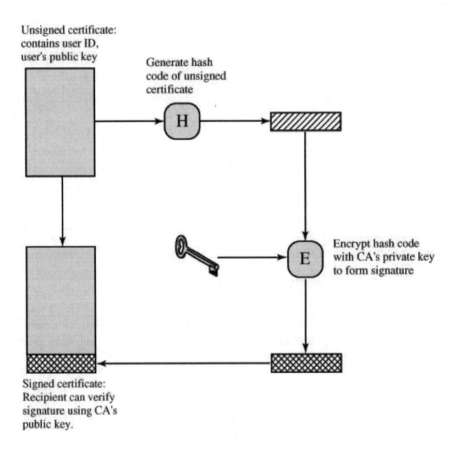

Figure 4.20: Public Key Cerificate Use.

Figure 4.21 shows the general format of a certificate, which includes the following elements:

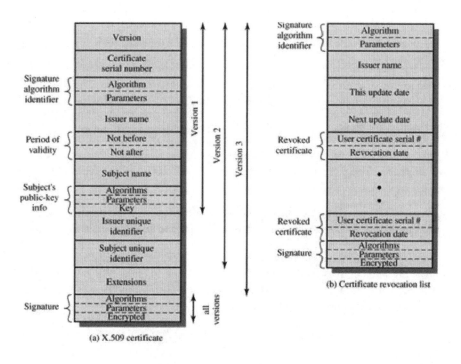

(a) X.509 certificate

Figure 4.21: X.509 Cerificate.

Version: Differentiates among successive versions of the certificate format: the default version is 1. If the Issuer Unique Identifier or Subject Unique Identifier are present, the value must be version 2. If one or more extensions are present, the version must be version 3.

Serial number: An integer value, unique within the issuing CA, that is unambiguously associated with this certificate.

Signature algorithm identifier: The algorithm used to sign the certificate, together with any associated parameters. Because this information is repeated in the Signature field at the end of the certificate, this field has little, if any, utility.

Issuer name: X.500 name of the CA that created and signed this certificate.

Period of validity: Consists of two dates: the first and the last on which certificate is valid.

Subject name: The name of the user to whom this certificate refers. That is, this certificate certifies the public key of the subject who holds the corresponding private key.

Subject's public key information: The public key of the subject, plus an identifier of the algorithm for which this key is to be used, together with any associated parameters.

Issuer unique identifier: An optional bit string field used to identify uniquely the issuing CA in the event the X.500 name has been reused for different entities.

Subject unique identifier: An optional bit string used to identify uniquely the subject in the event the X.500 name has been reused for different entities.

Extensions: A set of one or more extension fields. Extensions were added in version 3 and are discussed later.

Signature: Covers all of the other fields of the certificate; it contains the hash code of the other fields, encrypted with the CA's private key. This field includes the signature algorithm identifier.

The unique identifier fields were added in version 2 to handle the possible reuse of subject and/or issuer names over time. These fields are rarely used. The standard uses the following notation to define a certificate:

$$CA << A >> = CAV, SN, AI, CA, TA, A, Ap \qquad (4.1)$$

where

$$Y << X >> = certificate of user X issued by certification authority Y \qquad (4.2)$$

YI= the signing of I by Y. It consists of I with an encrypted hash code appended The CA signs the certificate with its private key. If the corresponding public key is known to a user, then that user can verify that a certificate signed by the CA is valid.

Obtaining a User's Certificate

User certificates generated by a CA have the following characteristics:

1. Any user with access to the public of the CA can verify the user public key that was encrypted.

2. No party other than the CA can modify the certificate without this being detected.

Because certificates are unforgeable, they can be placed in a directory without the need for the directory to make special efforts to protect them.

If all users subscribe to the same CA, then there is a common trust of that CA. All user certificates can be placed in the directory for access by all users. In addition, a user can transmit his certificate directly to other users. In either case, once B is in possession of A's certificate, B has confidence that message it encrypts with A's public key will be secure from eavesdropping and that messages signed with A's private key are unforgeable.

If there is a large community of users, it may not be practical for all users to subscribe to the same CA. Because it is the CA that signs certificates, each participating user must have a copy of the CA's own public key to verify signatures. This public key must be provided to each user in an absolutely secure (with respect to integrity and authenticity) way so that the user has confidence in the associated certificates. Thus, with many users, it may be more practical for there to be a number of CAs, each of which securely provides its public key to some fraction of the users. Now suppose that A has obtained a certificate from certification authority X1 and B has obtained a certificate from CA X2. If A does not securely know the public key of X2, then B's certificate, issued by X2, is useless to A. A can read B's certificate, but A cannot verify the signature. However, if the two CAs have securely exchanged their own public keys, the following procedure will enable A to obtain B's public key:

1. A obtains from directory, the certificate of X2 signed by X1. Because A securely knows X1's public key, A can obtain X2's public key from its certificate and verify it by means of X1's signature on the certificate

2. A then goes back to the directory and obtains the certificate of B signed by X2. Because A now has a trusted copy of X2's public key, A can verify the signature and securely obtain B's public key

A has used a chain of certificates to obtain B's public key. In the notation of X.509, this chain is expressed as

$$X1 << X2 >> X2 << B >> \qquad (4.3)$$

In the same fashion, B can obtain A's public key with the chain:

$$X2 << X1 >> X1 << A >> \qquad (4.4)$$

This scheme need not be limited to a chain of two certificates. An arbitrarily long path of CAs can be followed to produce a chain. A chain with N elements would be expressed as

$$X1 << X2 >> X2 << X3 >> XN << B >> \qquad (4.5)$$

In this case, each pair of CAs in the chain (Xi, Xi+1) must have created certificates for each other. All these certificates of CAs by CAs need to appear in the directory, and the user needs to know how they are linked to follow a path to another user's public-key certificate. X.509 suggests that CAs are arranged in a hierarchy so that navigation is straightforward. Figure 4.22, taken from X.509, is an example of such a hierarchy. The connected circles indicate the hierarchical relationship among the CAs; the associated boxes indicate certificates maintained in the directory for each CA entry. The directory entry for each CA includes two types of certificates:

■ **Forward certificates:** Certificates of X generated by other CAs.

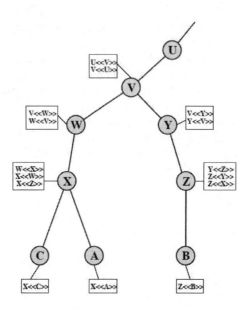

Figure 4.22: X.509 Certificate hierarchy.

◼ **Reverse certificates:** Certificates generated by X that are the certificates of other CAs.

In this example, user A can acquire the following certificates from the directory to establish a certification path to B:

$$X << W >> W << V >> V << Y >> Y << Z >> Z << B >> \qquad (4.6)$$

When A has obtained these certificates, it can unwrap the certification path in sequence to recover a trusted copy of B's public key. Using this public key, A can send encrypted messages to B. If A wishes to receive encrypted messages from B, or to sign messages sent to B, then B will require A's public key, which can be obtained from the following certification path:

$$Z << Y >> Y << V >> V << W >> W << X >> X << A >> \qquad (4.7)$$

B can obtain this set of certificates from the directory, or A can provide them as part of its initial message to B.

Revocation of Certificates: Recall from Figure 4.22 that each certificate includes a period of validity. Typically, a new certificate is issued before the expiration of the old one. In addition, it may be desirable on occasion to revoke a certificate before it expires, for one of the following reasons:

1. The user's private key is assumed to be compromised.

2. The user is no longer certified by this CA.

3. The CA's certificate is assumed to be compromised.

Each CA must maintain a list consisting of all revoked but not expired certificates issued by that CA, including both those issued to users and to other CAs. These lists should be posted on the directory. Each certificate revocation list (CRL) posted to the directory is signed by the issuer and includes Figure 4.21 the issuer's name, the date the list was created, the date the next CRL is scheduled to be issued, and an entry for each revoked certificate. Each entry consists of the serial number of a certificate and revocation date for that certificate. Because serial numbers are unique within a CA, the serial number is sufficient to identify the certificate. When a user receives a certificate in a message, the user must determine whether the certificate has been revoked. The user could check the directory each time a certificate is received. To avoid the delays (and possible costs) associated with directory searches, it is likely that the user would maintain a local cache of certificates and lists of revoked certificates.

Authentication Procedures: X.509 also includes three alternative authentication procedures Figure 4.23 that are intended for use across a variety of applications. All these procedures make use of public-key signatures. It is assumed that the two parties know each other's public key, either by obtaining each other's certificates from the directory or because the certificate is included in the initial message from each side. These procedures are treated as strong contrary to simple authentication procedures in which a client is authenticated to a server by sending him its identifier and password in clear or hashed together with a timestamp and nonce.

One-Way Authentication: One-way authentication involves a single transfer of information from one user (A) to another (B), and establishes the following:

1. The identity of A and that the message was generated by A.

2. That the message was intended for B.

3. The integrity and originality (it has not been sent multiple times) of the message.

   Note that only the identity of the initiating entity is verified in this process, not that of the responding entity. At minimum, the message includes a timestamp, a nonce and the identity of B and is signed with A's private key. The timestamp consists of an optional generation time and an expiration time. This prevents delayed delivery of messages. The nonce can be used to detect replay attacks. The nonce value must be unique within the expiration time of the message. Thus, B can store the nonce until it expires and reject any new messages with the same nonce. For pure authentication, the message is used simply to present credentials to B. The message may also include information to be conveyed. This information, sgnData, is included within the scope of the signature, guaranteeing its authenticity and integrity. The message may also be used to convey a session key to B, encrypted with B's public key.

Two-Way Authentication: In addition to the three elements just listed, two-way authentication establishes the following elements:

4. The identity of B and that the reply message was generated by B.

5. That the message was intended for A.

6. The integrity and originality of the reply. The reply message includes the nonce from A, to validate the reply. It also includes a timestamp and nonce generated by B. As before, the message may include signed additional information and a session key encrypted with A's public key.

Three-Way Authentication: Here, a final message from A to B is included, which contains a signed copy of the nonce. The intent of this design is that timestamps need not be checked: Because both nonces are echoed back by the other side, each side can check the returned nonce to detect replay attack. This approach is needed when synchronized clocks are not available. It is not shown in Figure 4.23, but the response from A also includes B to counter meet-in-the middle attack when opponent C intercepts messages between A and B

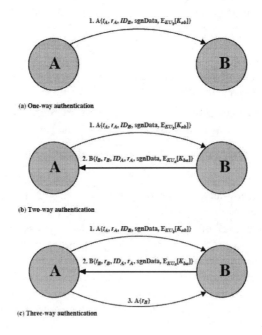

Figure 4.23: X.509 Authentication procedures.

MD5 Message Digest Algorithm

MD5 was developed by Ron Rivest at MIT in 1991. Until 1996, when a flaw was found in it, MD5 was the most widely used secure hash algorithm. In description, we follow Stallings *Cryptography and Network Security textbook.*

MD5 Logic: The algorithm takes as input a message of arbitrary length and produces as output a 128-bit message digest. The input is processed in 512-bit blocks. Figure 4.24 depicts the overall processing of a message to produce a digest. The processing consists of the following steps:

1. **Append padding bits:** The message is padded so that its length in bits is congruent to 448 modulo 512

$$(length \equiv 448 mod 512) \tag{4.8}$$

. That is, the length of the padded message is 64 bits less than an integer multiple of 512 bits. Padding is always added, even if the message is already of the desired length. For example, if the message is 448 bits long, it is padded with 512 bits to a length of 960 bits. Thus, the number of padding bits is in the range of 1 to 512. The padding consists of a single 1-bit followed by the necessary number of 0-bits.

2. **Append length:** A 64-bit representation of the length in bits of the original message (before the padding) is appended to the result of Step 1 (least significant byte first). If the original length is greater than 2^{64}, then only the lower-order 64 bits of the length are used. Thus, the field contains the length of the original message, modulo 2^{64} . The outcome of the first two steps yields a message that is an integer multiple of 512 bits in length. In Figure 4.24 the expanded message is represented as the sequence of 512-bit blocks , so that the total length of the expanded message is bits. Equivalently, the result is a multiple of 16 32-bit words. Let M[0..N-1] denote the words of the resulting message with N an integer multiple of 16. Thus, N= L*16.

3. **Initialize MD buffer:** A 128-bit buffer is used to hold intermediate and final results of the hash function. The buffer can be represented as four 32-bit registers (A,B,C,D). These registers are initialized to the following 32-bit integers (hexadecimal values):

   A=67452301 B=EFCDAB89 C=98BADCFE D=10325476

   These values are stored in little-endian format, which is the least-significant byte of a word in the low-address byte position. As 32-bit strings, the initialization values (in hexadecimal format) appear as follows: Word A: 01 23 45 67 Word B: 89 AB CD EF Word C: FE DC BA 98 Word D: 76 54 32 10

4. **Process message in 512-bit (16-word) blocks:** The heart of the algorithm is a compression function that consists of four "rounds" of processing; this module is labeled in Figure 4.24, and its logic is illustrated in Figure 4.25. The

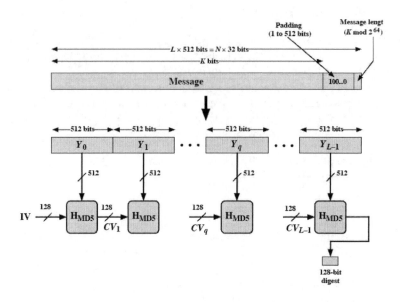

Figure 4.24: Message Digest Generation using MD5.

four rounds have a similar structure, but each uses a different primitive logical function, referred to as F, G, H, and I in the specification.

Each round takes as input the current 512-bit block being processed (Y_q) and the 128-bit buffer value ABCD and updates the contents of the buffer. Each round also makes use of one-fourth of a 64-element table T[1..64], constructed from the sine function. The i-th element of T, denoted T[i], has the value equal to the integer part of $2^3 2 * abs(sin(i))$, where i is in radians. Because $abs(sin(i)) \in [0, 1]$, each element of T is an integer that can be represented in 32 bits. The table provides a "randomized" set of 32-bit patterns, which should eliminate any regularities in the input data. The output of the fourth round is added to the input to the first round (CV_q) to produce (CV_{q+1}). The addition is done independently for each of the four words in the buffer with each of the corresponding words in CV_q, using addition modulo 2^{32}.

5. **Output:** After all L 512-bit blocks have been processed, the output from the L-th stage is the 128-bit message digest.

We can summarize the behavior of MD5 as follows:

$$CV_0 = IV CV_{q+1} = SUM_{32}(CV_q, RF_I(Y_q, RFH(Y_q, RF_G(Y_q, RF_F(Y_q, CV_q)))))) MD = CV_{L-1}$$
(4.9)

Where IV- initial value of the ABCD buffer, defined in Step 3 Y_q - the q-th 512-bit block of the message L the number of blocks in the message (including padding and

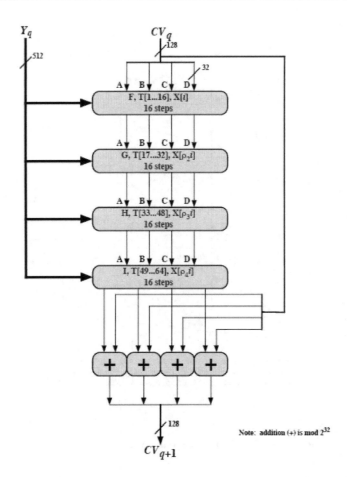

Figure 4.25: MD5 Processing of a Single 512 bit Block.

length fields) CV_q - chaining variable processed with the q-th block of the message RF_x - round function using primitive logic function x MD - final message digest value SUM_{32} - addition modulo performed separately on each word of the pair of inputs

MD5 Compression Function Let's look in more detail at the logic of the four rounds of the processing of one 512-bit block. Each round consists of a sequence of 16 steps operating on the buffer ABCD Figure 4.26. Each step is of the form

$$a \leftarrow b + ((a + g(b,c,d) + X[k] + T[i]) << lS) \qquad (4.10)$$

Where a,b,c,d the four words of the buffer, in a specified order that varies across steps g one of the primitive functions F,G,H,I ¡¡l S circular left shift (rotation) of the 32-bit argument by s bits X[k] M[q *16+k] k-th 32-bit word in the q-th 512-bit of the message T[i] the i-th 32-bit word in matrix T + - addition modulo2^32

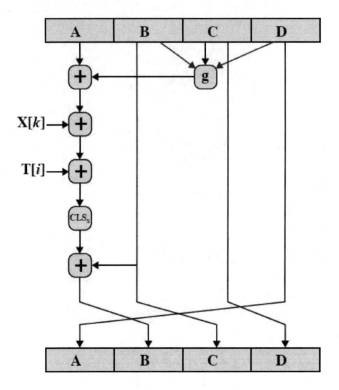

Figure 4.26: Elementary MD5 operation (single step).

The order in which the four words (a,b,c,d) are used produces a word-level circular right shift for each step. One of the four primitive logical functions is used for each of the four rounds of the algorithm. Each primitive function takes three 32-bit words as input and produces a 32-bit output. Each function performs a set of logical operations; that is, the n-th bit of the output is a function of the three inputs. The functions can be summarized as follows:

Table 4.5: MD5 Function

Round	Primitive Function (g)	g(b,c,d)
1	F(b,c,d)	$(b \wedge c) \vee (\overline{b} \wedge d)$
2	G(b.c,d)	$(b \wedge c) \vee (c \wedge \overline{d})$
3	H(b,c,d)	$b \oplus c \oplus d$
4	I(b,c,d)	$c \oplus (b \vee \overline{d})$

The array of 32-bit words X[0..15] holds the value of the current 512-bit input block being processed. Within a round, each of the 16 words of X[i] is used exactly once, during one step; the order in which these words are used varies from round to round. In the first round, they are used in the original order. The following permutations are defined for rounds 2 through 4:

$$\rho_2(i) = (1+5i) \, mod \, 16 \qquad (4.11)$$

$$\rho_3(i) = (5+3i) \, mod \, 16 \qquad (4.12)$$

$$\rho_4(i) = 7i \, mod \, 16 \qquad (4.13)$$

$$consider \, permutation \, \rho_2 \qquad (4.14)$$

Table 4.6: Permutation ρ_2

0	1	2	3	4	5	6	7	8	9	10	11	12	13	14	15
1	6	11	0	5	10	15	4	9	14	3	8	13	2	7	12

Each of the 64 32-bit word elements of T is used exactly once, during one step of one round. Also, note that for each step, only one of the 4 bytes of the ABCD buffer is updated. Hence, each byte of the buffer is updated four times during the round and then a final time at the end to produce the final output of this block. Finally, note that four different circular left shift amounts are used each round and are different from round to round. The point of all this complexity is to make it very difficult to generate collisions (two 512-bit blocks that produce the same output).

Public-Key Infrastructure

RFC 2822 (Internet Security Glossary) defines public-key infrastructure (PKI) as the set of hardware, software, people, policies, and procedures needed to create, manage, store, distribute, and revoke digital certificates based on asymmetric cryptography. The principal objective for developing a PKI is to enable secure, convenient, and efficient acquisition of public keys. The Internet Engineering Task Force (IETF) Public Key Infrastructure X.509 (PKIX) working group has been the driving force behind setting up a formal (and generic) model based on X.509 that is suitable for deploying a certificate-based architecture on the Internet. This section describes the PKIX model. Figure 4.27 shows the interrelationship among the key elements of the PKIX model. These elements are

■ End entity: A generic term used to denote end users, devices (e.g., servers, routers), or any other entity that can be identified in the subject field of a public key certificate. End entities typically consume and/or support PKI-related services.

■ Certification authority (CA): The issuer of certificates and (usually) certificate revocation lists (CRLs). It may also support a variety of administrative functions, although these are often delegated to one or more registration authorities.

■ Registration authority (RA): An optional component that can assume a number of administrative functions from the CA. The RA is often associated with the end entity registration process, but can assist in a number of other areas as well.

■ CRL issuer: An optional component that a CA can delegate to publish CRLs.

■ Repository: A generic term used to denote any method for storing certificates and CRLs so that they can be retrieved by end entities.

PKIX Management Functions PKIX identifies a number of management functions that potentially need to be supported by management protocols. These are indicated in Figure 4.27 and include the following:

■ Registration: This is the process whereby a user first makes itself known to a CA (directly, or through an RA), prior to that CA issuing a certificate or certificates for that user. Registration begins the process of enrolling in a PKI. Registration usually involves some offline or online procedure for mutual authentication. Typically, the end entity is issued one or more shared secret keys used for subsequent authentication.

■ Initialization: Before a client system can operate securely, it is necessary to install key materials that have the appropriate relationship with keys stored elsewhere in the infrastructure. For example, the client needs to be securely initialized with the public key and other assured information of the trusted CA(s), to be used in validating certificate paths.

■ Certification: This is the process in which a CA issues a certificate for a user's public key, and returns that certificate to the user's client system and/or posts that certificate in a repository.

■ Key pair recovery: Key pairs can be used to support digital signature creation and verification, encryption and decryption, or both. When a key pair is used for encryption/decryption, it is important to provide a mechanism to recover the necessary decryption keys when normal access to the keying material is no longer possible, otherwise it will not be possible to recover the encrypted data. Loss of access to the decryption key can result from forgotten passwords/PINs, corrupted disk drives, damage to hardware tokens, and so on.

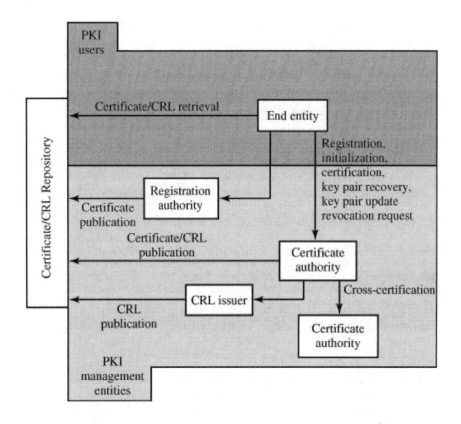

Figure 4.27: PKIX Architectural Model.

Key pair recovery allows end entities to restore their encryption/decryption key pair from an authorized key backup facility (typically, the CA that issued the end entity's certificate).

■ Key pair update: All key pairs need to be updated regularly (i.e., replaced with a new key pair) and new certificates issued. Update is required when the certificate lifetime expires and as a result of certificate revocation.

■ Revocation request: An authorized person advises a CA of an abnormal situation requiring certificate revocation. Reasons for revocation include private key compromise, change in affiliation, and name change.

■ Cross certification: Two CAs exchange information used in establishing a cross-certificate. A cross-certificate is a certificate issued by one CA to another CA that contains a CA signature key used for issuing certificates.

PKIX Management Protocols: The PKIX working group has defined two alternative management protocols between PKIX entities that support the management functions listed in the preceding subsection. RFC 2510 defines the certificate management protocols (CMP). Within CMP, each of the management functions is explicitly identified by specific protocol exchanges. CMP is designed to be a flexible protocol able to accommodate a variety of technical, operational, and business models.

RFC 2797 defines certificate management messages over CMS (CMC), where CMS refers to RFC 2630, cryptographic message syntax. CMC is built on earlier work and is intended to leverage existing implementations. Although all of the PKIX functions are supported, the functions do not all map into specific protocol exchanges.

The most commonly used PKI management protocols are

■ PKCS#10

■ PKCS#7

■ Certificate Management Protocol (CMP)

■ Certificate Management using CMS (CMC)

■ Simple Certificate Enrollment Protocol (SCEP)

PKCS#10 and PKC#7 protocols are a part of the Public Key Cryptographic Standards (PKCS) that define various standards for PKI cryptography. Some of the standards that are part of PKCS are

❖ PKCS#2: This standard has now been incorporated into PKCS#1

❖ PKCS#3: Diffie-Hellman Key Agreement Standard

❖ PKCS#4: This standard has now been incorporated into PKCS#1

❖ PKCS#5: Password-Based Cryptography Standard

❖ PKCS#6: Extended-Certificate Syntax Standard

❖ PKCS#7: Cryptographic Message Syntax Standard

❖ PKCS#8: Private Key Information Syntax Standard

❖ PKCS#9: Selected Attribute Types

❖ PKCS#10: Certification Request Syntax Standard

❖ PKCS#11: Cryptographic Token Interface Standard

❖ PKCS#12: Personal Information Exchange Syntax Standard

❖ PKCS#13: Elliptic Curve Cryptography Standard

❖ PKCS#14: Pseudorandom Number Generation Standard

❖ PKCS#15: Cryptographic Token Information Format Standard

Before discussing each of the PKI management protocols in detail, let us first look at a basic criterion for evaluating these protocols. These evaluation criteria should be kept in mind while implementing these protocols and can also be used to compare different protocols.

The evaluation criteria for PKI Management protocols are listed below:

■ These protocols must support the creation and publication of certificates and CRLs. In other words, they should allow entities to make certificate and revocation requests.

■ These protocols should be extensible, so that they can be used over disparate systems. They should also be able to address the needs of the organizations local network.

■ They should support both two-party and three-party transactions. The design of the protocol should facilitate the use of a single protocol by the entities irrespective of whether they are interacting with a CA or an RA.

■ These protocols should be algorithm-independent. Since organizations might need to use different algorithms for their key pairs, these protocols should have the ability to recognize the type of algorithm that is used. Some of the common algorithms that are used in cryptography are MD5, RSA, and DSA.

■ PKI management protocols must support different transport mechanisms, such as HTTP, FTP, and TCP/IP.

Having looked at the evaluation criteria, let us now look at each of the PKI management protocols in detail.

PKCS#10: PKCS#10, or Certificate Request Syntax Standard, defines the syntax for certificate requests. According to the PKCS#10 standard, a certificate request comprises the following three elements:

■ Certificate request information

■ A signature algorithm identifier

■ A digital signature on the certification request information

The certificate request information is composed of the Distinguished Name (DN) of the entity, the public key of the entity, and some other attributes that are optional. These attributes contain additional information about the entity, such as the postal address to which the signed certificate should be returned if electronic mail is not available. These attributes may also contain a challenge password which the entity can use when requesting for the revocation of the certificate at a later stage. Suppose a user requests the AllSolv CA for a certificate. Now to request for a certificate according to PKCS#10, the user needs to perform the following steps:

1. Generate a CertificateRequestInfo value as per the PKCS#10 specification from his public key and user name. As already discussed, this CertificateRequestInfo value consists of the distinguished name of the entity, in this case Bob, and the public key of the entity.

2. After generating the CertificateRequestInfo value, Bob needs to sign this value with his private key.

3. Finally, Bob needs to generate a CertifcateRequest value as per PKCS#10 from the CertificateRequestInfo value and his signature.

CertificateRequestInfo comprises the following components:

■ Version: Represents the version number so that it is compatible with any future modifications. As can be seen from the preceding example, the version number is 0.

■ Subject: Represents the distinguished name of the subject of the certificate.

■ SubjectPublicKeyInfo: Represents the public key information of the subject of the certificate, which is to be certified.

■ Attributes: Represents additional information about the subject of the certificate such as the subject's common name and the organization name.

PKCS#10 is the most common standard for certificate requests. Since most of the PKI applications have become Web-enabled, certificate requests can be made online. However, PKCS#10 does not support HTTP protocols. When a certificate request is made over the Web by using HTTP, the CA is unable to authenticate the entity. Therefore, PKCS#10 is used most commonly with the Secure Sockets Layer (SSL) for making certificate requests.

Generally, PKCS#10 and SSL are used in a three-party transaction; in which an RA authenticates the request after an entity has submitted it to the CA. The following process takes place in a third-party transaction when PKCS#10 is used with SSL:

1. An SSL connection is established between the client and the CA.

2. The client submits a PKCS#10 request to the CA.

3. The CA sends the request to the RA for verification.

4. An SSL session is established between the RA and the CA.

5. Based on the verification of the information, the RA processes the request. The RA can approve or deny the request.

6. If the RA approves the request, the CA issues a certificate.

Note: The request for comments for this protocol are in RFC 2314. Although PKCS#10 is the most widely used certificate format, it suffers from some inherent limitations.

Limitations of PKCS#10- A few limitations of PKCS#10 are:

■ PKCS#10 is not algorithm-independent. Just like an RSA algorithm, it also assumes that the private key might be used for creating the digital signature.

■ The digital signature on a PKCS#10 request does not provide all the information that a CA needs to authenticate the users. In addition, there is no well-defined mechanism to ensure that a certificate request has not been altered during its transit.

■ PKCS#10 defines the syntax for only one message type, which is a certificate request, and not for the complete protocol. It does not specify the syntax and protocol for any other types of messages such as certificate revocation requests. Hence, messages other than certificate requests have to be implemented by using other protocols, such as HTTP.

Consequently, PKCS#10 is considered the industry standard for certificate requests.

PKCS#7: PKCS#7 or cryptographic message syntax standard defines the syntax for cryptographic data, such as digital signatures. PKCS allows for authentication of attribute information in addition to authenticating the content of the messages. Some of the important uses of PKCS#7 are

■ The CAs use the PKCS#7 standard as a response to the entity requesting a certificate.

■ It is used to authenticate the certificate messages sent to an entity.

■ It provides complete information to the CA for processing certificate requests.

■ It is used by many protocols such as S/MIME for providing security.

PKCS#7 stipulates that the format of a message must consist of two fields:

■ Content type
■ Content

Let us look at each of these fields in detail.

Content Type The content type field outlines the specifications for the format of the content and is referred to as an object identifier. The six content types defined by PKCS#7 are

■ Data
■ Signed data
■ Enveloped data
■ Signed and enveloped data
■ Digested data
■ Encrypted data

■ Content types can also be classified into two classes

■ Enhanced: The content types other than the data content type fall in this class.

We will discuss only the signed data content type because it is used most commonly for PKI cryptography.

Signed Data: The fields that are included in the signed data content type are:

■ Version: It is the version number of the content.

■ Digest algorithms: These are the encrypted message digest algorithms of the content.

■ Content Info: It is the digitally signed content.

■ Certificates: These are the set of X.509 certificates and/or PKCS#6 certificates. This is an optional field.

■ CRLs: This is also an optional field and contains a set of CRLs.

■ Signer Info: The signer info field contains the following information:

[l]The version of the certificate

[l] The issuer and serial number

[l]Authenticated attributes

[l] Digital signature algorithm

[l] Digital signature

[l] Unauthenticated attributes

The following steps take place for creating a signed data content type:

1. A message digest for each user is calculated based on a signer-specific message digest algorithm.

2. The user's private key encrypts this message digest and the associated information. The encrypted message digest and other signer-specific information together form the signer info value.

3. After the signer info value has been generated, certificates and CRLs are collected.

4. Finally, for all of the users, the signer info values, certificates, CRLs, and message digest algorithms are collated to form the signed data content type.

In the previous section where we discussed PKCS#10, we looked at how Bob obtained a certificate by using PKCS#10. Let us now look at how Bob can use PKCS#7 to create a digitally signed message by using PKCS#7. Bob needs to perform the following steps to create a digitally signed message by using PKCS#7:

1. Encode a value of type ContentInfo as per PKCS#7 for the data that he wants to sign.

2. Digest the data to be signed as per PKCS#7.

3. Encode a value of type DigestInfo as per PKCS#7 from the message digest.

4. Encrypt the encoded DigestInfo with his private key.

5. Encode a SignedData type value as per PKCS#7 from the first ContentInfo value, the encrypted message digest, and other information such as his certificate and the message digest algorithm identifier.

6. Encode another ContentInfo type value from the SignedData value as per PKCS#7.

Limitations of PKCS#7 Similar to PKCS#10, PKCS#7 does not define any syntax for certificate revocation messages. However, combining PKCS#7 with PKCS#10 results in the formation of a complete and secure transaction model. Both of these protocols can be implemented easily since their formats are supported by most systems. PKCS#7 is highly extensible. Any information can be added to the format by using the authenticated and unauthenticated attributes. Two other protocols that are also often discussed are PKCS#11 and PKCS#12. Let us look at a brief description of these protocols. Note: The request for comments for PKCS#10 is included in RFC 2315.

PKCS#11: PKCS#11 was introduced to implement cryptography with the use of portable computing devices such as smart cards, PCMCIA cards, and smart diskettes as they provide a way to store the private key component of a public key/private key pair securely, under the control of a single user. In this protocol, the cryptographic application utilizes the device to perform the operations rather than performing cryptographic operations so that sensitive information such as private keys are never revealed. As more applications are developed for public key cryptography, a standard programming interface for these devices becomes increasingly valuable. This standard is used for a lower-level programming interface that abstracts the details of the devices and presents a common model of the cryptographic device to the application. These cryptographic devices are known as cryptographic token. There are different kinds of tokens, namely:

- Signing tokens: These tokens consist of a signing certificate and are used for signing objects, messages, and for SSL authentication.

- External key distribution tokens: These are used for distributing private keys.

- Signing and decryption tokens: Signing tokens do not support encrypted S/MIME, as they cannot decrypt messages. Hence, signing and decryption tokens are used for encrypted messages over the Internet.

- Multipurpose tokens: These tokens can perform several cryptographic functions and are similar to cryptographic accelerator cards.

PKCS#11 can be used for the resource sharing if needed and is also termed as a cryptoki.

PKCS#12: This is a standard, which describes the syntax for the transfer of personal identity information, including private keys, certificates, miscellaneous secrets, and extensions. Applications, browsers, and machines that support PKCS#12 allow users to import, export, and exercise a single set of personal identity information through them. This standard supports direct transfer of personal information under several privacy and integrity modes. There are four combinations of privacy modes and integrity modes. The privacy modes use encryption to protect personal information from exposure, and the integrity modes protect personal information from tampering. The privacy modes are

- Public key privacy mode: Personal information is enveloped on the source platform by using a trusted encryption public key of a known destination platform. The envelope is opened with the corresponding private key.

- Password privacy mode: Personal information is encrypted with a symmetric key derived from a user name and a privacy password. If password integrity mode is used as well, the privacy password and the integrity password may or may not be the same.

The integrity modes are

- Public key integrity mode: Integrity is guaranteed through a digital signature on the contents of the PFX Protocol Data Unit (PDU), which is produced using the source platforms private signature key. The signature is verified on the destination platform by using the corresponding public key.

- Password integrity mode: Integrity is guaranteed through a Message Authentication Code (MAC) derived from a secret integrity password. If the password privacy mode is used as well, the privacy password and the integrity password may or may not be the same.

Note: The most secure of the privacy and integrity modes require the source and destination platforms to have trusted public/private key pairs usable for digital signatures and encryption, respectively. PKCS#12 also supports lower-security, password-based privacy and integrity modes for those cases in which trusted public/private key pairs are not available.

RSA Algorithm

It is known by the initials of the three discoverers (Rivest, Shamir, Adleman): RSA. It has survived all attempts to break it for more than 30 years and is considered very strong. Much practical security is based on it. For this reason, Rivest, Shamir and

Adleman were given the 2002 ACM Turing Award. Its major disadvantage is that it requires keys of at least 1024 bits for good security (vs. 128 bits for symmetric-key algorithms), which makes it quite slow. The RSA method is based on some principles from number theory. We will now summarize how to use the method:

1. Choose two large primes, p and q (typically 1024 bits).

2. Compute n = p q and z = (p 1) (q 1).

3. Choose a number relatively prime to z and call it d.

4. Find e such that e d = 1 mod z.

With these parameters computed in advance, we are ready to begin encryption. Divide the plaintext (regarded as a bit string) into blocks, so that each plaintext message, P, falls in the interval 0 P ¡ n. Do that by grouping the plaintext into blocks of k bits, where k is the largest integer for which 2k ¡ n is true.

To encrypt a message, P, compute $C = P^e \pmod{n}$. To decrypt C, compute $P = C^d \pmod{n}$. It can be proven that for all P in the specified range, the encryption and decryption functions are inverses. To perform the encryption, you need e and n. To perform the decryption, you need d and n. Therefore, the public key consists of the pair (e, n) and the private key consists of (d, n).

The security of the method is based on the difficulty of factoring large numbers. If the cryptanalyst could factor the (publicly known) n, he could then find p and q, and from these z. Equipped with knowledge of z and e, d can be found using Euclid's algorithm. Fortunately, mathematicians have been trying to factor large numbers for at least 300 years, and the accumulated evidence suggests that it is an exceedingly difficult problem.

According to Rivest and colleagues, factoring a 500-digit number would require 10^{25} years using brute force. In both cases, they assumed the best known algorithm and a computer with a 1-μsec instruction time. With a million chips running in parallel, each with an instruction time of 1 nsec, it would still take 10^{16} years. Even if computers continue to get faster by an order of magnitude per decade, it will be many years before factoring a 500-digit number becomes feasible, at which time our descendants can simply choose p and q still larger.

A trivial pedagogical example of how the RSA algorithm works is given in Figure 4.28. For this example, we have chosen p = 3 and q = 11, giving n = 33 and z = 20. A suitable value for d is d = 7, since 7 and 20 have no common factors. With these choices, e can be found by solving the equation 7e = 1 (mod 20), which yields e = 3. The ciphertext, C, corresponding to a plaintext message, P, is given by $C = P^3 \pmod{33}$. The ciphertext is decrypted by the receiver by making use of the rule $P = C^7 \pmod{33}$. The figure shows the encryption of the plaintext "SUZANNE" as an example.

Because the primes chosen for this example are so small, P must be less than 33, so each plaintext block can contain only a single character. The result is a monoalphabetic substitution cipher, not very impressive. If instead we had chosen p and

Plaintext (P)			Ciphertext (C)		After decryption	
Symbolic	Numeric	P3	P3 (mod 33)	C7	C7 (mod 33)	Symbolic
S	19	6859	28	13492928512	19	S
U	21	9261	21	1801088541	21	U
Z	26	17576	20	1280000000	26	Z
A	01	1	1	1	01	A
N	14	2744	5	78125	14	N
N	14	2744	5	78125	14	N
E	05	125	26	8031810176	05	E

Sender's computation   Receiver's computation

Figure 4.28: An example of RSA algorithm.

$q \approx 2^{512}$, we would have $n \approx 2^{1024}$, so each block could be up to 1024 bits or 128 eight-bit characters, versus 8 characters for DES and 16 characters for AES.

It should be pointed out that using RSA as we have described is similar to using a symmetric algorithm in ECB mode–the same input block gives the same output block. Therefore, some form of chaining is needed for data encryption. However, in practice, most RSA-based systems use public-key cryptography primarily for distributing one-time session keys for use with some symmetric-key algorithm such as AES or triple DES. RSA is too slow for actually encrypting large volumes of data but is widely used for key distribution.

Chapter 5

Authorization —Future Internet Architecture

5.1 Introduction

Authentication and access control are closely related to each other which are the two main aspects of security. Authentication deals with passwords, biometrics, certificates, etc., to verify the user and access control grants the permission to perform the operations on an application. By enforcing the access control mechanism, we gain confidentiality. We have discussed in detail the authentication where the issue is to identify the entities in the architecture where the authorization deals with the situation where the entities are already authenticated. We discuss various mechanisms of access control that can be enforced on the authenticated entities which are present in current Internet and suitable for future Internet. A detailed case study has been considered stating a mechanism that suites the architecture.

5.2 Need of Authorization

Access control is the fundamental principle of security and it deals with the restrictions posed on the authenticated users. Authorization is the part of access control which is one aspect and the authentication is another aspect of security. This uses peer entity authentication and some rules to allow access or deny the access for the requested service. It is paramount for protecting the private and confidential information from various attacks. Authorization was treated as the heart of information security in the old ages, and during times it has been considered as a quaint notion. We are enforcing the restrictions on the authenticated users. Over the decades, several models were developed to enhance the principles of security, i.e., confidentiality, Integrity, availability or the administration flexibility. Without authorization, the services cannot be owned, created, destroyed, altered, observed, executed, appended or searched. The classic methods that restrict the access control of the entities are the access control list and the capabilities. Multilevel security is provided in Mandatory Access Control mechanisms to layout the essential security requirements of a system. For the Public Key Infrastructure (PKI) based applications, Role Based access control along with some tokens should be considered.

The usage of the available data based on the access list stored in the system should be maintained by a trusted third party. Access to the services stored in the system must be controlled by some means of authentication. The association of the individual entity with the certificate cannot be denied by the entity. The system identifies the entity accessing the services based on some identification like digital certificates which certifies their identity. The system identifies the entity based on the assumption, the system has entity records which are stored locally or remotely and accessed by the trusted third party. The importance of authorization has increased with the integrated data, new entities who require access to the required data [14]. This approach require some other security services like Identification, Authentication, Authorization and Accountability when invoked.

In Future Internet architectures access control is more than requiring authentication when the principals want to access the resources from the available system or from the network. Access is nothing but the ability of the principal (entity) to perform some action like read, write, execute, update, delete, modify, etc. It is the information flow between the principals/entities and the services. Access control is the control flow of information between the principals and the resources which communicate and interact with each other and this consists of three core components which work together to provide a secure environment and these are found in applications, routers, databases and much more [173] [175].

a Identification: For the effective access control, the system must provide some kind to identify for the entities of the system. If the identification is weak, there is a possibility of malicious entites to get identified and access permissions may be allocated to the malicious entites which cause severe damage. The label can be an ID (identifier), complete name along with surname, smart card or the biometric that is mapped to the entity within the security database. The identification of the principals is performed using the sourceID of the entities like UserID, IP address to protect the applications from potential attacks.

b Authentication: The process of identification is performed using authentication to prove authenticity of the user. The widely used mechanisms are **something the entity knows:** The entity knows or has some identity that they can remembered like password, passphrase or other unique authentication code such as PIN. *Password* is a private word or a combination of the characters that the entities know and should be difficult to guess and easy to remember. *passphrase* is a combination of characters, longer than password from which virtual password is derived. **Something the entity has:** The entity has something and can produce when asked for like smart cards, ATM cards, tokens etc. *Smart cards* contains a chip that will verify the data and validate the number of pieces of information instead of PIN. Token is also a chip and a liquid crystal that shows a computer generated number. Synchronous tokens are synchronized with the server and works based on the time based database and asynchronous tokens require no server, tokens maintain time setting, uses challenge-response system.**Something an entity is:** It deals with entity characteristics like fingerprints, palm prints, retina, etc, and this method of dealing with characteristics is called as biometric authentication. Some systems require ATM and PIN called two-factor authentication as two separate mechanisms are used. The process of authentication is performed using the concept of PKI (For more details please refer to Chapter 4).

c Authorization: It is a matching between the identity of the entity and the access levels granted for that particular entity. This referring of the entity and the access levels are stored in the database. Authorization can be performed using any one of the three ways which issue access permissions for each user which becomes complex in sort time, issuing access permissions to a class of members who are authenticated is very common practice and finally access permissions across the multiple systems using a centralized authentication and access control system. Generally, it consists of read, write and execute permissions which are explained in detail in the following sections.

d Accountability: It is also known as auditability. This ensures all actions of access are attributed to an authenticated entity. It is often accomplished by means of system logs and database and auditing those in the database. The system log stores the information like the failed attempts toward the access of the files. It is simply a tracking system for a particular application.

5.3 Access Control Mechanisms

An important aspect of security is to protect the information from unauthorized disclosure or improper modifications (integrity) and ensuring availability of the services for the authorized users. Access to a system or a resource to be controlled by some process and this process we can call as access control mechanism. For the development of these, we require some regulations in the system. The development process takes places based on the following concepts.

Security Policy: SecuritypPolicy defines a set of rules which are regulated while implementing access control mechanism. The request is processed by mediating it to the data or the services maintained in the system and also determines whether to grant or deny. The mechanism is implemented using some regulations established by the policy. Different mechanisms can be applied based on the permissions, by different means of security assurances. A security model is implemented based on the formal representation of the policy and its related functions. The formal methods contain the proofs of the properties that are provided by the access control mechanism. They define low-level and high level functions that are imposed by the policy.

Security Model: The model provides a formal presentation of the access control policy and its working. It provides a formal proof of security properties being designed for access control system.

Security Mechanism: It defines the low level functions which implement the controls that are imposed by the policy.

The mentioned concepts correspond to the conceptual separation between the different levels of the design and provides multilevel software development. The separation is between the policies and mechanisms applied on the services. It is possible to discuss the protection requirements based on the policies, compare different access policies and mechanisms and the enforcement of these policies on the entities involved in the communication. It should also provide tamperproof information, non-bypassable, confined to a limited part of the system and apply rigorous verification methods. The various access control mechanisms are discussed in the following sections.

5.3.1   Access Control Matrix (ACM)

The view of access control mechanism started with Lampson's matrix in 1969. This matrix contains all the information required by a system to make decisions about the entities which are allowed to do what with the various services. These attributes define the access rights of the services provided by the system. In order to protect the services which are shared to various systems among various entities we use access control mechanism. The entity is defined as a user (may not be a human sometimes may be a server in the network) and the service is the resource or the application which is made available to the entity. The fundamental concepts of access control in the field of authorization is Access Control List (ACL) and the capabilities. These two are derived from the Lampson access control matrix that contains a row for each entity and a column for every service provided by the system. Access control matrix is an ACL in the form of table. The entities and the services are identified and the permissions are granted and their combination is presented in the form of a matrix. The allowed access will be stored at the intersection of the row of entity (E) and the service (S). Generally a system allows read(r), write(w) and execute(e) privileges for the entities toward the services or the resources. ACM can be used to summarize the permissions of the entities and the services. This is extremely helpful in the service or application design to ensure the security for all entities throughout the process.

5.3.2   Access Control Lists (ACL)

Simplifying the access rights management is to store them in the form of access control matrix, a column at a time, along with the service to which the column refers.

This maintenance of the lists is called Access Control List (ACL). The network devices are configured with access lists which define the entity names or the IDs or the IP addresses associated and authorized to access the services. When we are using ACL in a network, IP address or the network designation will be the ID and the action consists of the instructions to allow or block the traffic that passes through. The service access can be changed only by the administrator. The ACL for a service or the application will be the entity ID or the Group ID and the actions which are allowed to access the requested service. These ACLs have their own advantages and disadvantages in the sense of security management. ACLs can be divided into general and specific properties depending on the importance of the services. These are used where users manage their own files and difficult to maintain in large environments and constantly changing environments or where the entities want to delegate their authority to another entity for a particular period of time. There are many action pairs in ACL and the system continues to search down the list until it finds a match. If a match is found, then permission is granted, or else the permission is denied or blocked by the system. The default action for the entity which is new to the system is based on the organization's overall security, i.e., it may be deined by default or permitted to by default. ACLs are often used for system provisioning permissions applied to the actions of an entity or to a group of entities. Within the system, the information is translated into an ACL, when access to a particular service is requested. As the entities and the services appear in the access control matrix, it stores all the relevant information on the authorization decisions to be considered on the entities. As the ACL is a large dataset and is difficult to manage, it can be partitioned into more manageable pieces. One way is to split the matrix into columns and store the column with its corresponding service. Another way is to store them in rows, where each row is stored with its corresponding entity. This kind of row-wise storage of the permissions is called capabilities or the C-lists. ACLs perform packet filtering to control the packet flow over a network. The use of ACLs in the network has some advantage over the IP like authenticate incoming remote shell and remote copy protocol requests, block unwanted traffic or the entities, access control over Telnet, limit the debug command output, classify the traffic, NAT control, reduce DOS attacks, restrict the routing content updates, trigger dial on demand calls, etc., [189].

Capabilities or C-lists: Capabilities built the association between the entities and the services are built within the system indicating the authorization whereas ACL uses a separate method for associating the entities to the files that are required. This is an inherent advantage of the capability. They are the dual approach to the ACLs. The matrix is stored in the form of rows which makes it easy to view all the access that is associated with the entities. These C-lists were developed in 1970s but couldn't prove their success. Although C-lists have several security advantages over ACL's the systems follow the ACL approach. The combined use of ACLs and capabilities is sufficient for an entity to gain the authorization. In the distributed network, repeated authentication is not required. This gives an opportunity to fetch the services from various providers without repeated authentication. Each provider in the network can use fine-grained access control using ACLs.

5.3.3   Identity-Based Access Control (IBAC)

Before allowing the entities to access the services, the authentication and their access right policies are to be publicized by the certificate authorities. The agents in the network can store the list of the authenticated entities and their permissions in the databases. The requests of the entities can be fulfilled by other databases, if it comes via an authenticated entity. The rules of the entities can be stored with the help of ACLs, i.e., the entry in the ACL specifies what each entity may perform within the network. The decisions based on the Identity is straightforward, consists of the problems like Information leakage, role exploration. delegation and revocation, building trust relationships and distributed identity management.

5.3.4   Authorization-Based Access Control (ABAC)

In identity-based access control, the entities are identified and their access control permissions are stored with the certificate authorities. If a service is requested by the entity, it is forwarded to the policy engine for determining the authorizations and reports back to the entity. The service is allocated to the entity on the basis of its authorization but not on the identity. The identity of the entity is sent to the policy engine and we get back a set of permissions which the entity is allowed to do. Entity requests the service by including the rights it wants to access. This small change results in a more manageable, evolvable and secure system. Each domain or the system has a database of all the services available to its entities/principals along with a set of access permissions and the policies. While IBAC has a list of entities associated with the service, ABAC has a list of access permissions for each entity. A policy language can be used to store which entity gets which rights. This has an advantage over IBAC as each database has the details about its own entities, no problem of distributed identity management. If one entity changes the duties to another, the access permissions are simply changed in that database and can revoke that are not appropriate. No need to inform other databases about the changes, as no other database is involved and no information leakage about the organization as the structure of the database is not revealed to another. Easy delegation of the permissions from one to another without informing the authorities. This mechanism makes easy upgrade of the system. The system leads to a scalable as each database is responsible for its own entities, more evolvable as the service has to interpret the contents of authorization. It is more private as there is no information leakage, manageable due to easy delegation of the permissions to one another and secure as the encryption and signature are used to protect the request from the attacks.

5.3.5   Rule-Based Access Control (R-BAC)

In this system, the access to the services is based on the list of predefined rules for the access to be granted. The rules are created or authorized by the owners, privileges are granted based on the specific condition that is met. In the ACL, the matrix can specify which entity is allowed to access what, whereas in rule-based system conditions are applied for the access of a particular application. Rule-based controls are the common form of DAC, as the system owner develops the rules based on the needs of the organization. Rules are enforced using a mediation mechanism which ensures the access by intercepting each and every request comparing with the access permissions of the entity.

5.3.6   Policy-Based Access Control (PBAC)

Policy based access control verifies whether an entity is authorized to access a service according to the policies defined by the policy repository and agreed by the entity. The activities are regulated by the policies with various granularities within an organization. The security policies are dependent on the role the entity plays within an organization. All these policies are enforced by different levels of supervisors or the owners of that particular department. The policies are to be described in a different syntaxes and difficult to have a global view of the policies and how they apply to a specific case. Sometimes two policies may conflict and there is no way to combine them. In short, enforcing these rules may be complex and error prone as there is no clear idea of applying the rules for a request. The solution for the problem is to enforce the pre-defined rules in a consistent way and keep track of the access rules, always keep them up to date. It should allow a wide variety of mechanisms to implement, the access status should be made clear and no direct access to the services. All these rules are to be considered and some meta information to combine them for taking a final decision. A policy will specify how these rules are to be combined, a composite aggregate rules using a composite pattern are considered. All the applicable rules are to be stored in a unique repository of the organization in a centralized fashion.

5.3.7   Discretionary Access Controls (DAC)

Discretionary access control is a very early form of authorization which are widely deployed in many architectures like UNIX, Linux etc., as it is flexible in nature. These are implemented on the option of the user. Now-a-day's these are used to manage the owners data in their own systems and the security of that files, OS as well as it is supported by Linux. The owner determines the privileges they can allocate for others. It is user-centric and the owner has the power to allocate the access and to whom based on the requirements. The owner can allow, in general, unrestricted access or they can allow specific entity or set of entities to access the service. The owner of the service has full control regarding the access of the owned service by other entities and such controls are called discretionary. The matrix gets updated when the service and the entities are added or deleted. These are inadequate for enforcing the information policies. The policies govern the access of the entities to the services on the basis of the identity of the entity and the access permissions specified, for individual entity or a class of entities which are allowed. If the access permission is related to the service, the access is granted or else denied. The problem with this approach is that there is no constraint on copying the information from owner service to other. As well it does not provide real assurance for the flow of information and does not impose any restriction once the entity receives the service. The diffusion of the service is controlled in mandatory systems by preventing the information from high level to low level entities.

5.3.8 Mandatory Access Controls (MAC)

Mandatory access controls use data classification schemes, this mechanism gives limited access to the entities and the data owners. With DACs, the controls applied by the entity are free to their discretion but not based on the classification. Each set of service is given rates to specify the level of application that the entity can access. The ratings are collected and often referred to the sensitivity levels which indicates the confidentiality level of the service or the application. Each entity and the service is assigned a security level. The security level associated with a service reflects the sensitivity of the information contained in the service, verifying the potential damage that could result from unauthorized disclosure of the information. MAC itself requires a system to manage the access control with the security policies. MAC is used for the systems and the services which are highly sensitive, where the owner does not want others to bypass the mandated access control. MAC provides a multilayered service processing. Based on the information provided by the owner like the level of control and the system makes the decision control, allows the access for a service. For this, the service needs to be labeled according to the classification, depending on the permissions, the entity or the group of entities are granted. The security level associated with an entity, also called clearance, reflects the entities trustworthiness not to disclose sensitive information to other entities who are not authorized. Security level is an element of hierarchical ordered set. It consists of TOP SECRET, SECRET, CONFIDENTIAL and UNCLASSIFIED. The multilevel security model was first developed by David Elliott and Len LaPadula in 1973 for the defense applications that describe a set of rules that uses the label on the applications and the clearance for the entities in the system. This multilevel security is required when the entities and the services at various levels use the same system applications. The main purpose of this is to enforce a form of access control by restricting the entities on the services for which they have the necessary permissions. Each security level dominates itself and all others below the hierarchy. Access to a service is granted only if there exists a relationship between the security level associated with the entity and the service. It can be stated as each entity's clearance must dominate the security level of the service being read and an entity's clearance must be dominated by the security level of the service being written. These two state the properties of read down and write up which will prevent the information flow from high level services to low level services. A variation in this model is called Lattice-based access control where entities are assigned a matrix of permissions for particular services. The level of access control varies with the authorization classified based on the services possessed by the individual in each class. The lattice access control contains the entities, services and the boundaries associated with each pair. This structure specifies the level of access each entity has toward each service. The column-based attributes of the ACL are considered for this type of model. The problem with this access control mechanism is that it couldn't solve the Trojan Horse completely [116].

MAC enforces security labels to its entities and the services whereas DAC enforces authorization to a service on the basis of the permissions granted by the owner. RBAC, is an independent component of the access control along with MAC and DAC. If the system uses DAC, MAC and RBAC, then the access is allowed based on the permissions granted by these mechanisms. In some cases, RBAC is used by itself. RBAC [176] is a policy neutral by itself and some have mandatory flavor while others have a strong discretionary flavor.

Nondiscretionary controls are strictly-enforced versions of MACs that are managed by a central authority in the organization and can be based on an individuals role–role-based controls –or a specified set of tasks (subject- or object-based)–task-based controls. Role-based controls are assigned to a role the user performs in an organization, and task-based controls are to a particular assignment or responsibility. The role and task controls make it easier to maintain the controls and restrictions associated with a particular role or task, especially if the individual performing the role or task changes often. Instead of constantly assigning and revoking the privileges of individuals who come and go, the administrator simply assigns the associated access rights to the role or task, and then whenever individuals are associated with that role or task, they automatically receive the corresponding access. When their turns are over, they are removed from the role or task and the access is revoked.

5.3.9   Role-Based Access Control (RBAC)

Role-based access control mechanism has been widely accepted by many due to its low cost and complexity for securing large networked systems. It was poineered in the 1970s for the online systems which has begun with multi-user and multi-application environment. Later, again introduced in 1992 by David Ferraiolo and Rick Kuhn. It is not directly concerned with the policy but has been accepted as a security model and enforces the access control mechanism in an organizational way. This has greatly simplified the management of permissions. The access control is allocated based on the roles the entities are assigned by the organization of a network. The owner governs what the roles can access and how they can access the services as in DAC or Policy-based or as with MACs. It regulates entity access to the information on the basis of the activities entities execute in the system and its own access capabilities. Role-based policies require the identification of the roles in the system. A role can be defined as a set of actions and responsibilities connected by the entity's activities. Services are associated with a role that will inherit the privileges assigned to that role. Entities can be reassigned from one role to another. It directly supports the three security principles: *least privilege* which allocates only those permissions required for the tasks conducted by members of the role that has been assigned. *Separation of duties* is ensured by invoking the mutually exclusive roles to complete a particular service/task. *Data abstraction* issues an abstracted permissions to the entities rather than the read, write, execute which are allocated by the operating system. The adoption of this model has several advantages like authorization management, roles hierarchy and separation of duties. This allows better management by separating the entity assignment to the roles and the access control to the roles. It allows better static/dynamic constraint enforcement that restricts the number of roles allowed for a given privilege. This is true even for a group of entities and the roles the entities play in various groups [31]. When we look at the meaning of a group, it is a list of principals which have the same access permissions for a period of time using some defined procedures. It includes the capability to establish the relationships between the roles and the permissions as well as entities and roles. Roles can take the inheritance relations like the one role inherits the permissions assigned to a different role. To enforce the security policy which even includes the separation of duties and even takes care of authority delegation. It even deals with role-role permission, user-role relationship along with role-role relationships. There are four RBAC architectures based on the variations on how they can be applied within the system [176].

- Non-RBAC: It is as simple as the traditional mapping, i.e., the matrix as in ACLs. There are no roles associated with mapping, other than any identified by a particular user.

- Limited RBAC: This is achieved when roles are mapped with entities within a single service rather than as a whole. Entities in this are also able to access the non-RBAC based services. This is based on the entity defined within a service and not necessarily based on the role the entity is playing in an organization. An entity can play multiple roles in several services, can have direct access to another service in the system with a different role.

- Hybrid RBAC: This introduces the use of role that is applied to several services based on the entity's specific role within an organization. In this, the entity can be assigned to roles defined solely within an organization for specific applications, complimenting the larger, or more encompassing the organizational role used by other systems.

- Full RBAC: The systems are controlled by roles defined by the organization's policy and access control infrastructure, applied to the services and systems across the network. The services and associated data apply permissions based on the enterprise definition, not one defined by a specific service.

The main advantage of the RBAC access system is that it can be easily modeled based on the organization functional structure. The roles are in the form of hierarchy of an organization, so they have roles in the functional hierarchy of an information system.

For the future Internet architectures, the flexible certificate mechanism along with flexible access controls are required along with a strong security. The access can be granted or denied based on the authorizations of the entities which can use different access models. In reality, they use a combination of the mechanisms to implement a smooth access control in the system. The rules can be called policies for the information sharing over the network. A distributed policy is to be implemented, to achieve reliability where the nodes are not stable. Policy decision points are considered to invoke the local copy of the policy for making a decision. It is noted that the policy rules may change during the service lifetime dynamically. These rules are changed to overcome the risk assessment and the changed rules must be distributed immediately to all the databases. To overcome the continuous request for a set of services, and getting authorized each time, we use authentication mechanism with the server at a single point. For the certification, IDs can be built by the devices and access mechanism to be provided with the help of trusted third parties CAs. On the basis of authentication, the entity is allowed to use the services which are allowed. The entities involved in a service have to get authenticated for the exchange of services [97].

5.4 SONATE —Access Control Mechanism Model for Distributed Networks Case Study

The access control mechanism provides a solution of who can access what services provided by SONATE. The prerequisites of the access controls are as follows:

☞ The mechanism should support access control, for sharing the services with a group of users.

☞ It should offer proper access to the user, i.e., make sure the information is not elsewhere used without knowledge of the owner.

☞ The mechanism must be able to generate notifications about the usage of the services to the owner.

☞ The broker should have appropriate access control to offer privacy, for both services and relationships between the user and services.

☞ The mechanism must be able to define access control constraints based on the rules. It should support fine-grained access control policies for the services.

☞ It must be able to facilitate users to define access control policies not only based on predefined constant properties but also based on dynamic properties of the services or entities.

☞ It should offer the options to the users that allow specific operations on services, such as read/write/execute.

☞ The mechanisms must be transparent for the authorized users.

The services provided by the SONATE architecture are flexible and loosely coupled which are vulnerable to attacks. Some defense mechanisms need be provided for access of these services by the entities/principals of the system. The access controls need to be provided for the protection of the services from the access attacks. The access control in the system considers whether to grant the access to the services requested by the consumer. In SONATE, the purpose of access control is to restrict the access of the entities for the services/applications. This is the first line of defense to protect the applications/services of the system. These are developed to enforce the rules of a security policy and to dictate how the principals can access the applications. There are several models available [121] for the development of access control mechanism. For the development of any access control system the three abstractions are required to be considered and these are *Access Control Policies, Access Control Models, and Access Control Mechanisms*. The *Access Control Policies (ACPs)* deal with how the access is managed and who can access what resources, access control list is a *Access Control Mechanism (ACM)* and the gap between the policies and mechanism is built using the *Access Control Model* based on the security levels and the properties.

Access control is a way for managing the access of the resources by the users. When an entity tries to access some resource and it is asked for identification is the access control. The Access Control List (ACL) based mechanism is not so complex to get installed on the routers, brokers of the network. These are fine grained providing flexibility to the file owners for assigning the access permissions to a Group. Role Based Access Control (RBAC) mechanism is used as the entities play different roles for performing a task. It provides easy determination of the services who can access them and easy for revoking the access toward the services. The entites of SONATE, Consumer/user, broker, Provider fall under different groups which requires different permissions for the access of the services for providing authorization. The broker analyzes the data passing, compares it with the data stored in its repository for the restriction or permission of the access. These act as network filters when installed in routers and system filters when stored in the repository of the broker for the avoidance of vulnerable attacks. Mandatory Access Control (MAC) model is used to define the security levels of the entities and the services. The matrix of the privileges are stored in the repository of the broker to make easy verification of the entity whenever a request is delivered.

5.4.1   Role-Based Access Control (RBAC) to suite SONATE:

This model allows the principals/ entities to control the access to the services and the operations to be performed on the services by the principals based on their identity provided to the system. In this security labels are not used and it is usually implemented using Access Control list (ACL). Many modern operating systems typically considers ACL-based approach which are developed based on the principals requirement [69][165]. These govern the access based on the user's identity and access permissions they specify for each service for which the principals are allowed. The basic access modes are read, write, execute and these are stored in the form of access table where each application is associated with a list of the actions that can be performed by the principal. The access list is stored in the repository of the service broker in the form of a matrix called the access matrix (Table 5.1), which can be represented by m_{ij} where "m" is the matrix, i is the ith principal in the matrix and j is the jth application of the matrix. This specifies the permission level that must be granted to the principals with respect to the protected resource.

Table 5.1: Acces Matrix

Principals	Service (P_1)	P_2
s_1	Read	Write
s_2	Read and execute	
s_3		Read
s_n	Read	Append

ACL restricts the grants for the access of the services according to the privileges. This specifies the permission level that must be granted to the principals with respect to the protected resource assigned to the network as well as to the individual system. Permissions specify the operations that the entities can perform on specific applications/ services. Every principal is assigned a level of access for each application based on the role they play in the network. The principals/entities of the system are provider, broker and consumer/users represented by "S". There exist two types of user principals based on the group they belong and they are technical and non-technical / normal role of the user principals and all the principals are authenticated. "S" is the range of the entities/ principals which are unlimited and given by S = $s_1 \cdots s_i \cdots s_n$. To find provider principals, s_p in the set then it is identified by $s_p = s - s'$. Permission read (r) is assigned to brokers, normal users as well to the users who can read and view the contents and its properties for the acceptance or the rejection of the resources. Principals with write (w) permissions can alter, update the existing service Building Blocks, and sometimes can delete the resources from the pool and even alter the access rights of the principals in the network. Execute (x) permission allows the principals to execute the services that were allotted to the principals. The meaning of the access attribute is not at all constrained; rather each access mode is analyzed and paired with the access principal that matches the privilege (Table 5.2).

Table 5.2: Principals with their Permissions

Role of the Principals	Privileges
Technical user	Read, write, execute
Non-technical user	Read and execute
Brokers	Read only
Providers	Read, write, execute

The permissions are accessed by the principals based on the group they belong to such as owner, group and public. The services are fetched from the providers which are available in the network via brokers who communicate and interact with others on the network. The owner of the service will contain full access rights like read, write, execute but not always, as the ownership can be transferred to others by removing its permissions on the services that were provided to other brokers of the network. The authenticated principals belong to a group of those who work with the same permissions on the network. In SONATE, a set of brokers who transfer and fetch the information from others can be considered as one group. Brokers contain read only permissions for the acceptance or rejection of the service. The permissions of the users vary when they play distinct roles, i.e., from technical to nontechnical roles. Nontechnical users are treated as public who access the Internet or utilize the resources whose permissions are to read and execute the services. Let us take an example for the issue of permission to the user where the user is a nontechnical user, broker and provider. A request from the user will be checked for the privileges of the principal as illustrated (Table 5.2) and these ACL's are to be present with the brokers for services to be accepted and in the network for the flow of services from one system to another system. All privileges are not allowed by all the principals of the network. For the access permissions the principals must be authenticated and some levels of security are to be permitted and these must be verified with the security levels of the applications. After the verification of these the services are allotted to the user else a negative acknowledgment is sent to the principals. The access control permissions can be granted to the authentication principals using the security levels of principals and services. The access privileges change if the security level of application is higher than the security level of the principal and vice versa.

5.4.2 *Mandatory Access Control (MAC) to suite SONATE:*

In this model, the system compares the principal's authority for the access of the security levels of the services/applications based on the classification of the principals and their access to the services [69] [165]. Every service is associated with the security label which includes the classification of the services based on the information. The hierarchy related to the security levels of the services was discussed by the author in the paper [171] with respect to SONATE. The hierarchy consists of microlevel security that provides top level security for the services like the information related to military affairs like top secrets documents related to missiles, bombs, and so on. This level provides top level security for highly confidential applications. Medium level secuirty is provided to the services which are just below the top secret, i.e., to the secret and confidential applications like financial transactions, etc. And finally, macro level security which is provided to unclassified services which are communicated over the network. Three levels of security are provided in the form of security modules for the purpose of secure communication over the network and for the protection of flexible services. Different combinations provide various levels of security for the services by enabling secure communication (Figure 5.1). A process of selection and composition (S & C) is used for the selection of the best suitable services among those available.

    A.   Micro level

    B.   Medium level

    C.   Macro level

    A.   **Micro Level Security:** The fine-grained protocol modules that perform the

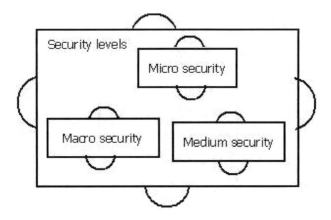

Figure 5.1: Security level modules.

functions in reality for the fulfillment of the demands of the user are called Building Blocks (BBs). These BBs are atomic in nature and their functions varies from network functionality to encryption, decryption, retransmission, congestion control, etc. A building block should be a well-defined set that satisfies the requirements and the collection of these BBs provides different services for the user. In simple words, a service is an abstract representation of a building block.

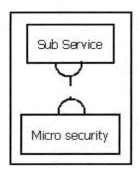

Figure 5.2: Micro Level security module.

For critical applications like financial, business, bank transactions, etc., require security very crucially. For these types of applications, a micro level security that can be called top level security is addressed where a security code is embedded into the module itself (Figure 5.2). Formation of a service with a combination of BBs and encrypting them provides a high level security which disables an intruder to break the critical service. This uses more memory because the security code is used in each and every BB but yields good results.

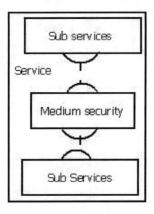

Figure 5.3: Medium level security module.

B. **Medium Level Security:** The security modules are developed and inserted into the service module at the time of formation of the protocol graph (Figure 5.3). The combination of BBs for the formation of a service results from simple to very complex services. The security modules are developed in the pool of services. According to the requirements of the user the security modules are selected and included in the service for the purpose of secure communication. The security module that is used in the formation of a protocol graph service will describe the quality of the security provided to the service. This type of security is provided for the services which are below the critical/top level applications.

C. **Macro Level Security:** Formation of protocolgraph with the combination of a set of protocols results in a service. Macro level security is provided to the services which are of least priority, i.e., a minimum level of security is provided to the requested services of the system. In this level security protocols are incorporated after the formation of a protocol graph with the required modules (BBs) (Figure 5.4). Minimum level of security is provided for the protection of services being provided to the users.

Each security level dominates itself and all others below it. Access to these services is permitted if there exists a relationship between the security levels associated with the principals and the applications. Access to these services are permitted if there exists a relationship between the security levels associated with the principals and

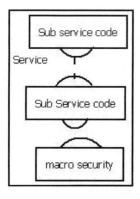

Figure 5.4: Macro level security module.

the applications/services. And this can be represented as "Z" where $Z = z_1, \cdots z_p$. Similarly, the applications can be classified on the basis of security levels is denoted by "q" where $q = q_1 \cdots q_n$, and "e" be the grant categories alloted for the principals that range from $e = e_1, \cdots, e_r$

The relation between "Z"" and "q" and the access grants "e" is given by $z_i = (q_i, e_i)$ where $e_i \in e$ & $q_i \in q$

In this framework the access control permissions are granted to the group instead of an individual of the network. The security levels are regulated based on the roles the principals/entities play and the activities and the responsibilities they perform in the system. For the allocation of security levels, the principals must be identified which is performed by the process of authentication mechanism and a role of an entity can be defined based on the actions and responsibilities they deliver for a particular task. For example, the security level of the bank manager of a bank for accessing the files will be more than the access permissions of the clerk of the bank. Therefore, the micro level security will be allocated to the file and its access permissions will be more for the manager principal and medium level security and a minimum security permissions are provided for the clerk. In SONATE, the main principals are the users who play two roles in the network, i.e., one for the utilization of the applications and one for developing those applications/protocols in the network, brokers who accept the request of the user and deliver the service to the user and the provider who stores and provides the services to the various users of the network. A principal's role reflects the operations performed by the principals for an application.

The permissions will be accessed by the principals based on the group they belong to such as owner, group, public and the role they play in the network. The services are fetched from the providers avaiable in the network via brokers who communicate and interact with others of the network. The owner of the service will contain full access rights like read, write, execute but not always as the ownership can be transferred to others by removing its permissions on the services that were provided to other brokers in the network. The authenticated principals belong a group those who work with same permissions in the network, In SONATE a set of brokers who transfers and fetches the information from others can be considered as a group. The brokers contain read only permissions for the acceptance or rejection of the service.User principals who belong to technical group permissions vary from the users who belong to normal user groups. The nontechnical/normal users are treated as public who access the Internet or utilize the resources whose permissions are to read and execute the services. Let us take an example for the issue of permission to the user where the user is nontechnical user, broker and provider. A request from the user will be checked for the privileges of the principal and these ACL's are to be present with the brokers for services to be accepted and in the network for the flow of services from one system to other system. All privileges are not allowed by all the principals of the network. For the access permissions the principals must be authenticated, belong to a role group and security level of the principals are verified with the security levels of the applications.

The policy list is stored in the repository of the broker in XML format and the details are stored by the service provider. And these policies are implemented using a policy enforcement point in the security domain. Before granting the access of an application the user must authenticate and then the privileges are to be assigned according to the fundamental conceptual model of security (Table 5.2). The levels are discussed for the services and the principals/entites of the architecture are based on Mandatory Access Control (MAC), the privileges are granted to the principals using the Discretionary Access Control (DAC), based on the roles they play in the system and these roles were decided based on Role-Based Access Control (RBAC). These access control privileges are maintained in the repository of the brokers and the servers of the system. After receiving the request from the user, broker checks in its repository for its authentication and the assigned privileges for granting the access to the principal.

5.5   Access Control Operations for SONATE

The permissions are granted based on the roles of the principals they play in the current system of the network. The permissions of each application is interlinked with different principals of the system. The primitives of the provider are derived from high level user (technical user) specifications. The access rules of the models are being translated into separate functions such as one for each read, write, execute. An application is made up of protocols "P" and access modes of the functions are given as PF1, PF2 and so on. The access control lists consist of 9 bits: the first 3 bits are allocated for the access mode privileges and the next 3 bits for the group where the application/ protocols/file belongs to and the last 3 bits are for other users in the network. The advantage of using bits is that the ACLs can be represented in small vectors.

Appropriate protocols are used by applications during its operation and only one medium is used for communication at any time. The system is considered to follow the properties:

- The nodes/entities of the network are deployed with appropriate software and are homogeneous in nature.

- Any principal/entity may act as a consumer.

- Service provider tries to satisfy the request if the service permissions allotted belongs to the user.

- Service consumer requests for ervice through a propagation channel on a hop basis.

- Communication link is ideal.

The passive entities of SONATE are called applications which are denoted by 'A' supported by service oriented network architecture and it is given by

$$A \in a_1, a_2, \cdots, a_x \tag{5.1}$$

Different information carried by applications is broadly classified into two categories as mandatory information (M) and additional information (K) which are represented as a service, i.e., S = {M + K}. In general, an application can be expressed as

$$A = \Sigma_{i=1}^{n} M_i + \Sigma_{j=0}^{m} K_j \tag{5.2}$$

where mandatory information is given by

$$M \in \{m_1, m_2, \cdots, m_n\} \tag{5.3}$$

and that of additional/optional information is given by

$$K \in \{k_1, k_2, \cdots, k_m\} \tag{5.4}$$

In case of "$j = 0$" application interaction is similar to the interaction of the current application where the user has minimal facility of interaction, and in the case of '$j = 1$' application is coarse tuned, and as the value of "j" increases better the tune of the application. The application uses different protocols for communication and also there are many applications which can work with different protocols.

These applications are a set of BBs which contain mandatory services that require security access permissions which are grated using access privileges "ap" and the policies which include user identification, key exchange certificate, digital signature, X.509 certificates, etc., for the requested services/applications. There is no restriction for the increment of the entities that may be active or passive of the system. When an entity role is treated as vigorous then that entity can be constrained by the treatment of the principals in the system.

The applications which are a set of BBs are represented by

$$BB \in BB_1, BB_2, \cdots, BB_n[152] \tag{5.5}$$

and protocols $P \subset BB's$, protocol graph $pg \subset BBs$

Let "P" be the total number of protocols available and it is given by

$$P \in p_1, p_2, \cdots, p_z \tag{5.6}$$

To satisfy the user request with an application, a protocol graph is formed which is set of BBs and

$p_{ai} > p_{ai+1}$, and $a_k = BB/P$

where BB/P can be $802.x, TCP, IP \cdots$

For performing a secure communication, there is a requirement of security services which exist as BB's in the pool of the provider

$$BB_f = B_{f1}, \cdots B_{fs}, \cdots, B_{fm} \tag{5.7}$$

$$a_f = P_f | P_f \subset P \tag{5.8}$$

then the set "P" contains

$$P = P_1 \cup \cdots P_{TCP} \cup P_{IP} \cup P_{MD5} \cup P_{AES} \cup \cdots P_n \tag{5.9}$$

A protocol graph is nothing but a service which consists of Building blocks. If a protocol graph follows abc format then it is presented as $(P_a \cup P_b \cup P_c)$

This graph contains root BB, left BB, right BB and represented as $\{a_l \cup b_{ri} \cup c_r \cdots\}$ where "l" = left, "ri" = right, "r" = root A service can be written as

$$S = \Sigma_{i=1}^n a_{lr} + \Sigma_{i=1}^n b_{lr} + \Sigma_{i=1}^n c_{lr} \tag{5.10}$$

where a_{lr} = left root of "a", similar for "b" and "c"

The access control list identifies the individual users or groups of users who may access the file. Because all the access control information is stored in the repository and is clearly associated with the file, identifying who can access a file, and add or delete names can be performed very efficiently. An ordered set of protocols used for an application a_k is given by

$$p_k = \{p_{a1}, p_{a2}, \cdots, p_{al}\} \tag{5.11}$$

where $p_{ai} > p_{ai+1}$, $a_k = \{p_k | p_k \subset P\}$ i.e. TCP, IP, Ethernet, 802.x etc., are sequence of protocols used for its functionality. Similarly "p_f" is a set of protocols supported for an application 'a_f' to function properly, i.e., where

$$a_f = p_f | p_f \subset P \tag{5.12}$$

and $P \supset p_f$ and p_k. The universal protocol set "P" consists of all protocols and it can be written as

$$P = \{P_1 \cup \cdots \cup P_{TCP} \cup P_{IP} \cup \cdots \cup P_n\} \tag{5.13}$$

where all protocols are of ordered subset. If p_i follows "xyz" protocol format then it is written as $p_i = \{P_{xyz}\}$ similarly any other protocols can be represented by this, e.g. $p_k = \{P_{TCP} \cup P_{IP}\}$ means TCP/IP protocol suit.

For satisfying the various access permissions the system must satisfy some rules and conditions. Let us take a variable "c" c = (S, A,am) which is a secure state where $am \in r,w,x$, $S \in s'$ and $c* = (C \cup (S,A,am))$ and security functions which describes the application current security level, maximum security level of the principals in the network and current level of the pricipals and it is given by "F" and

$$F = (F_S, F_A, F_q) \, if \, and \, only \, if \, E_S > F_q; F \leq z^S * z^A \tag{5.14}$$

5.5.1 Access Control Conditions

Condition 1: Suppose W= (c,m, F,P) is an authenticated state which contains variable c, application/protocol matrix, security function and the protocol/application, $(S,A,am) \notin c$ and $c* = c \cup S,A,am$ and $W* = (c*,m,F,P)$ then W* is also an authenticated state if

    (a) (am = x or am = r+w) or

    (b) (am = r or am = w) and $F_S(S) > F_A(P)$ then $A \in c*(S:r,w) \Rightarrow$ $F_S(S) > F_A(P)$ by definition. If w is an authenticated then W* also does. Therefore 1 and 2 hold good.

Condition 2: Let W = (c,m,F,P) is a state that satisfies authentication and applies some security level to the application and the principal, i.e., $S \subset s'$, $s' \in S$, $c \notin (S,A,am)$, $c* = c \cup S,A,am$ and $W* = (c*,m,F,P)$ If W* satisfies any one of the security level then

    (a) if am = w then $F_q(S) = F_A(S)$ or $F_A(P) > F_q(S)$ or

    (b) if am = r then $F_q(S) > F_A(P)$

If W* satisfies the security level applied to S,A, and (S,A,am) then it yields 1,2 conditions.

Condition 3: Suppose W= (c,m,F,P) that satisfies a security level, $(S,A,am) \notin c$ but $c* = c \cup (S,A,am)$ and $W* = (c*,m,F,P)$ then W* fulfills the satisfaction of security level if $am \in m_{ij}$.

Inference: If W = (c,m,F,P) is a secure state and $(s_i,a_i,am) \notin c$, $c* = (c \cup (s_i,a_i,am))$ and $W* = (c*,m,F,P)$ then W* is a secure state if and only if

    (a) $s_i \in s_p$ and condition 1 and 3 are met or

    (b) $s_i \in s'$ and the conditions 1, 2 and 3 are met.

5.5.2 Access Control Functions

The access control functions for the system are derived using the rules given by Bell Lapudla [22].

5.5.2.1 Function (PF1): Read

A request is sent by the principal to get the permission for reading an application. The request contains (get access, user_id, Protocol_id, access mode(r)) , i.e., $R_e = (g, s_i, p_i, r) \in (S * A * am)$.

1. The request is received by the broker principal from the other principal and checks in its reposity for the request to get fulfilled and

2. If the request is correct, i.e., principal_id, application and the permission as read then check the principal authentication, if not authenticated then check the security level of the principal must dominate the security level of the application.

If the above two conditions are satisfied, then the request is fulfilled by fetching it from the provider or else a negative response is sent to the principal via the other principal, i.e., may be user/ broker which is given by

$$PF1(R_e, W) = \{ \ (yes, c \cup (s_i, p_i, r), m, F, P) \qquad \text{if value}$$

$$value = [R_e \in PF1] \wedge [r \in m_{ij}] \wedge [F_S(s_i) > F_A(p_i)] \wedge [s_i \in s'] \vee [F_q(s_i) > F_A(p_i)]$$

Proof: Suppose W is a secure state that satisfies the authentication of the principal and security level of the application and $R_e \in PF1$. $PF1(R_e, W) = (D, W^*)$ where D is the decision of yes or no with

1. $W* = W$

2. $W* = (c \cup (s_i, p_i, r), m, F, P)$ W^* is a secure state so as W from 1 and if $(s_i, p_i, r) \in c$ then $W = W*$ as above. If $(s_i, p_i, r) \notin c$ then according to PF1 $F_S(s_i) > F_A(p_i)$, W^* satisfies the secure state from condition 1 and if $s_i \in s'$ then $F_q(s_i) > F_A(p_i)$, W^* satisfies the security relation from condition 2 and $r \in m_{ij}$ and, W^* satisties the 3rd condition. Therefore, from inference it is proved that PF1 maintains a secure state for delivering the service to the user via broker.

5.5.2.2 Function (PF2): Write

A request is sent by the principal to get written permission for an application. The request contains (get access, user_id, Protocol_id, access mode(w)), i.e., $R_e = (g, s_i, p_i, w) \in (S * A * am)$.

1. The request is received by the broker principal from the other principal and checks in its reposity for the fulfillment of the request and

2. If the request is correct then check the principal authentication, if not authenticated then check the security level of the protoco,l i.e., $F_q(p_i)$ must be dominated by the security level of the application $F_S(s_i)$. The principal must play a technical role to get permission for writing an application.

If 1 and 2 are satisfied, then the request gets fulfilled by fetching it from the provider or else a negative response is sent to the principal.

$$PF2(R_e, W) = \{ \ (yes, c \cup (s_i, p_i, w), m, F, P) \qquad \text{if value}$$

$$value = [R_e \in PF2] \wedge [w \in m_{ij}] \wedge [F_S(s_i) > F_A(p_i)] \wedge [s_i \in s'] \vee [F_q(s_i) = F_A(p_i)]$$

Proof: Suppose W is a secure state that satisfies the authentication of the principal and security level of the application and $R_e \in PF2$.*If* $(s_i), p_i, w) \notin c$ *and* $W* = (c \cup (s_i, p_i, w)m, FP)$ *then accordingto PF2,* $F_S(s_i) > F_A(p_i)$, $W*$ satisfies the secure state from condition 1 and if $s_i \in s'$ then $F_q(s_i = F_A(p_i)$, $W*$ satisfies the security relation from condition 2 and $w \in m_{ij}$ and, W* satisfies condition 3. Therefore, from inference it is proved that PF2 maintains a secure state for delivering the service in write mode.

5.5.2.3   Function (PF3): Get Execute

A request sent by the principal to get execute permission for an application. The request contains(get access, user_id, Protocol_id, access mode(x)), i.e., $R_e = (g, s_i, p_i, x) \in (S * A * am)$.   This function is useful for the execution process which consists of many number of steps. It is a procedure for the execution of an application. The request is received by the broker principal and checks in its reposity for the request to satisfy rule 1 and if temporary pointer points to the application with access mode 'x' then the permission is granted for the requested application via the broker or else a negative response is sent to the principal via the other principal.

$$PF3(R_e, W) = \{ \ (yes, c \cup (s_i, p_i, x), m, F, P) \qquad \text{if value}$$

$$value = [R_e \in PF3] \wedge [x \in m_{ij}]$$

Proof: Suppose W is a secure state and $R_e \in PF3$. Let $W* = (c \cup (s_i, p_i, x), m, F, P)$ and $(s_i), p_i, x) \notin c$ then W* satisfies the authentication by condition 1 and W* satisfies s' by condition 2 and $x \in m_{ij}$ according to PF3, W* satisfies condition 3 therefore from inference it is proved that PF3 maintains a secure state.

5.5.2.4   Function (PF4): Cancel the Access Permissions (am)

The request contains (cancel access, request_Id, receiving_id, protocol_id, access mode) i.e $FP4 : R_e = (s_h, r, s_i, p_i, am) \in (S_h * g/r * S_i * A * am)$, $am \in (r, w, x, a)$

1. The requested protocol is allotted to other brokers in the network for the usage of an application and these are not the original owners of the application but act as owner for a particular session of time. The write permission is allowed for the original owner, and

2. The protocol_id is the root application of the provider or is inferior to the root and if requesting a principal is allowed to cancel the access permissions for an application in the current state, i.e., transferring the ownership of the BB from one system to the other system.

The transferred permission for an application expires with the principal then the access mode of that particular protocol is made off and it is removed from the ACL of the broker and if no other modes are left for that application/protocol, then it will be removed from the providers pool.

$$PF4(R_e, W) = \{ \quad (yes, c - (s_i, p_i, am), m|m_{ij} - am, F, P) \qquad \text{if value}$$

$$value = [R_e \in PF4] \land [p_i \neq p_j] \land [A_{s(j)} \in c(s_h : w)] \lor [p_i = p_j] \land [cancel(s_h, p_j, W)]$$

Proof: Let W be a secure state and $W* = W$ or $W* = (c - (s_i, p_i, am), m|m_{ij} - am, F, P)$. Suppose $c* \supseteq c$, $m*_{ij} \supseteq m_{ij}$ and $F* = F$ for all i, j. If $(S, A, am) \in c*$ with $am = r$ or $w \Longrightarrow (S, A, am) \in c$ then FP4 is authenticated and considers some security level for application. Therefore, $W*$ is a secure state and FP4 can rescind an application from the pool along with the access permissions, i.e., $(r, w, x) \in am$.

5.5.2.5 Function (PF5): Development of an Application

For the development of a new application, a request is sent by authenticated principal and if access permission is write then it is allowed for the generation of an application. A Protocol_id and the security level are allotted for the new application. It can be represented as (generate leaf protocol, principal_id, protocol_id, security level), i.e., $PF5 : R_e = (g, s_i, p_i, z_k) \in (g/r/ * S * A * Z)$ The request is forwarded to the broker. The broker checks in its repository for the registration details of the request, if exists it and

1. If the security level of the principal dominates the security level of the application, then the new application ID is stored with the broker and the application is stored in the provider pool. If any problem occurs, then the user receives a negative acknowledgement.

$$PF5(R_e, W) = \{ \quad (yes, c, m, F|F_A \leftarrow F_A \cup (A_{new(p)}, z_k), P \cap (p_i, A_{new(p)})) \qquad \text{if value}$$

$$value = [R_e \in PF5] \land [p_i \in c(s_i : w, a)] \land [z_k > F_A(p_i)]$$

Proof: Let W be a secure state and from above $c* = c$ and $m* = m$. If $(s_h, A_{new(P)}, am) \notin c$ for any $s_h \in S$ and $am \in (r, w, x, a)$, then $W*$ is a secure state. Therefore, PF5 preseves a secure state.

5.5.2.6 Function (PF6): Deletion of an Application

$PF6: R_e = (s_i, p_i) \in (S*A)$. This results in deleting the protocols and all the inferior protocols related to an application from the protocol graph. It is almost equal to cancel of access permission but in this the application is removed from the pool.

$$PF6(R_e, W) = \begin{cases} (yes, c - am(p_i), , m|m_{uv} \leftarrow \phi : z \leq u \leq n, \\ p_v \in inferior(p_i, F, P - subtree(p_i))) \end{cases} \quad \text{if value}$$

$$value = [R_e \in PF6] \wedge [p_i \neq p_k] \wedge [p_{s(i)} \in c(s_i : w)]$$

Proof: W is a secure state and if $(s_i, p_{i'}, am) \in c*$ then $am \in m_{ii'}$ so W* is a secure state and deletion of an application/protocols occurs in this secure state.

5.5.2.7 Function (PF7): Change Security Level of an Application

$R_e = (r, s_i, p_i, z_u) \in (g/r/ * S * A * Z)$ principal s_i request that the security level of an application p_i be changed (reclassification) then the z_u conditions that are to be considered are $s_h \in s'$, and $[(s_h, p_i, a) \in c \Rightarrow F_q(s_h) < z_u] \wedge [(s_h, p_i, w) \in c \Rightarrow F_q(s_h) = z_u] \wedge [(s_h, p_i, r) \in c \Rightarrow F_q(s_h) > z_u]$ then

$$PF7(R_e, W) = \{ (yes, c, m, F|F_A(p_i) \leftarrow z_u, P) \quad \text{if value}$$

$$value = [R_e \in PF11] \wedge [s_i \in s_p \wedge F_q(s_i) > F_A(p_i) \vee F_q(s_i) > z_u > F_A(p_i]$$

$$\wedge [fors \in s[(p_i \in c(S:r, w)) \Rightarrow F_S(s_i) > z_u]]$$

$$\wedge [the\ above\ condition] \wedge [compact(W, p_i, z_u)] \wedge [change(W, p_i, z_u)]$$

Proof: If $F* \neq F$ then $F* = F|F_A(p_i) \leftarrow$ and if the condition is true then W* is a secure state the same as W. Therefore, the security level of an application can be changed.

5.5.2.8 Function (PF8): Change Current Security Level of Principal

$PF8: R_e = (s_i, z_v) \in (S*Z)$ If the principal got the write permissions and request for change for its current security level, then the security levels are to be changed, i.e., the security level can be changed if and only if $[p_i \in c(s_i : a) \Rightarrow F_A(p_i) > z_v] \wedge [p_i \in c(s_i : w) \Rightarrow F_A(p_i) = z_v] \wedge [p_i \in c(s_i : a) \Rightarrow F_A(p_i) < z_v]$ these conditions are true.

$$PF8(R_e, W) = \{ (yes, c, m, F|F_q(s_i) \leftarrow z_u, P)) \quad \text{if value}$$

$$value = [R_e \in PF10] \wedge [F_S(s_i) > z_u] \wedge [s_i \in s_p \vee the\ above\ conditions]$$

Proof: If $F* \neq F$, then $F* = F|F_q(s_i) \leftarrow z_u$ and the condition above is true then the principal gets permission to change its current security level.

5.6 Convergence of Services

If

$$E(X - A)^2 = 0 \tag{5.15}$$

then X = "A" with probability 1 or X converges to "A" with probability 1. User wants to get done an application "A" to a tolerance limit of ε (i.e., liberty of not satisfying some request of $\Sigma_{j=1}^{m} K_j$). Let σ_x^2 be variability of measurement. According to Chebyshev inequality it is given as

$$P\{|X - A| \le \varepsilon\} \ge 1 - \frac{\sigma_x^2}{\varepsilon^2} \tag{5.16}$$

If σ_x is much smaller than ε then observed variable X is between $(A - \varepsilon)$ and $(A + \varepsilon)$ which is almost certain and one measurement of X is sufficient. However if σ_x is not sufficiently smaller compared to ε, then the result will not be of sufficient accuracy. To improve the accuracy of the estimate, 'A' need to take 'n' measurements corresponding to "n" random variables $\{X_i, = 1, \cdots, n\}$ with mean "A" and noise random variable Y_i given by

$$X_i = A + Y_i \qquad i = 1, \cdots, n \tag{5.17}$$

Average of "n" random variables represented as

$$\hat{X} = \frac{X_1 + X_2 + \cdots + X_n}{n} \tag{5.18}$$

where mean of $\hat{X}$ is "A" and variance is $n\sigma_x^2$ and corresponding Chebyshev inequality is given by

$$P\{|X - A| < \varepsilon\} \ge 1 - \frac{\sigma_x^2}{n\varepsilon^2} \tag{5.19}$$

The verification of permissions are performed by the broker then the services are selected and composed. The services/applications gets fulfilled for the user with a tolerance limit. For the accuracy of fulfillment of the services, a selection and composition process is performed and a service which is best satisfying the priorities of the user is selected out of "n" possible services.

5.6.1 Pointwise Convergence of Service Request

Discrete sequence of random variables $\{X_1, X_2, X_3, \cdots, X_N, \cdots\}$ converges to a limiting random variable X iff for any $\varepsilon > 0$; however, for smaller find a number "n_0" such that

$$|X_n(\xi) - X(\xi)| < \varepsilon \tag{5.20}$$

for every $n > n_0$ and every ξ if it is right for variables but highly restrictive for random variables.

5.6.2   Almost Sure Convergence of Service Request

A sequence of random variables $\{X_n\}$ converges almost surely to the random variable X, if for every ξ point in the same space S satisfies the following criterion:

$$\lim_{n \to \infty} |X_n(\xi) - X(\xi)| < \varepsilon \to 0 \qquad (5.21)$$

with probability 1. This can also be written as

$$P(X_n \to X) = 1 \quad as \quad n \to \infty \qquad (5.22)$$

The service selection and composition process helps in making a decision by evaluating the priorities among various alternatives for the selection of the best suitable service among the "n" available services with a maximum acuracy for the fulfillment of the request of the user.

5.7   Secure Service Compositon - Read permission

A simple example with read permission is discussed for the composition of the services using the above properties which is tested on the testbed of SONATE and the results are satisfactory. In SONATE, various combinations of BB's produce different services which require a process of selection of the best service after the composition process is performed using the ANP process [152]. Before, this selection and composition the service user/consumer need to satisfy the mandatory conditions of the security such as the security level of the user, authentication of the user by providing identification and access permission of the user for the secure communication. A simple file transfer with "Read permission" is discussed in detail which is as follows:

- The first step is to fetch the requirement of the service from the user.

- Check for authentication, and identify the service requirements of the entity of the system.

- If the entity is identified as authenticated, check for the requested service in the repository along with the access permission of the user.

- If the permission is read as requested by the user, then fetch the file from the provider.

- The provider searches for the file in its repository, if the file matches the requirements, then it delivers to the broker, or else the description of the file is parsed for the identification of the available self composition alternatives.

- The service/BB should at least satisfy the mandatory properties of security like the security level of the service must be lower than the security level of the user (for more details please refer Section 5.5) .

■ After obtaining all the possible alternatives along with the optional properties, the best service is selected with *"Read"* permission and delivered to the user.

■ If the user tries to perform a "Write" operation on the obtained service, the system displays a message to the user *"File exists with Read only Permission"*

Thus, if the user is restricted to perform any changes on the services, file transfer with *"Write"* permission can be performed as in Algorithm 5.1.

Algorithm 5.1
Perform write operation

1. *Send Request as* **Write**

2. *Check authentication, permission*

3. *If Permission = no*

4. *Return not permitted*

5. *Else*

6.   *Check If Write = Create type matches*

7.   *Generate ProtocolProtocol_id, security level*

8.   *Else not permitted*

9.   *If Write = Delete type matches*

10.   *Check**Application***

11.   *Exists then Delete the Application*

12.   *And Delete the Security Level Application*

13.   *Else not permitted*

14.   *If Write = change Security Level type*

15. *For Services*

16.   *Allow reclassification if (current security level of the entity < the security level of the service) then*

17.   *Permit to change*

18. *For Principals/ Entities*

19.   *Allow if (current security level of the entity > the security level of the service) then*

20.   *Permit to change*

21.   *Else not permitted*

5.8   Summary

In this chapter, various authorization mechanisms were discussed. Access control based on access control list is proposed for the avoidance of access attacks and discussed especially in the case study of SONATE. The access permissions vary from one group to the other group based on the role the entities play in the communication. The functions and operations discussed in this work are deployed and tested for the feasibility by considering a real scenario. For the conduction of experiment, a standalone and another distributed system is considered. The verification is performed using the authentication mechanism and the process of access permissions is verified using the access control permissions. The results are satisfactory as the system allows only the authorized users to access the services. An inherent attack for the voilation of permissions is purposefully considered and verified during the service delivery. The experiment is conducted by considering various types of data starting with a simple and small text file, to very big files like an audio clip, video clip, image files, compressed files, etc. It is observed that the system does not allow the entities to violate the permissions. If the entities violate the permissions, then a message was displayed. The combination of both authentication and authorization provides secure communication in SONATE and the results are satisfactory in both the scenarios.

Table 5.3: Security Evaluation Results

	Replay Attack	Data Tampering	Impersonation	Repudiation
PKI authentication mechanism	Yes	Yes	Yes	Yes
Access control mechanism	Yes	Yes	Yes	Yes

*Appendix—5A

Access Permissions

Permissions are Linux's method of protecting files and directories. Every file or directory is owned by a user and assigned to a group. The owner of a file has the right to set permissions in order to protect the file from being accessed, modified or destroyed.

File ownership is an important component of Unix that provides a secure method for storing files. Every file in Unix has the following attributes–

Owner permissions –The owner's permissions determine what actions the owner of the file can perform on the file.

Group permissions –The group's permissions determine what actions a user, who is a member of the group that a file belongs to, can perform on the file.

Other (world) permissions –The permissions for others indicate what action all other users can perform on the file.

The Order of the Permissions

When testing for permissions, the system looks at the groups in order. When Unix checks permissions, the order is this:

■ If the file is owned by the user, the user permissions determine the access.

■ If the group of the file is the same as the user's group, the group permisson determines the access.

■ If the user is not the file owner, and is not in the group, then the other permission is used.

If you are denied permission, Unix does not examine the next group.

Symbolic method: The symbolic method is useful for changing just one or two permissions. Following the chmod command, you specify three items: whose permission you wish to change, whether you want to add or remove the permission, and the permission itself. The following chart illustrates the possibilities:

Table 5.4: Symbol Methods

Who	Operand	Permission
u (user/owner)	-(remove)	r(read)
g(group)	+ (add)	w(write)
o(other)		x(execute)
a(all three)		

Typical Permissions

Most of the time permissions fall into three cases:

- The information is personal. Many people have a directory or two they store information they do not wish to be public. Mail should probably be confidential, and all of your mailbox files should be in a directory with permission of 700, denying everyone but yourself and the system administrator read access to your letters.

- The information is not personal, yet no one should be able to modify the information. Most of my directories are set up this way, with the permission of 755.

- The files are managed by a team of people. This means group write permission, or directories with the mode 775.

Changing Permissions While creating an account, the system assigns an owner ID and a group ID to each user. All the permissions mentioned above are also assigned based on the owner and the groups. Only the person who owns the file (and the root user) can change the file's permissions. There are two methods of changing the permissions on a file: symbolic and octal. Two commands are available to change the owner and the group of files

- chown: The chown command stands for "change owner" and is used to change the owner of a file.

- chgrp: The chgrp command stands for "change group" and is used to change the group of a file.

File Access Modes

The permissions of a file are the first line of defense in the security of a Unix system. The basic building blocks of Unix permissions are the read, write, and execute permissions, which have been described below:

Read Grants the capability for the user to read the contents. The user can look at the filename inside the directory or the file.

Write Grants the capability to modify or remove the content of the file.

Execute User with execute permissions can run a file as a program.

The permissions are broken into groups of threes, and each position in the group denotes a specific permission, in this order: read (r), write (w), execute (x). The first three characters (2-4) represent the permissions for the file's owner. For example, - rwxr-xr- represents that the owner has read (r), write (w) and execute (x) permission. The second group of three characters (5-7) consists of the permissions for the group to which the file belongs. For example, -rwxr-xr– represents that the group has read (r) and execute (x) permission, but no write permission.

The last group of three characters (8-10) represents the permissions for everyone else. For example, -rwxr-xr– represents that there is read (r) only permission.

Determining Permissions

To determine the permissions of a file, use the ls -l command. The first character of the output of the ls -l command specifies the file type. The next nine characters represent the permissions set on the file. There are three types of permissions: r (read), w (write), and x (execute). These permissions have different meanings for files and directories.

The first three permissions are for the user owner, the second three are for people in the group, and the last three are for everyone else (others). Therefore, in the preceding example, the owner of the file (steve) has read and write permissions, the members of the group (staff) have read permission and everyone else has read permission.

Group accounts Groups were invented to provide more flexibility when issuing permissions. Every user is a member of at least one group (a primary group) and may be a member of additional (secondary) groups. To see the group's you belong to, type the group's command. Permissions have different meanings on files and directories. The following chart illustrates the differences:

Table 5.5: File Permissions versus Directory Permissions

Permission	Symbol	Meaning for Files	Meaning for Directories
Read	r	Can view or copy file	Can list with ls
Write	w	Can modify file	Can add or delete files in the directory(if execute permission is also set)
Execute	x	Can run file like a program	Can add to that directory. Can also use that directory in a path

Chapter 6

Intrusion Detection and Prevention Systems—Future Internet Architecture

6.1 Introduction

The protection of information assets not only relies on people as on technical controls, technical solutions, guided by policy and properly implemented, are an essential component of an information security program. Chapter 5 has discussed the importance of access control mechanisms for the Future Internet. This chapter describes more advanced technologies–intrusion detection and prevention systems and avoidance of DDos attacks with a technique which has been applied on one of the Future Internet architecture called SONATE. DoS attack is a serious threat commonly found in Current Internet and various attempts are made to find solutions but could not succeed to avoid it permanently. The protection of the services and the entities while communicating becomes an important issue and the measures to be considered are detection of the attack, prevention of the attack and recovery from the attack. The purpose of a prevention technique is to protect the services from being damaged. Detection allows to detect how, when and the cause of damage whereas recovery of the system allows the system to restore the repository, services that are damaged. In a DoS attack, a large number of spoof packets are sent to the victim machine to affect the operations performed by that system by making it busy in handling the requests of the user. The main function of the DoS attack is to malfunction the normal operation of the service providers so that it is unable to provide services to the user. The central element of the architecture for the communication over the network with other entities is the service agent. Various intrusion detection and prevention techniques are discussed along with a mechanism for the avoidance of the DoS attack in the Future Internet architecture.

6.2   Intrusion Detection and Prevention System (IDPS)

Intrusion is defined as an attempt by the attacker to gain access to an authorized service with an intension to perform some action or disrupt the normal operations within the system or with the system itself. Some systems are self propogated like a virus, always instigated by some entity whose intension is to harm the resource or the organization. In simple words, we can say misuses of the resources by an entity can be treated as an intruder. These intruders can be originated from outside or from inside of an organization. An intruder can perform the attacks based on their skills they obtained. The attacker uses the breached system as the base to launch malicious activities on the entire network. For detecting the unauthorized anamolous activities in a system performed by the intruders is defined as intrusion detection and the system which detects these intrusions are called an Intrusion Detection System (IDS). It is a mechanism which monitors the network with the help of some procedures to identify the intruders. IDS is like a security guard which looks at the traffic that is in progress. It is traditionally used to detect the suspicious activities inside the organization or the traffic arriving to the network from outside. This system came into existence in the late 1990's commercially which acts as an alarm system when a suspicious activity or a rule is violated. The static filtering rules for the traffic arriving at the system is applied by the firewalls present in the system. Antivirus can be treated as a best example for the intrusion detection system. The detection system is updatable or adoptable dynamically for dynamic filtering. It can be a software or a hardware that can be used to detect an attack. Some IDS detect the attacks and some others try to block the attack. These IDS can be used to detect the anamolous activity on an individual host system or on a network as part of a network device. IDS detect the attacks based on malicious signature or using an anamoly detection with no prevention techniques. These provide a evidence of an attack, can't take an action on the issues detected. When an intrusion is detected, the actions that are taken by an organization is the reaction to that intrusion called *Intrusion Reaction*. The restoration of the activities or the services to the normal state and tries to identify the source along with the method applied for an intrusion which is known as *Intrusion Correction*. Once the method is known, some preventive steps are to be taken in order to prevent the same type of attacks are known as *Intrusion Prevention*. The system that takes a prevention against intrusion is called as Intrusion Prevention System (IPS). IPS not only detects the intrusion but also prevents the intrusion from attacking the services in an organization by means of a response. IPSs are the proactive mechanisms used to detect malicious packets introduced into the network to stop intrusions before they perform any damage. It can change the security environment by reconfiguring it in a firewall or a router or in a switch to prevent the access of unauthorized entity. This system helps in minimizing the manual handling of the alerts and decreases the amount of false negatives. The IDS provides real time information when suspicious activity is found. IDS detects but cannot prevent an attack, in contrast IPS monitors like IDS, automatically invokes a preventive action based on the event occured. IPS provides a predetermined set of functions and actions to be performed on a network or a system that helps to block the unwanted activity. IPS is considered as the access control, enforcement of techique whereas IDS as network monitoring and auditing techonology. Some IDS adopt preventive measures that allow them to act more proactively in implementing policy. IPS incorporate detection methods and makes it easy and simple to block the activities which are of no interest using "Block" option. As the detection system as well as prevention system works simultaneously, in general terms Intrusion Detection and Prevention system (IDPS) used which consists of anti-intrusion technologies.

6.3 Why to Use Intrusion Detection and Prevention System (IDPS)

An attack can cause a large loss to confidentiality, integrity and availability of the services. To protect the services from this loss we require IDPS. The service owners don't want anyone to breach the system with malicious intensions and carry out the various attacks by endangering not only the system but the whole network. We require some system that alerts us about these activities and allows us to take some action upon such incidents by eliminating the root cause of that incident. IDPS helps in detecting the attacks, security violations that are not prevented by other security mechanisms. It examines and documents the existing threat of an organization. It acts as a quality control for security design in large and complex networks of an organization. It allows improved diagnosis, recovery and correction of the errors that occur due to attacks. In other words, we can say that they increase the fear in attackers and are less likely to attempt or compromise a system. As it is not easy to stop attacks, it is better to take precautions to detect and prevent the attacks, maintain the attack document for future purpose. It is capable of detecting the early warnings who try to enter the system using doornob rattling. IDPS helps in responding to the changing environment which is due to threat. It also helps in assisting the administrator in after-attack review by starring the information on how the attack has occured and which methods the attacker has used. It has a capability of changing the security control configuration to stop an attack. It can even replace the attack content by removing the infected portions or files. It can even act as proxy and helps in normalizing the request to discard some attacks. IDPS has its own mechanisms to detect intrusions that are applied to prevent the various attacks and decrease the damage of the resources states the requirement of IDPS.

6.4 IDPS Methods

The IDPS comes into existence once it detects a suspicious activity. If configured according to interact with the system for the restriction of the traffic and allows to collaborate itself with any IDS or the access control systems. The IDPS can inject new access control list in the routers, VPN, switches to restrict or block the traffic. There are different types of IDPS present and used for various purposes.

6.4.1 Host-Based Instrusion Detection and Prevention System (HIDPS)

Host-based intrusion detection system is an intrusion detection system that is installed on a server or on an individual system. This is used to analyze the activities directly at the network interface of a particular host. This is normally a software deployed on a local host that monitors the event logs, root kit detection, policy enforcement and other attacks which are going to happen to the system. Once installed, the system activity is understood, a baseline is created then the HIDS will be deployed in prevention mode. The system functionality depends on the logs and evidences that are obtained. There are plenty of approaches to deploy the software into the system. One way to deploy is TCP wrapper where it wraps the various host services of the network in an extra layer that interprets the packet request for various services. The second approach is to deploy the agents which run as seperate process and monitor each and every request coming to the host. These two methods are effective in detecting the misuse or any suspicious activity in the system. It helps not only monitoring the stored files like .ini, .dat. and so on but also works on the change management by recording the size of files, locations, etc., of the system. HIDS classifies the files into various categories by itself and sends the notifications when the change occurs. HIDS works only if the system generates logs and match the pre-defined policies. If the hackers break the HIDS server then it is of no use. The agents of HIDS monitor the changes occured in critical system and the system changes occured in the privileges. It effectively detects the objectionable activities as the IDS runs on the host directly. The main disadvantage of HIDS is it orders to report an intrusion to the management in real time where information has to flow over the network. If the host itself is under attack then the system is of no use. In order to avoid this issue, it sends a beacon at regular intervals to the management system with an assumption that the correct system does its work correctly. This approach works good for a lesser number of systems but does not yield a complete solution. If the intruders manage to turn off the log systems although the agent is running, it will not trigger any alerts. The HIDS monitors not only the specific system but can identify the attacks on non-network based systems. The usage of switched network protocols will not effect HIDPS. HIDPS produces false positive alarm only when an authorized change occurs on a file which is being monitored. HIDPS poses the management issues, to operate than network based IDPS. HIDPS is not optimized to multihost scanning and is vulnerable to direct and host OS attacks. It is vulnerable to denial of Service (DoS) attacks. It uses a large amount of disk space to retain the host OS logs and may need to add disk capacity to the system. It may cause performance overhead and may reduce system performance below the levels which are acceptable. To overcome the problems of HIDPS we move to Network-based IDPS.

6.4.2 Network-Based Instrusion Detection and Prevention System (NIDPS)

Network-based intrusion detection and prevention system is incorporated into the network of a passive architecture, with access to the network. It monitors and analyzes the pattern in real time, reports to the management on detecting a malicious activity. It has a visibility to every packet moving in that network segment. As NIDPS examines the packet headers, it detects Denial of Service attacks. If the traffic increases, then the effectiveness of this technique decreases.It monitors all the traffic traveling through the device, if the load is more than it begins to drop the packets. If the packet in the traffic is encrypted, then it provides adequate monitoring. The encrypted packets provide confidentiality but reduce the ability of IDS to inspect. The IDS gains visibility if only the data portions of the packet are encrypted. Other information like header information including session information, protocol ports and the participants in communication are in cleartext. If IDS tries to gain more information, it fails as the information is encrypted. Many newer technologies are allowing to breach the session encryption and then re-establish it. As IDS analyzes each and every packet and its contents, it does not interfere in existing communication but when an IPS is unable to perform automated responses, it tries to terminate the connection. IDS can be integrated with firewalls, routers to facilitate dynamic rules to block specific protocols, IP address with unwanted communications. IDS and IPS work together, to monitor IDS is used and to take desisions of blocking/dropping of packets is performed by IPS. This IPS also helps in correcting CRC errors, fragmented packets, etc. Before the deployment of switches, a hub was used for connecting the networks. Hubs were used to receive traffic from one node to others. The disadvantage of hub is anyone connected to the hub can monitor the traffic. To overcome this, in the early 1990s switches were used. Switches provide a dedicated point to point links between their ports. NIDPS measures the activity based on the signatures stored in the database. TCP/IP reassembles the packets and applies protocol stack, application protocol verification and other comparison techniques. In the Protocol stack, it checks for invalid packets, i.e., malicious packets under the rules of TCP/IP protocol. DoS and DDoS rely on the malicious packets that take advantage of weaknesses in the protocol stack. In the application protocol, the verification is performed on the high order protocols. These high order protocols like HTTP, FTP, etc., are monitored for unexpected behavior of the packets, voilations in the packet structure to perform some actions for the avoidance of intrusions. NIDPS is not suitable for the attacks that occur directly but sometimes are not detectable by intruders. If the IDPS itself is malfunctioned, it may become unstable and stop functioning. The administrator has to be engaged to evaluate the results as the NIDPS cannot reliably ascertain if an intrusion is successful or not. The broad use of switches instead of hubs serves as the solution, but still some are not capable of providing appropriate data for analysis by

NIDPS. Even though switches have monitoring ports, they may not be able to mirror all the data within a reliable time.

6.4.3 Signature-Based Detection

It is also known as knowledge-based IDS or misuse detection IDPS or expert system based IDPS or Model based IDPS. This system is used to recover the system from known attacks. The best example which works in the same fashion as signature-based is anti-virus. The anti-virus software maintains a pattern of signatures in the database which matches with incoming packets of those signatures. These are widely used to stop many attacks which are predefined that have clear and distinct signature patterns. It just compares the traffic with the stored patterns, if a pattern is matched then a signal of alert is generated or else traffic flows as normal. To detect the attacks correctly, the database has to be updated constantly, on a daily basis if possible by the labs like McAfee, AVG, etc. It is mostly interested in honey trap. Many techniques are used to make this technique more robust. For a host-based, signature detection monitors the key strokes for gathering the pattern of attacks. It even involves reviewing the files for changes almost like a virus scanner. String signature searches for text string pattern that causes a possible attack. When the ports are monitored, signature-based, host-based compares the various audit files for common techniques. The TCP connection failures to the well known ports can be treated as an indication that someone is scanning the ports, if there is a large number of SYN-ACK packs indicates that is system is under SYN flooding attack. In network-based signatuures based IDS, the packets are examined on the network. If the packets are found suspected, i.e., matched with the signature then they are prevented using some action. The protocol stack is examined in the network to find any packets that violate the TCP/IP protocol. Ping- of-death is an example for a known pattern. It also examines the protocol headers for illegal combinations. If a signature notices the header consists of both SYN and FIN flag set at a time then this can be an indication of the system that it is under attack. This IDS has less false alarm rates as they watch for specific strings, patterns and signatures. If the database is not up to date or a slight change in the pattern will fail to detect the attacks. The signature-based rely solely on its own database to detect attack, if the attack details are available then the packets are allowed into the system. As a result, they are useless to new techniques that are emerging for attack. This mechanism is not effective to passive attacks like network sniffing, session hijacking, sequence number of spoofing and redirects.

6.4.4 Anamoly Detection

Denning has found a real time intrusion by monitoring and analyzing the audit records to find abnormal patterns in 1987. From then, this anamoly detection has become an area of research beceause of its ability to detect unknown attacks.This constructs a baseline using the normal traffic flow at peak hours, nonpeak hours, night hours, etc., and the activities occuring according to organization requirements. The baseline is constructed based on the mean and variance of the statistics. As mean gives the statistical norm and variance gives a way to measure the distribution of data about mean. The baseline normal must be adopted according to the changes evolve, else there will be more false alarms. This even gets activated if it notices many Telnet sessions on a single day or a heavy traffic of SNMP. To avoid these, the baseline should be robust that covers the whole organizations network segments. The baseline must be able to cover all traffic, can vary from simple to comprehensive content based on the characteristics of the network. The biggest challenge is developing an effective baseline for functioning of the system in a smooth way. This baseline is generated by training the profile based on the traffic pattern over a period of time. Once this baseline is developed based on training, the detection mode is started. If an attack exists in the network while creating a baseline, the activity becomes a part of baseline and it goes by undetected. This means it does not detect all unknown attacks. There are different anamoly detection methods and some of them which are mostly in use are Protocol anamoly detection, Traffic anamoly detection, Statistical anamoly, Stateful protocol anamoly detection.

6.4.4.1 Protocol Anamoly-Based Intrusion Detection

This detection tries to identify the abnormal behavior in the network protocols. This method works well with well-defined protocols of the organization. Some modules are to be added for the unsual use of the available standard protocols. If the IDS is aware of valid protocols, the system works well. It refers to the anamoly in protocol format and behavior with respect to the defined standards. If an HTTP session is being monitored, the attributes present in the session are trying to deviate the standard session, IDS treats it as a malicious activity. There are many aspects that are to be monitored like TCP header, various flags of IP header, etc.

6.4.4.2 Traffic Anamoly-Based Intrusion Detection

The traffic pattern is observed, if any unexpected pattern is detected by the IDS then it is intimated to the administrator. When a session is established, the traffic pattern is observed until the session is terminated. This relies on the ability to establish"Normal" patterns of traffic and behavior of the system, network and its applications. Defining these parameters in a dynamic environment may be dynamic.

6.4.4.3 Stateful Protocol Anamoly Based Intrusion Detection

This is anamoly-based IDS except that the vendors/manufacturers define a set of rules that are accepted universally. It keeps track of the state of the protocol both in network and application layers. This protocol is aware of the protocols how they work like FTP, therefore, it detects intrusion activity. Sharing the relevant data that is collected in a session can be used to detect various intrusions that involve request and responses, helps in detecting multisession attacks. This process is called deep packet inspection, examines packets closely to application layer to find possible attacks. It also examines authentication session for malicious activity as well as the unexpected sequence of commands like issuing the same command continuously, etc. It requires heavy processing overhead to track multiple connections, increases the analytical complexity of the sessions. Until a protocol violates the behavior, the method fails to detect an attack.

6.4.4.4 Stateful Matching Intrusion Detection System

This technique of pattern matching takes the detection to the next level. The signature in a stream of traffic or overall system behavior is scanned rather than individual packet activities. The attacker can send large amounts of information to the system from various locations with long waiting time between each transmission to confuse the signature-based IDS. If the IDS is tuned to record and analyze traffic over a long period of time, the attack is identified. As the signatures are used, it must be updated regularly.

6.4.4.5 Statistical Anamoly Based Detection

This is also called behaviour-based IDS. It collects the traffic information, performs statistics and observes the normality of the traffic. The evaluation of the information establishes a baseline. Once the baseline is established, the IDS collects the samples periodically, uses statistical methods and compares with baseline. If the activity is out of baseline, an alert is sent to the administrator. This can help in detecting new attacks, once it notices abnormal activity in the system. But this type of system requires more and more overhead and signature-based IDS compares the patterns constantly against the baseline. This system develops a model for normal patterns for the activity and behavior by collecting the information. These models are based on historical information which are used to compare, validate the ongoing application. This system does not rely on a predefined set of known attacks like in knowledge based IDS. This system suits good at a high level, considering the characteristics, behaviour and acting against baseline. If the traffic is more in dynamic environment, it is difficult to define normal traffic. It may not be able to detect minor changes that occured and may generate false negatives. It is able to detect attacks that occur by the privileged users of an organization. This is not so effective due to the high number of false alarms, user profile development is difficult if the users have irregular schedules. The statistical IDS must be flexible that allows modifications to the model, gives a chance to intruders also. SIDS will not recognize the attacks that are learned to be normal, i.e., if the activity is not abnormal, it will not detect it. The attribute determination is difficult to create a normal baseline. Many of the SIDS use neural networks to train the data using large amounts of data. These neural networks collect millions of transactions to identify anamolys. The baseline is set for different protocols and different users accordingly.

6.5   Log File Monitor (LFM)

LFM is similar to NIDPS which reviews the log files generated by the servers, even IDPS, looks for the signatures and patterns that lead to an intrusion. In host-based, it monitors only individual systems whereas LFM is able to examine multiple log files from various number of systems. The intrusions can be found based on the recorded events of an entire network. This approach requires considerable resources as it involves the collection of resources observing the movements of those events, storage of the event information and analyzing the large amount of data.

6.6   Intrusion Detection and Prevention System (IDPS) Response

IDPS's response performs in a different way, it is based on the configuration and its functional properties. Some of them respond in an active way while others apply passive ways. When it responds in an active way, it even modifies the network environment itself or some action is taken against the intrusion. In a passive way, it sends alarms or notifications to the administrator by collecting passive data using Simple Network Management Protocol (SNMP) traps. The administrator takes an action after performing the analysis on passive data. IDPS can be configured to execute when it detects specific types of intrusions. They block or detect the attacks. They block the traffic if they detect a suspected IP address of the attacker. This blocking can be for a certain period of time, once the period expires then the system is set to normal rules. It may even block TCP or UDP port traffic if it detects some suspicious activity. It can even terminate a session or a connection based on the observation. Once the action is taken, the system is set back to the normal state. In the passive response, most commonly implemented, although they have active systems, these are disabled by default.

The commercial IDPS generates a routine detail of the reports at regular intervals. Some requirements are to be considered like the system environment, security goals and objectives are to be described based on the organization requirements, restrictions from outside and its related constraints. Most of IDPS are misuse detectors, the product value depends on the signature database and should get updated to analyze the events captured.

NIDPS and HIDPS can be used together to cover both individual systems that can connect networks. In order to avoid the damage to the whole organization, these should be implemented using phase stratergy. Once NIDPS is configured and found running without any issue, HIDPS can be implemented to protect from critical systems. When both are installed, the administrator scans the network for attacks that originate from outside. It can identify problems in the network firewalls and can detect large amounts of network traffic. The effectiveness of IDPS can be measured based on the threshold value which specifies a maximum acceptance level. These threshold values are mostly used in stateful and anamoly based detections for analysis. The generation of blacklists by the IDPSs can help to block the malicious activity.

These attacks are assigned high priority that match with the blacklist. The white list is generated to reduce the false positives. These black and white lists are used in signature-based detection and stateful analysis.

IDPS can detect attacks, identify the attacks occuring location in the network, useful as evidence to detect the attacks and can take corrective measures to avoid malicious activities. It can miss some intrusions and doesn't work well on high speed network with heavy traffic. As it notices this, it generates false alarms. It cannot perform some security mechanisms on the message or on packet like identification and authentication system consists of encryption, access control, virus detection, etc. It cannot detect and respond instantaneously when network traffic is heavy and more processing load on the system or a network. It can't establish newly published attacks without signature analysis update. Some attacks are performed by the malicious agents to trip the organizers and IDPS, making the administrator to conduct its own DoS attack by overreacting to the attacks which are caused normally. The DDos attack made possible to connect many hackable systems. There are plenty of methods to detect the attacks which are disscussed in the above sections. Now-a-days, spoofing-based detection has come into existence to overcome some of the problems that were not solved by the above methods. When this method is applied in a firewall, the packets are passed or dropped but flagged as possibily spoofed. In this system, packets are believed to have spoofed source addresses and they generate alerts for use by IDPS. This method uses a combination of methods. This first finds out whether the packet is suspicious or not using passive techniques then using active probes. Different techniques are used to determine whether the packet is spoofed or not. If the packet is not spoofed, the system updates the database with new values. With this, the IDS will be able to detect new attacks and these methods are based on on-demand adjunct to primary IDS. Basically, it is used to detect spoofed packets. A case study is performed on one of the Future Internet architectures explained in detail which uses the spoofed packets and wakes up the prevention system once it detects the suspicious events. Before discussing this method in detail, we must know about the DoS and DDoS attack possibility in the network.

6.7 DoS and Types of DoS Attacks

The principle objective of security to fulfill the request in a timely manner is called availability. Code Laws of U.S of Information Security defines as "Availability as ensuring timely and reliable access to and use of the information." We define availability as "ensuring the presence of desired service in a timely manner." DoS is an attack that violates the availability of the services in a system. It is executed by a malicious entity to stop the utilization of the resources of others in the network in an intended time.

Denial of Service (DoS) attack is a serious threat in the network communication of the current network and may be an issue even in the future. The available methods become more sophisticated, effective and powerful to detect these attacks [118]. In DoS, a large number of spoof packets are sent to the victim machine to affect the operations performed by that system. The system becomes busy in handling the requests sent by the victim and couldn't be able to fulfill the additional user's requests for the services. It not only affects the victim system but also other hosts, routers and the entire network itself. The attacker on the victim machine blocks the services offered by that system which ultimately stops the proper functioning of the system. Some of the effects caused by a DoS attack are

1. The performance of the system degrades.

2. System resources like CPU, memory, buffer and bandwidth are blocked.

3. Authorized users are unable to access the services offered by the victim machine.

A DoS attack can be performed in two ways. First by consuming system resources such as CPU, memory and network bandwidth and second by using system vulnerabilities like the TCP handshaking, etc. There are various types of attacks which use a different type of technique to perform attacks [7]. In a typical DoS attack, a sender sends a huge number of packets to the victim machine. These packets are spoofed, i.e., these packets dont have an actual source address, rather they contain spoofed addresses. These are generated randomly by the attacker and make the system busy which ultimately results in unavailability of the services to other users of the network.

6.7.1 Semantic Attacks and Flooding Attacks

DoS attacks can be classified broadly as vulnerability-based attacks which otherwise can be called semantic attacks and flooding attacks/Brute force attacks. *Semantic attacks* are caused due to the exploitation of one or more policies which has some flaw in it or bug that implements the target system, sending continuous requests to consume excessive amounts of resources on the targeted system [7]. A *brute force attack* of DoS aims to deny a service to an authenticated user by invoking a large amount of service requests which are valid and tries to exhaust the key resources [134].

6.7.2 DoS/ DDoS Attacks

A **Denial of Service (DoS) attack** is one of the dangerous attacks [119] as it is not only able to affect the victim but also other host, router and network. In a DoS attack, the attacker sends a large number of spoof packets to the victim machine in order to block the services offered by that machine. There exist various approaches for performing DoS attacks.

1. SYN attack: In SYN attack method attacker uses the system vulnerabilities to perform the attack [143] which use TCP handshaking process [199].

2. Flood attack: In this method attacker sends a large number of packets to flood the victim. for example-ICMP attack, UDP attack [143], TCP attack [44].

3. Reflector attack: In this method the attacker sends packets to intermediary nodes such as a router which requires a response. These packets have a source address set to the victim's address. Routers send response packets to a victim. As a result, these packets can flood the victim [44][126].

4. Scripting attack: In this attack, the attacker sends database queries to the victim which consumes database resources [143].

In a **Distributed Denial of Service (DDoS) Attack,** attack is not made on the victim but uses other systems over the network to perform this attack. For this, it searches for less secured machines and installs its DoS attacking code in those machines. Thereafter, an attacker attacks using a controller machine. Controller machine gives the instructions to the zombie machine for performing the attack. Zombie machine sends a large number of spoof packets to the victim machine for flooding the victims resources. The volume of malicious traffic is so high that a victim cannot handle it and denies providing normal network services by flooding a great number of malicious traffic. In DoS attack the source IP addresses of the malicious packets are spoofed. When an attack is performed, then a large number of packets appear in nearby router of the victim which results in congestion [118][143] [205] [182] [215]

In DoS/DDoS, the attacker hides behind the network (compromise of controller and zombie systems) and uses spoof packets to send the request resulting a difficulty in identifying the real attacker. The attacker can perform network scanning many times in search of zombie systems to hide itself and perform the task. After collecting sufficient zombie systems it performs the attack [7]. In most of the DoS/DDoS attacks spoof IP addresses are used by the attacker as source address [205]. DDoS attacks with IP spoofing are much more difficult to defend.

DoS defense techniques can be further classified on the basis of the deployment and use of network elements. There are two types of solutions available to detect or block the attack on the network [205].

1. Router-based and

2. Host-based.

The router-based approach requires support from the network elements such as routers, etc., Cordination among the network elements results in success of these methods. This approach requires cost and time for widespread deployment of the defense mechanism in routers or network element. In host-based way, defense mechanism is installed at the victim location to detect/block the attack.

Host-based approach is fast and doesn't require network support for the deployment of the approach. The attack is detected and prevented at the end host. Host based approaches can be deployed rapidly when compared with router-based approaches.

6.7.3 DNS Reflector Attack

DNS reflector attack comes under the category of amplification and reflector attack. The basic technique of this attack is to send a request for a large DNS file with the source IP address spoofed. Attackers send DNS query requests to the DNS servers with a spoofed source address. The source address is set as the address of the victim. The response sent from the DNS server can be 73 times larger than the request it receives [7]. The DNS server can response in two ways: either by sending multiple response or in the form of sending a large file to the requester. Nonetheless, in both cases response is sent to a victim and it is very large. In this way, the DNS server unknowingly gets involved in the attack and the attacker amplifies the magnitude of the attack. Because of this, bandwidth of the victim is consumed and is unable to communicate with the other systems on the Internet. In the reflector attack, more than 32,000 name servers are involved which tremendously magnifies the attack volume.

6.7.4 Permanent Denial of Service Attack (PDoS)

PDoS damages the system permanently which gets recovered only by the replacement of the hardware. Working on PDoS attack depends on security loopholes on the target computers. The attacker uses the vulnerabilities of the system and replaces the device's firmware with the attacker's own code. This process is also known as flashing. This code makes the device or the computer unable to work properly until it is repaired or replaced. The PDoS is a pure hardware targeted attack which is faster and requires fewer resources than using a botnet in a DDoS attack. Because of the quick response, great attack potential and high probability of security exploits on Network Enabled Embedded Devices (NEEDs), this technique has come in the notice of numerous hacker communities.

6.7.5 DoS Targets

Generally the targets for DoS attacks are the end systems, routers or the entire network. DoS attacks can occur at the various layers of the Internet architecture including the operating system, router, communication link or on the whole architecture itself. There is a possibility of attack on IDS and firewalls, on the protocols of the layers separately like on the application layer protocols: Telnet, SMTP, IMAP XMPP, IRC, BGP, BOOTP, SIP, etc. Likewise, the protocols of the network and transport layer such as UDP Flood, TCP SYN, ICMP, and so on.

6.7.6 Recent Attacks

Recently many popular websites have faced DDoS attacks. Some attacks are very dangerous in the history of DoS attack. Attackers are using new techniques and intelligence for performing these attacks. The number of computers involved in an attack are increasing very often. Some of the recent attacks performed on popular websites are described below:

1. Anti-spam website spamhaus has recently experienced the biggest DoS attack in the history of a DoS attack. Spamhaus supplies the list of IP addresses for servers and computers on the net linked for the distribution of spam [134].

The blacklists supplied by the nonprofit organizations are used by ISPs, enterprises and spam blocking software developers to block the worst sources of junk mail before other spam filtering measures are brought into play. The latest attack was started on the spamhaus website on 18 March 2013 with the largest malicious attack traffic of 300 GB per second. First, the attack made the spamhaus disconnect from the rest of the Internet. It is the largest attack of its kind which was performed through Open DNS resolver. It is a DNS reflector attack [187].

In spamhaus attack, the attacker sends the requests for the DNS zone file to open DNS resolvers and the attacker spoofed the CloudFlare IPs and used it as the source address to perform their DNS queries. Open DNS servers responded with DNS zone file by generating approximately 75 Gbps of attack traffic collectively to send to the victim's source address. The requests were likely approximately 36 bytes long and the response was approximately 3000 bytes long which makes it nearly 100 times bigger than the request [187].

2. From 19th September 2012 to a month, long time period, a major DoS attack was performed on Bank of America, JPMorgan Chase, Wells Fargo, U.S. Bank and PNC Bank. They all suffered slowdown of the servers for many days and became unreachable to bank customers. The attacker performed a DoS attack on Bank of America first, then performed on others too. This attack was one of the biggest attacks, as a huge volume of packets were routed to bank servers. According to researchers, the volume of traffic was 10–20 times larger than the previous record of a DoS attack. In a DoS attack, attackers got control of thousands of powerful application servers and used them to generate high volume of traffic directed toward the server of the bank's websites. In this attack, no data were stolen or even ATM network was also working fine as the attacker's aim was to block the bank website temporarily and stop the public access. Such type of attack requires months of preparation because taking control of very high end application servers is not so easy when it is known that the servers are secured by a very efficient security system. Behind this attack superior level of intelligence was applied so that attacks lasted for a long time.

3. CNN News website was attacked a couple of times by a DoS attacker in April 2008 [53] [219]. The CNN website went down within 3 hours of the attack. CNN fixed the consequences of the attack by limiting the number of users who could access the site from specific geographical locations. A tool named DIY DDoS was used in the attack. Few experts say that there are more tools like Supper DDoS tool, which were used in the CNN attack.

Recent attacks on various network services have shown that the DoS attack is more dangerous. These attacks become more powerful and hard to resist. Attackers use a combination of size and intelligence in the attack. In most of the previous DoS attacks, the attacker used a maximum of 1 Gbps traffic but the new attack traffic was between 60–100 Gbps or more than that. Simultaneously the attacker uses a very large number of zombie computers. Attack on bank websites had involved

2000–3000 computers and most of them were influential business machines. Attackers used spoof source addresses to hide their identity, perform attacks on victim websites by sending a large number of requests, after that they used DNS servers to perform DoS reflection attack.

However, most large enterprises use high end security software like firewall, intrusion detection software to secure their data and important resources, but such a huge attack which involves more than 2000 high end business machines and attacker traffic of more than 100 Gbps, make them surrender. Attackers target large bank websites, military and government websites rather than the small enterprises to demonstrate their superior technical knowledge. Most importantly, the present Internet is not secure as a lot of computer systems are connected to it. The Internet is open to all and the information flow from one system to another is not secure. It can be easily accessible by third-party software and can be misused by them. An attacker uses network vulnerabilities to prepare for an attack. Unsecured communication and computers are their primary target for the attack. Therefore, there is an urgent need for the development of a new security protocol and a secure architecture in order to cope with various security issues especially like DoS.

6.7.7   Classification of Defense Techniques of DoS

There are various types of DoS attacks found which have already been discussed above. To resolve these, some techniques were proposed for the detection and prevention of the attacks which are discussed below:

6.7.7.1   Detection Techniques

Detection techniques are utilized for the detection of DoS attacks. Detection techniques monitor network traffic and analyze the behavior of the network for the detection of malicious activity. These techniques monitor network traffic and if there is a sudden rise in traffic than the detection method is used for the detection of DoS attack. Working of detection technique relies on the attack mechanism, e.g., in a DDoS attack, in which an attacker sends a large number of ICMP requests in the preparation phase of a DDoS attack. Detection techniques can monitor an astonishing increase in the number of ICMP packets, analyze them for the possibility of an attack. If there is an attack, there is a possibility of identifying the source system of DoS attack and necessary measures can be taken to resist a DoS attack. Detection-based techniques are also classified into two categories:

1. Signature based: Signature-based techniques rely on the knowledge of DoS attack mechanism. Every attack method has some specific pattern. If such a pattern is visible, then it can be analyzed that there is a possibility of DoS attack in the network can be analyzed easily. Techniques in this category detect the DoS attack by monitoring the system. These techniques analyze the network to find the pattern for the cases like a sudden increase in traffic of a particular type of packet, variation in the traffic, increase of traffic on any specific link or

subnet of the network. Such parameters for signature-based techniques, able to detect known types of attacks.

2. Anomaly-based detection techniques: Anomaly-based detection techniques monitor the network for normal behavior and if found any noteworthy deviation from the normal behavior then it is treated as a possibility of DoS attack [118]. These techniques are helpful in finding unknown DoS attacks. The best example of such a technique is SYN Flood detection technique.

6.7.7.2   DoS Prevention Techniques

Prevention techniques attempt to filter the traffic or prevent attack by blocking the attacker's IP address. First, it identifies then blocks the entire malicious subnet. Action of prevention techniques depend on the analysis of the detection techniques. Strong detection techniques offer more chances to prevent the DoS attack. Prevention techniques involve techniques to filter out the spoof packets [205], router-based packet filtering [7], and network level filtering of packets, hop count filtering techniques, etc. Filtering of spoof packets depends on identification of spoof and bogus IP address. Once spoof address is known then every packet from that source is dropped. Router-based techniques require support from the router. This technique uses routing information to identify the attacker. Generally Border Gateway Protocol (BGP) is used to filter packets coming from a spoofed source.

A   Network level filtering: This type of filtering technique filters traffic at the network level. These techniques control the traffic which enters or leaves over the network. Working of these techniques depends upon the information about the packets along with the expected source address. If source addresses are known and are within the expected source address record, then the traffic is allowed to leave or enter the network. Ingress/egress filtering techniques are the examples of such technique. Ingress filtering means filtering of traffic expected to enter in the network. Egress filtering means filtering of traffic going outside the network [213].

B   Response techniques: These techniques are nearly the same as prevention techniques. These are used after a DoS attack was detected. These techniques provide an immediate solution to minimize the impact of a DoS attack. These techniques use filtering and traffic control techniques to overcome the damage of a DoS attack.

C   Tolerance techniques: These techniques try to minimize the effect of a DoS attack without differentiating the legitimate traffic and malicious traffic. These techniques refer to utilize good policies in implementation of various network level protocols and generally these are implemented as part of the infrastructure. Example of a tolerance technique is congestion control policies [134]. Congestion policies are used to balance the traffic load in the communication links. If there is any abrupt increase in any link, then traffic is diverted or congestion control policies are used. If congestion policies are implemented in view of DoS, then it can be minimized [213].

6.8   DoS Attack in SONATE

Development of SONATE is divided into eight phases as discussed in future work (For more details please refer to Section 2.6.17). It provides backward compatibility to TCP/IP protocols due to its flexible and loosely coupled nature of the architecture. Currently this framework uses TCP/IP network for communication with other systems containing SONATE (in Phase 3). In Phase 3 of the architecture, the framework is deployed over the TCP/IP network as an overlay and it is using Type 2 packet formats to send messages (refer to Chapter 4) from one system to the other. Service consumer submits a service request using the application programs. The service broker receives the demand and searches for the suitable building blocks in its repository. If the required building blocks are available, then the broker composes the service using selection and composition process [152]. The broker adds the building blocks in the workflow and service requests to get fulfilled. If the broker doesn't have the desired BBs in the repository, it communicates with others and demand for the desired Building Blocks. After receiving the desired BBs from the other brokers of the network, the service broker adds them to the workflow and services are offered to the service customer.

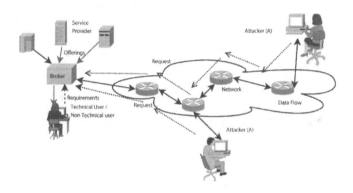

Figure 6.1: Communication system under DoS attack.

Service brokers are the primary targets for the attacker because if the broker is unable to communicate, as the communication is impossible among the service consumer and service provider. In SONATE, a node (A) will respond to other node (B) if and only if a node requests for a service (Figure 6.1). In TCP/IP-based network, the scenario is different. A node can communicate and send data to other nodes without any demand. Use of the TCP/IP network for communication may lead to DoS attack in the architecture. In the future, there is a possibility of an attack when TCP/IP is provided as a service. This can be made by keeping the broker too busy for the fulfillment of the requested resources and not allowed to perform other actions. Therefore, there is a requirement of a method that can make the resources available to the user in a timely manner and if any malfunction occurs, able to detect and prevent it from that attack. Prevention of this attack is impossible and achieves a robust and resilient behavior of the architecture. Several issues need to be concerned in order to defend these attacks. Basically there are three types of attacks like the alteration of the information related to the configuration, alteration of the network components, or the consumption of non-renewable resources.

This presents a robust method that inspects incoming IP packets at a victim machine without any network support. Proposed method will verify the authenticated packets by filtering the spoofed packets. The idea is to use packet's header information to distinguish spoofed packets from the legitimate packets. This method is using the hop count and MAC address to identify the legitimate packet. Hop count information can be obtained by time to live field (TTL) of the IP packet. This information is further used to identify the packets. When router forward packets to the next router it decrements TTL value by one. The MAC address is the address of the system which is used by the source of the packet. A methodology has been proposed in the next section in which the following tasks were identified.

1. Validation of incoming packets.

2. Detection of spoof packets by inspecting every incoming packet.

3. Prevention from the DoS attack by filtering spoof packets so that the broker is available for communication and service provider is able to provide service to authenticate users.

6.9 DoS Detection and Prevention Mechanism for SONATE

A methodology has been proposed for the detection and prevention of DoS attack in the architecture of SONATE. The detection state is used to validate the source address using hop count and the identification of the spoofed packets. If a hop count of the incoming packet is not consistent with the stored hop count, then the packets are assumed to be spoofed. These packets are filtered in the prevention state. In the prevention state, the spoofed packets are identified using the algorithm of the detection state then the MAC address is extracted from the captured packet which is compared with the stored MAC address. If the received packets are consistent, the packet is not discarded otherwise, the packet is filtered out.

Using a case diagram for the system shows that the system has three main components namely service consumer, service broker and service provider. The broker has two main causes which are detection and prevention. Detection case is again having sub use cases which are validation, capture packet, valid IP table creation and identification of spoof packets. Prevention case is related to filter of spoof packets (Figure 6.2).

The static structure of the system is described using a class diagram which will show system's classes, their attributes, their methods and relationship between them.

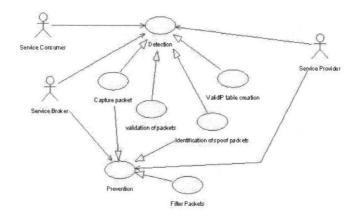

Figure 6.2: Use case diagram for detection and prevention states.

The class diagram consists of six classes (Figure 6.3). The main class is the class which starts the application and creates the work flow and adds building blocks in the workflow. After that it executes the workflow. Application building block class is implementing the application building block required to start the DoS_Availability service using applicationStart method. It also implements up and down the port for the application building block. DoS_Detection Building Block uses an alert class to implement diverse functionalities which include capturing of packets, validation of packets, and detection of spoof packets. The value class is used by the alert class to store values for source address in it. JPcaptor class provides methods to capture the packets. It provides a method to identify the network interface card and a method to process the packets.

6.9.1 Detection State

In the architecture of SONATE when a DoS attack occurs, the broker starts functioning by waking up the DoS Detection Building Block (DDBB). The detection state is used to validate the source address using the hop count of the incoming packets which helps in detecting the spoof packets. The detection state monitors the incoming packets and if it detects the spoof packets, then it calls the filtering building block which is used for filtering the spoof packets. Functioning of the detection BB is to be validated using the following, where it first validates the packets using the validIP table. This table consists of authenticated users list which is used for validating the incoming packets that are going to be received by the broker of the system. For the verification of the packet, the algorithm captures the incoming packets and extracts its source IP address, TTL value and the MAC address. After the extraction process, it computes hopcount(H_n). The hop count is obtained by subtracting the TTL value

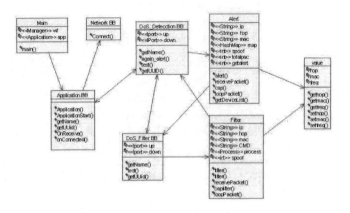

Figure 6.3: Class diagram for detection and prevention of DoS.

from the initial TTL value which is obtained using the if else ladder (Algorithm1). The algorithm compares (H_n) with the stored (H_s) of the validIp table. If both of them are the same, then it is treated as a valid packet from a valid source address of the network. Sometimes there is a possibility of the packet was spoofed even if H_n is equal to H_s. If such a situation arises, when it is necessary to verify the IP address of the source along with the MAC address of the incoming packet. Thus, the validIP table consists of source IP address, MAC address, hop count and frequency count.

In the algorithm (Figure 6.4), a variable spoof has been initiated to zero, used to count the suspicious packets. A monitoring window of specified packet size is considered for the inspection of the packets. The variable spoof increments by one when the incoming packet is identified as a malicious one. If the malicious packets exceed a threshold, then the system is considered under DoS attack. If the system is found under DoS attack, a call for the prevention BB is made. If the packets are below a threshold, then the algorithm of detection runs for investigating the incoming packets.

The table is important for the validation of the packet and for the filtration of the packets. The reason behind the consideration of this ladder (Chapter4) is the most modern OS uses only selected initial TTL values and they are 30, 32, 60, 64, 128 and 255 [205]. To get the final hop count this TTL value is used. After obtaining the hop count it extracts the IP address and MAC address of the system. These values are stored in a table called ValidIP table.

The alert object is created which implements Validate_Packet algorithm after the DDBB adds the application BB to workflow. Thus, DDBB implements a single functionality to validate packets continuously. Since this BB is required to secure the broker therefore it should be in memory for continuous validation of packets (Figure 6.5).

The sequence diagram (Figure 6.6) shows the interaction among various objects and the validation of those packets. Main class creates a workflow which adds ap-

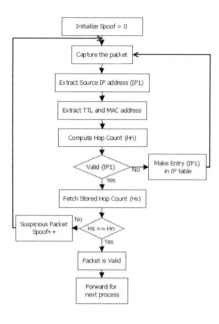

Figure 6.4: DoS detection algorithm.

plication, network and DoS_detection building block to it. After addition of building blocks, DoS_Detection calls alert class instance for capturing the packets. The packets are captured by the method provided by JPcapCaptor class. As soon as the packet is received, source address, TTL field and MAC address are extracted from the packet and compared with the stored value of the TTL and a MAC address corresponding to receive source address. If comparison is positive then packet is valid packet coming from the authenticated source and the packet is accepted. Otherwise the packet is considered as malicious packet.

When a new packet is captured by jpcap captor class then a hash table is created to store the IP value pair in it. Here the value is an object which stores corresponding values of source address. This hash table is populated with the stored validIP table stored in secondary media. Hash table can be updated when a new packet which is not stored in validIP table is captured (Figure 6.7). Before storing the new address its hop value and the MAC address is verified more than one time by sending packets to it and by receiving an acknowledgement packet from that source address.

A sequence of messages exchanged during the creation of the table is shown in (Figure 6.8). In the process of table creation, six objects are considered as in communication. This algorithm is applied on every incoming packet. In this algorithm, a variable spoof is initialized to zero which counts the number of suspicious packets. A monitoring window of specified packet size is chosen to inspect the packets. When a packet is identified as malicious then variable spoof is incremented by one. If a number of malicious packets is above a predefined threshold, it is concluded that there is

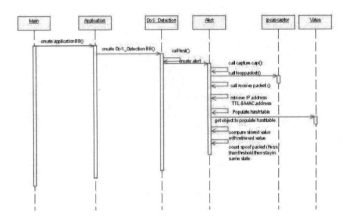

Figure 6.5: Sequence diagram for detection and prevention of DoS.

a DoS attack. In this situation, DDBB switches its state from detection to prevention by calling the DoS_Filter building block. If the number of malicious packets is below the threshold, then this algorithm continues to run in the detection state.

The whole process has been implemented in Java language and Jcap library is used for capturing the incoming packets. It itself uses a libcap library which is a native library of Windows OS. A detailed description of Jcap has been explained in Appendix.

6.9.2 Prevention State

The prevention state is used for the prevention of the system from a DoS attack after detecting the attack by the detection BB of the broker. A filtering algorithm has been used for the prevention of the attack on the system. This algorithm blocks the spoof address and drops the packets originating from the spoof address. The MAC address is considered as important for the confirmation of the true identity of the user. When a packet is suspected as spoofed or malicious, it is inspected again using the machine address. If the received (MAC_n) is the same as the stored MAC (MAC_s), it is treated as a valid packet reaching the destination via a different route; otherwise, it is treated as spoofed and the source address is blocked for further loss. Using this BB the broker can block the whole subnet if the entire subnet is involved in the attack (Figure 6.9). The algorithm uses a method drop_packet() to block the source IP address using Windows firewall. The Windows firewall is a powerful tool for managing the firewall related tasks. It provides a rich set of methods and commands to generate rule, update rule, allow an IP address or deny an IP address for managing the firewall. It applies the rules for blocking one or more IP addresses. The drop_packet() method maintains a buffer to hold the blocked IP address list by the name Block_IP for the filtration of the packet. Once the rule for Block_IP is generated, every packet from that IP is

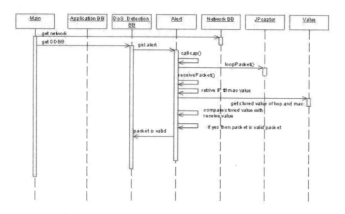

Figure 6.6: Sequence diagram for Validation of the packets.

filtered out. As the algorithm detects no spoof packets in the network, it changes its state by clearing the list of blocked IP addresses and allowing them to receive the packets from the network.

In the prevention state, the algorithm doesn't allow to add a new entry in the valid IP table as the address may be a spoofed address.

A sequence diagram (Figure 6.10) for the DoS prevention presents the switching of the states from DoS_detection to DoS_Filter BB. State is changed when the number of spoofed packets is above the upper threshold T1. If the numbers of spoof packets are above the upper threshold, then it indicates that the system is under denial of service attack and requires to call the filter BB for the prevention of the attack. The collaboration diagram (Figure 6.11) also represents switching of the states, i.e., from DoS_detection to DoS_Filter BB. It shows the sequence of messages exchanged during switching of the states. The switching occurs using the six objects in the communication and a total of eight messages are involved to perform the desired task. As soon as the detection state detects the attack, it sends the information to alert state which invokes the filter BB for the prevention of the attack.

The sequence diagram (Figure 6.12) explains the working of the filter state when DDBB call DFBB. This BB is required when the system is under attack. As soon as there is no attack, i.e., the number of spoof packets is below the lower threshold then it switches again to detection state. DFBB is invoked for filtering and is implemented by filtering BB in SONATE. To locate the IP address in valid IP table, both building blocks use a hashing technique. Hashing makes the searching of the IP address in the table very fast.

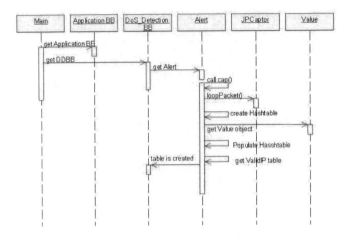

Figure 6.7: Sequence diagram for the Validation of IP

Threshold Values

Two threshold values T1 and T2 are used to switch the system from detection state to prevention state. T1 is used for the detection of the attack and T2 value is used for the prevention of the attack. If the number of suspicious packets above T1, DDBB calls DFBB for filtering the spoofed packets and if the number of spoof packets is less than the threshold T2, it switches its state to DDBB from DFBB. The value of the T1 and T2 depends upon the application on which this method is used. An algorithm (Algorithm 6.1) has been explained by considering the window size of 100 packets and they are decremented in every iteration. The variable spoof is initiated to zero when a new window starts which is used to count the spoof packets in the window.

Algorithm 6.1
Switching of the States

      1.   *In DDBB*

  2. If(window size == 0 && spoof < T1)

      3.   *stay in the Detection state;*

      4.   *else*

      5.   *call DFBB*

      6.   *In DFBB*

  7. If(window size == 0 && spoof < T2)

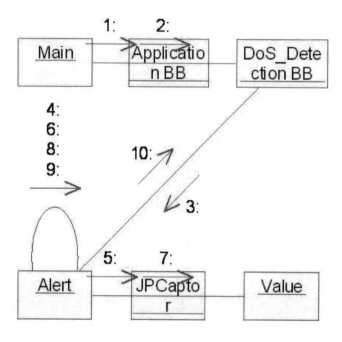

Figure 6.8: Collaboration diagram for ValidIP table

8.   *call DDBB*

9.   *stay in the Filtering state;*

The diagram (Figure 6.13) explains the switching of the system from one state to the other. The shift of the state occurs when the number of spoofed packets below a lower threshold T2. The lower threshold indicates that the system is not under the denial of service attack. Therefore, there is a need to switch back to the detection state.

6.10   Discussion and Results

Two building blocks are developed and deployed to test the performance namely one for DoS detection BB (DDBB) and another for DoS filter BB (DFBB). Hash function is used for the searching operation of the IP addresses. As soon as the system detects the attack it calls the DFBB building block for the filtering of the spoof packets. When the spoof packets are below the threshold as shown in the algorithm it will switch back to the detection state from the filtering state. The mechanism captures

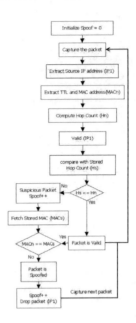

Figure 6.9: DoS prevention algorithm.

the incoming packets, inspects them and identifies the spoof packets. This algorithm not only validates incoming packets but also identifies spoof packets. This method starts in the detection state using DDBB to inspect the packets. If the number of spoofed packets increases above the upper threshold, then DFBB is called. DFBB filters the spoof packets.

For the experiment on the testbed, a frequency of spoof packet 100 packets per window is considered (window size is used in implementation for monitoring the packets). It is observed that there is a sudden increase in spoof packets immediately after the 43 window. An attack model is considered for the verification of the Building Blocks. By analyzing this method in an actual work environment (ie., In SONATE), it is proved that the method is very effective to detect and prevent DoS attack. Various test cases are considered and various results are obtained within the test bed of SONATE. A total of 98 windows is considered along with an attacker in the testbed and each window is of 100 packets for the experiment and sent over the systems of the testbed. The tests are performed when the system is not deployed with the prevention algorithm and only capturing of the packets is performed. The graphs are plotted when the UDP flooding attack is performed using a single thread with low speed, the same with 5, 10 threads with varying speed in the network. The experiment is performed for checking the proper functioning of the prevention algorithm by changing the IP, MAC, IP and MAC address in the network of systems and various graphs are obtained.

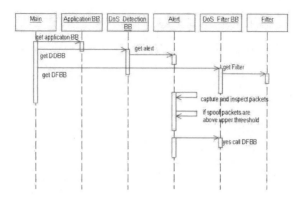

Figure 6.10: Sequence diagram for DoS prevention.

6.10.1   DoS Detection Building Block (DDBB) Class

DoS detection building block implements all the methods as implemented by the application building block. getName( ) method returns the name of the building block. GetUUID returns the ID of DoSDetection Building Block (DDBB). It also implements application specific methods which are as follows:

- Public void test( ): this method creates the alert object and calls the cap( ) method to start detection of the spoof packets.

- Public void again_alert( ): this method is called when there is switching from prevention to state to detection state. It happens when the filter class calls DDBB. Map instance is passed to the detection state to get the present state of the validIP table.

6.10.1.1   Alert Class

Alert class implements the functionalities performed by the detection state and it is in association with DDBB. Alert class implements methods for the following functionalities:

- ❖ Capture packet
- ❖ Validation of incoming packets
- ❖ Identification of spoof packets
- ❖ ValidIP table creation and update

Alert class implements the interface PacketReceiver and implements the following methods in it:

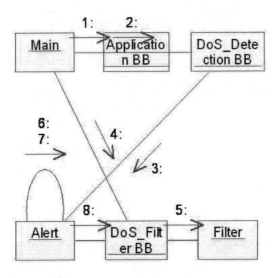

Figure 6.11: Collaboration diagram of DoS prevention.

a. Alert ( ): constructor to initialize the object of the class.

b. Alert (*Map* < *String, object* > *rmap*): constructor to initialize alert object when there is switching between state detection and prevention. This constructor populates the validIP table using rmap object.

c. Cap ( ): this method captures the incoming packets using JpcapCaptor class of Jpcap. It throws the IOException exception objects. It calls for the loopPacket method to repeatedly capture the packets. It also identifies network interface card which is using communication.

d. receivePacket(Packet packet): this method creates and updates the hash table. It validates the packet and checks for suspicious packets.

6.10.2 DoS Filter Building Block (DFBB)

DoS filter building block implements all the methods as implemented by the application building block. getName( ) method returns the name of the building block. getUUID returns the ID of DoS_Filter building block. It also implements application specific methods which are as follows:

Public void test( ): this method creates the filter object and calls the cap( ) method to start Detection of the spoof packets. DoS filter building block has two ports up and down. Action of these ports are also implemented as both ports provide communication with the other building blocks in the workflow.

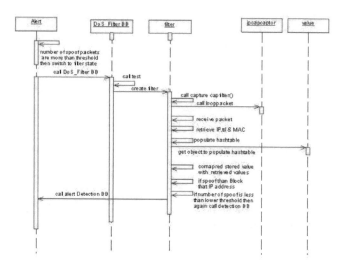

Figure 6.12: Sequence diagram for DoS filter mechanism.

6.10.2.1   Filter Class

Filter class implements the functionalities of the prevention state and it is in association with the DoS_Filter building block. Filter class implements the method to drop spoof packets. It creates filtering rules for the filter of the packets.

Filter class implements the interface packet receiver and implements the following methods in it:

a.   filter ( ): constructor to initialize the object of the class.

b.   filter (*Map < String, object > rmap*): constructor to initialize filter object when there is switching between state detection and prevention. This constructor populates the validIP table using rmap object.

c.   Capfilter(): capture the packets.

d.   receivePacket (Packet packet): it generates the rule for filtering spoof packets and filter the packets.

Figure 6.21 shows the reduction of the spoof packets on the victim machine when the DoS detection and prevention algorithm is implemented on the architecture of SONATE. The above line (Figure 6.22) represents a spoofed packet while the below line the valid packets when this algorithm is implemented in SONATE. It is clearly visible that count of spoof packet is below 20% and the average count is nearly 11% when this algorithm is used.

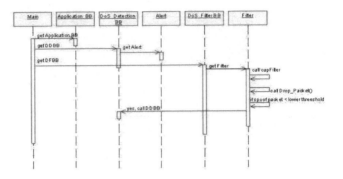

Figure 6.13: from DoS_Filter BB to DoS_Detection BB.

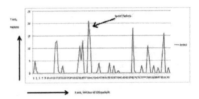

Figure 6.14: Graph showing the frequency of the packets before applying the detection algorithm.

6.11 Summary

Intrusion detection systems detect the intrusions but IPs not only detect intrusions but take the action to defend the network. NIDPS monitors the network traffic and notifies the administrator. A HIDPS works on the host system whereas knowledge-based IDPS examines the data traffic. Selecting IDPS that best suites the organization is a difficult task but once chosen it works fine up to a certain level. DoS attack is viable and obvious threat in any Future Internet environment and needs to be prevented. The architectures are flexible, loosely coupled and the agents of the network may get busy in fulfilling the demand of the malicious agents by avoiding the authenticated ones of the network. The DoS attack leads to congestion at the broker's end. In the case study, a mechanism is proposed and evaluated to avoid DoS attack. The mechanism is based on four parameters such as hop count, frequency count, IP address and MAC address. The results show that the proposed mechanism helps in fulfilling the request of the user in addition to prevention of DoS attack and related congestion. The proposed mechanism is very lightweight and easy to install.

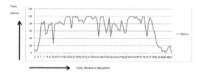

Figure 6.15: Graph obtained when UDP flooding attack is performed using five threads.

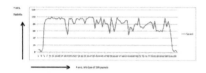

Figure 6.16: Graph obtained when UDP Flooding attack is performed using five threads.

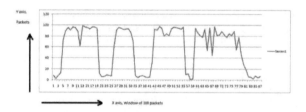

Figure 6.17: Communication with UDP Flooding attack using ten threads.

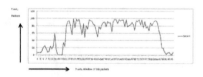

Figure 6.18: Graph obtained when IP address changed.

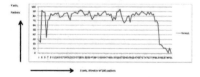

Figure 6.19: Graph obtained when MAC address changed.

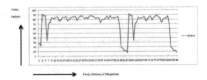

Figure 6.20: Graph showing both IP and MAC address changed.

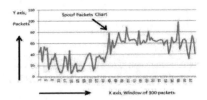

Figure 6.21: Graph obtained after prevention of DoS attack.

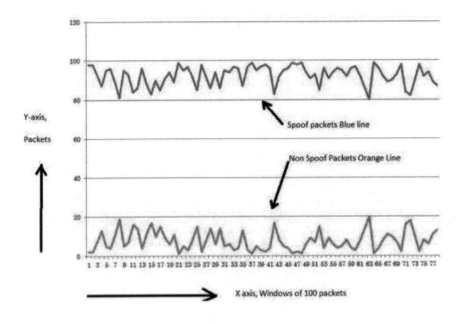

Figure 6.22: Graph after deploying Prevention Algorithm

Appendix-6A

Firewalls

The ability to connect any computer, anywhere, to any other computer, anywhere, is a mixed blessing. For individuals at home, wandering around the Internet is lots of fun. For corporate security managers, it is a nightmare. Most companies have large amounts of confidential information online-trade secrets, product development plans, marketing strategies, financial analyses, etc. Disclosure of this information to a competitor could have dire consequences. In addition to the danger of information leaking out, there is also a danger of information leaking in. In particular, viruses, worms, and other digital pests can breach security, destroy valuable data, and waste large amounts of administrator's time trying to clean up the mess they leave. Often they are imported by careless employees who want to play some nifty new game. Consequently, mechanisms are needed to keep "good" bits in and "bad" bits out. One method is to use IPsec. This approach protects data in transit between secure sites. However, IPsec does nothing to keep digital pests and intruders from getting onto the company LAN. To see how to accomplish this goal, we need to look at firewalls.

Firewalls are just a modern adaptation of that old medieval security standby: digging a deep moat around your castle. This design forced everyone entering or leaving the castle to pass over a single drawbridge, where they could be inspected by the I/O police. With networks, the same trick is possible: a company can have many LANs connected in arbitrary ways, but all traffic to or from the company is forced through an electronic drawbridge (firewall). No other route exists.

Firewall Design Principles

Information systems in corporations, government agencies, and other organizations have undergone a steady evolution:

- Centralized data processing system, with a central mainframe supporting a number of directly connected terminals

- Local area networks (LANs) interconnecting PCs and terminals to each other and the mainframe

- Premises network, consisting of a number of LANs, interconnecting PCs, servers, and perhaps a mainframe or two

- Enterprise-wide network, consisting of multiple, geographically distributed premises networks interconnected by a private wide area network (WAN)

- Internet connectivity, in which the various premises networks all hook into the Internet and may or may not also be connected by a private WAN

Internet connectivity is no longer optional for organizations. The information and services available are essential to the organization. Moreover, individual users within the organization want and need Internet access, and if this is not provided via their LAN, they will use dial-up capability from their PC to an Internet service provider (ISP). However, while Internet access provides benefits to the organization, it enables the outside world to reach and interact with local network assets. This creates a threat to the organization. While it is possible to equip each workstation and server on the premises network with strong security features, such as intrusion protection, this is not a practical approach. Consider a network with hundreds or even thousands of systems, running a mix of various versions of UNIX, plus Windows. When a security flaw is discovered, each potentially affected system must be upgraded to fix that flaw. The alternative, increasingly accepted, is the firewall. The firewall is inserted between the premises network and the Internet to establish a controlled link and to erect an outer security wall or perimeter. The aim of this perimeter is to protect the premises network from Internet-based attacks and to provide a single choke point where security and audit can be imposed. The firewall may be a single computer system or a set of two or more systems that cooperate to perform the firewall function. In this section, we look first at the general characteristics of firewalls. Then we look at the types of firewalls currently in common use. Finally, we examine some of the most common firewall configurations.

Firewall Characteristics

1. All traffic from inside to outside, and vice versa, must pass through the firewall. This is achieved by physically blocking all access to the local network except via the firewall. Various configurations are possible, as explained later in this section.

2. Only authorized traffic, as defined by the local security policy, will be allowed to pass. Various types of firewalls are used, which implement various types of security policies, as explained later in this section.

3. The firewall itself is immune to penetration. This implies the use of a trusted system with a secure operating system.

The four general techniques that firewalls use to control access and enforce the site's security policy are given below. Originally, firewalls focused primarily on service control, but they have since evolved to provide all four:

■ Service control: Determines the types of Internet services that can be accessed, inbound or outbound. The firewall may filter traffic on the basis of IP address and TCP port number; may provide proxy software that receives and interprets each service request before passing it on; or may host the server software itself, such as a Web or mail service.

■ Direction control: Determines the direction in which particular service requests may be initiated and allowed to flow through the firewall.

■ User control: Controls access to a service according to which user is attempting to access it. This feature is typically applied to users inside the firewall perimeter (local users). It may also be applied to incoming traffic from external users; the latter requires some form of secure authentication technology, such as is provided in IPSec.

■ Behavior control: Controls how particular services are used. For example, the firewall may filter e-mail to eliminate spam, or it may enable external access to only a portion of the information on a local Web server.

Before proceeding to the details of firewall types and configurations, it is best to summarize what one can expect from a firewall. The following capabilities are within the scope of a firewall:

1. A firewall defines a single choke point that keeps unauthorized users out of the protected network, prohibits potentially vulnerable services from entering or leaving the network, and provides protection from various kinds of IP spoofing and routing attacks. The use of a single choke point simplifies security management because security capabilities are consolidated on a single system or set of systems.

2. A firewall provides a location for monitoring security-related events. Audits and alarms can be implemented on the firewall system.

3. A firewall is a convenient platform for several Internet functions that are not security related. These include a network address translator, which maps local addresses to Internet addresses, and a network management function that audits or logs Internet usage.

4. A firewall can serve as the platform for IPSec. The firewall can be used to implement virtual private networks.

Firewalls have their limitations, including the following:

1. The firewall cannot protect against attacks that bypass the firewall. Internal systems may have dial-out capability to connect to an ISP. An internal LAN may support a modem pool that provides dial-in capability for traveling employees and telecommuters.

2. The firewall does not protect against internal threats, such as a disgruntled employee or an employee who unwittingly cooperates with an external attacker.

3. The firewall cannot protect against the transfer of virus-infected programs or files. Because of the variety of operating systems and applications supported inside the perimeter, it would be impractical and perhaps impossible for the firewall to scan all incoming files, e-mail, and messages for viruses.

Types of Firewalls

The three common types of firewalls are packet filters, application-level gateways, and circuit-level gateways.

Packet-Filtering Router

A packet-filtering router Figure 6.23 applies a set of rules to each incoming and outgoing IP packet and then forwards or discards the packet. The router is typically configured to filter packets going in both directions (from and to the internal network). Filtering rules are based on information contained in a network packet:

- **Source IP address:** The IP address of the system that originated the IP packet (e.g.,192.178.1.1)

- **Destination IP address:** The IP address of the system the IP packet is trying to reach (e.g., 192.168.1.2)

- **Source and destination transport-level address:** The transport level (e.g., TCP or UDP) port number, which defines applications such as SNMP or TELNET

- **IP protocol field:** Defines the transport protocol

- **Interface:** For a router with three or more ports, which interface of the router the packet came from or which interface of the router the packet is destined for

The packet filter is typically set up as a list of rules based on matches to fields in the IP or TCP header. If there is a match to one of the rules, that rule is invoked to determine whether to forward or discard the packet. If there is no match to any rule, then a default action is taken. Two default policies are possible:

- **Default** = discard: That which is not expressly permitted is prohibited.

■ **Default** = forward: That which is not expressly prohibited is permitted.

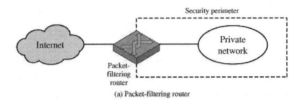

(a) Packet-filtering router

Figure 6.23: Packet level Firewall.

The default discard policy is more conservative. Initially, everything is blocked, and services must be added on a case-by-case basis. This policy is more visible to users, who are more likely to see the firewall as a hindrance. The default forward policy increases ease of use for end users but provides reduced security; the security administrator must, in essence, react to each new security threat as it becomes known.

One advantage of a packet-filtering router is its simplicity. Also, packet filters typically are transparent to users and are very fast. [WACK02] lists the following weaknesses of packet filter firewalls:

■ Because packet filter firewalls do not examine upper-layer data, they cannot prevent attacks that employ application-specific vulnerabilities or functions. For example, a packet filter firewall cannot block specific application commands; if a packet filter firewall allows a given application, all functions available within that application will be permitted.

■ Because of the limited information available to the firewall, the logging functionality present in packet filter firewalls is limited. Packet filter logs normally contain the same information used to make access control decisions (source address, destination address, and traffic type).

■ Most packet filter firewalls do not support advanced user authentication schemes. Once again, this limitation is mostly due to the lack of upper-layer functionality by the firewall.

■ They are generally vulnerable to attacks and exploits that take advantage of problems within the TCP/IP specification and protocol stack, such as network layer address spoofing. Many packet filter firewalls cannot detect a network packet in which the OSI Layer 3 addressing information has been altered. Spoofing attacks are generally employed by intruders to bypass the security controls implemented in a firewall platform.

■ Finally, due to the small number of variables used in access control decisions, packet filter firewalls are susceptible to security breaches caused by improper configurations. In other words, it is easy to accidentally configure a packet filter firewall to allow traffic types, sources, and destinations that should be denied based on an organization's information security policy.

Some of the attacks that can be made on packet-filtering routers and the appropriate countermeasures are the following:

- IP address spoofing: The intruder transmits packets from the outside with a source IP address field containing an address of an internal host. The attacker hopes that the use of a spoofed address will allow penetration of systems that employ simple source address security, in which packets from specific trusted internal hosts are accepted. The countermeasure is to discard packets with an inside source address if the packet arrives on an external interface.

- Source routing attacks: The source station specifies the route that a packet should take as it crosses the Internet, in the hopes that this will bypass security measures that do not analyze the source routing information. The countermeasure is to discard all packets that use this option.

- Tiny fragment attacks: The intruder uses the IP fragmentation option to create extremely small fragments and force the TCP header information into a separate packet fragment. This attack is designed to circumvent filtering rules that depend on TCP header information. Typically, a packet filter will make a filtering decision on the first fragment of a packet. All subsequent fragments of that packet are filtered out solely on the basis that they are part of the packet whose first fragment was rejected. The attacker hopes that the filtering router examines only the first fragment and that the remaining fragments are passed through. A tiny fragment attack can be defeated by enforcing a rule that the first fragment of a packet must contain a predefined minimum amount of the transport header. If the first fragment is rejected, the filter can remember the packet and discard all subsequent fragments.

Stateful Inspection Firewalls

A traditional packet filter Figure 6.24 makes filtering decisions on an individual packet basis and does not take into consideration any higher layer context. To understand what is meant by context and why a traditional packet filter is limited with regard to context, a little background is needed. Most standardized applications that run on top of TCP follow a client/server model. For example, for the Simple Mail Transfer Protocol (SMTP), e-mail is transmitted from a client system to a server system. The client system generates new e-mail messages, typically from user input. The server system accepts incoming e-mail messages and places them in the appropriate user mailboxes. SMTP operates by setting up a TCP connection between client and server, in which the TCP server port number, which identifies the SMTP server application, is 25. The TCP port number for the SMTP client is a number between 1024 and 65535 that is generated by the SMTP client.

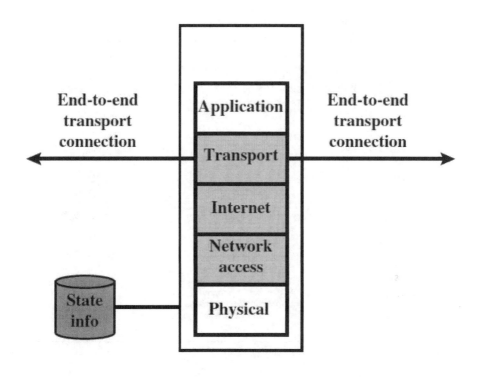

Figure 6.24: Stateful inspection Firewall.

In general, when an application that uses TCP creates a session with a remote host, it creates a TCP connection in which the TCP port number for the remote (server) application is a number less than 1024 and the TCP port number for the local (client) application is a number between 1024 and 65535. The numbers less than 1024 are the "well-known" port numbers and are assigned permanently to particular applications (e.g., 25 for server SMTP). The numbers between 1024 and 65535 are generated dynamically and have temporary significance only for the lifetime of a TCP connection.

A simple packet-filtering firewall must permit inbound network traffic on all these high-numbered ports for TCP-based traffic to occur. This creates a vulnerability that can be exploited by unauthorized users.

Application-Level Gateway

An application-level gateway, also called a proxy server, acts as a relay of application-level traffic Figure 6.25. The user contacts the gateway using a TCP/IP application, such as Telnet or FTP, and the gateway asks the user for the name of the remote host to be accessed. When the user responds and provides a valid user ID and authentication information, the gateway contacts the application on the remote host and relays TCP segments containing the application data between the two endpoints. If the gateway does not implement the proxy code for a specific application, the service is not supported and cannot be forwarded across the firewall. Further, the gateway can be configured to support only specific features of an application that the network administrator considers acceptable while denying all other features.

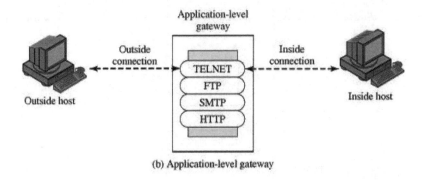

(b) Application-level gateway

Figure 6.25: Application Level Firewall

Application level gateways tend to be more secure than packet filters. Rather than trying to deal with the numerous possible combinations that are to be allowed and forbidden at the TCP and IP level, the application-level gateway needs only to scrutinize a few allowable applications. In addition, it is easy to log and audit all incoming traffic at the application level.

A prime disadvantage of this type of gateway is the additional processing overhead on each connection. In effect, there are two spliced connections between the end users, with the gateway at the splice point, and the gateway must examine and forward all traffic in both directions.

Circuit-Level Gateway

A third type of firewall is the circuit-level gateway Figure 6.26. This can be a standalone system or it can be a specialized function performed by an application-level gateway for certain applications. A circuit-level gateway does not permit an end-to-end TCP connection; rather, the gateway sets up two TCP connections, one between itself and a TCP user on an inner host and one between itself and a TCP user on an outside host. Once the two connections are established, the gateway typically relays TCP segments from one connection to the other without examining the contents. The security function consists of determining which connections will be allowed.

A typical use of circuit-level gateways is a situation in which the system adminis-

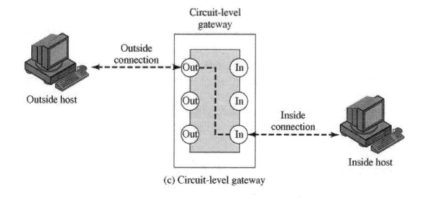

(c) Circuit-level gateway

Figure 6.26: Circuit level Firewall.

trator trusts the internal users. The gateway can be configured to support application-level or proxy service on inbound connections and circuit-level functions for out-bound connections. In this configuration, the gateway can incur the processing over-head of examining incoming application data for forbidden functions but does not incur that overhead on outgoing data.

An example of a circuit-level gateway implementation is the SOCKS package [KOBL92]; version 5 of SOCKS is defined in RFC 1928. The RFC defines SOCKS in the following fashion:

> The protocol described here is designed to provide a framework for client-server applications in both the TCP and UDP domains to conveniently and securely use the services of a network firewall. The protocol is conceptually a "shim-layer" between the application layer and the transport layer, and as such does not provide network-layer gateway services, such as forwarding of ICMP messages.

SOCKS consists of the following components:

- The SOCKS server, which runs on a UNIX-based firewall.

- The SOCKS client library, which runs on internal hosts protected by the fire-wall.

- SOCKS-ified versions of several standard client programs such as FTP and TELNET. The implementation of the SOCKS protocol typically involves the recompilation or relinking of TCP-based client applications to use the appro-priate encapsulation routines in the SOCKS library.

When a TCP-based client wishes to establish a connection to an object that is reach-able only via a firewall (such determination is left up to the implementation), it must open a TCP connection to the appropriate SOCKS port on the SOCKS server system.

The SOCKS service is located on TCP port 1080. If the connection request succeeds, the client enters a negotiation for the authentication method to be used, authenticates with the chosen method, and then sends a relay request. The SOCKS server evaluates the request and either establishes the appropriate connection or denies it. UDP exchanges are handled in a similar fashion. In essence, a TCP connection is opened to authenticate a user to send and receive UDP segments, and the UDP segments are forwarded as long as the TCP connection is open.

Bastion Host

A bastion host is a system identified by the firewall administrator as a critical strong point in the network's security. Typically, the bastion host serves as a platform for an application-level or circuit-level gateway. Common characteristics of a bastion host include the following:

- The bastion host hardware platform executes a secure version of its operating system, making it a trusted system.

- Only the services that the network administrator considers essential are installed on the bastion host. These include proxy applications such as Telnet, DNS, FTP, SMTP, and user authentication.

- The bastion host may require additional authentication before a user is allowed access to the proxy services. In addition, each proxy service may require its own authentication before granting user access.

- Each proxy is configured to support only a subset of the standard application's command set.

- Each proxy is configured to allow access only to specific host systems. This means that the limited command/feature set may be applied only to a subset of systems on the protected network.

- Each proxy maintains detailed audit information by logging all traffic, each connection, and the duration of each connection. The audit log is an essential tool for discovering and terminating intruder attacks.

- Each proxy module is a very small software package specifically designed for network security. Because of its relative simplicity, it is easier to check such modules for security flaws. For example, a typical UNIX mail application may contain over 20,000 lines of code, while a mail proxy may contain fewer than 1000.

- Each proxy is independent of other proxies on the bastion host. If there is a problem with the operation of any proxy, or if a future vulnerability is discovered, it can be uninstalled without affecting the operation of the other proxy applications. Also, if the user population requires support for a new service, the network administrator can easily install the required proxy on the bastion host.

■ A proxy generally performs no disk access other than to read its initial configuration file. This makes it difficult for an intruder to install Trojan horse sniffers or other dangerous files on the bastion host.

■ Each proxy runs as a nonprivileged user in a private and secured directory on the bastion host.

Firewall Configurations

In addition to the use of a simple configuration consisting of a single system, such as a single packet filtering router or a single gateway, more complex configurations are possible and indeed more common. We examine each of these in turn.

In the **screened host firewall, single-homed bastion** configuration Figure 6.27, the firewall consists of two systems: a packet-filtering router and a bastion host. Typically, the router is configured so that

1. For traffic from the Internet, only IP packets destined for the bastion host are allowed in.

2. For traffic from the internal network, only IP packets from the bastion host are allowed out.

The bastion host performs authentication and proxy functions. This configuration has greater security than simply a packet-filtering router or an application-level gateway alone, for two reasons. First, this configuration implements both packet-level and application-level filtering, allowing for considerable flexibility in defining security policy. Second, an intruder must generally penetrate two separate systems before the security of the internal network is compromised.

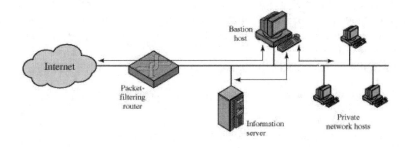

Figure 6.27: Screened host firewall, single-homed bastion network.

This configuration also affords flexibility in providing direct Internet access. For example, the internal network may include a public information server, such as a Web server, for which a high level of security is not required. In that case, the router can be configured to allow direct traffic between the information server and the Internet.

In the single-homed configuration just described, if the packet-filtering router is completely compromised, traffic could flow directly through the router between the Internet and other hosts on the private network. The **screened host firewall, dual-homed bastion** configuration physically prevents such a security breach Figure 6.28. The advantages of dual layers of security that were present in the previous configuration are present here as well. Again, an information server or other hosts can be allowed direct communication with the router if this is in accord with the security policy.

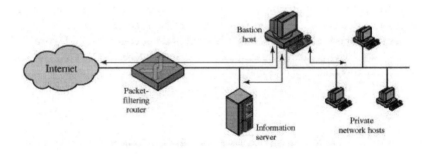

Figure 6.28: Screened host firewall, dual-homed bastion network.

The **screened subnet firewall** configuration of Figure 6.29 is the most secure of those we have considered. In this configuration, two packet-filtering routers are used, one between the bastion host and the Internet and one between the bastion host and the internal network. This configuration creates an isolated subnetwork, which may consist of simply the bastion but may also include one or more information servers and modems for dial-in capability. Typically, both the Internet and the internal network have access to hosts on the screened subnet, but traffic across the screened subnet is blocked.

This configuration offers several advantages:

■ There are now three levels of defense to thwart intruders.

■ The outside router advertises only the existence of the screened subnet to the Internet; therefore, the internal network is invisible to the Internet.

■ Similarly, the inside router advertises only the existence of the screened subnet to the internal network; therefore, the systems on the inside network cannot construct direct routes to the Internet.

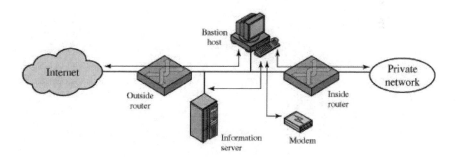

Figure 6.29: Screened subnet firewall.

Glossary

Access Control: Procedures and controls that limit or detect access to critical information resources. This can be accomplished through software, biometrics devices, or physical access to a controlled space.

Access Control Matrix: A table in which each row represents a subject, each column represents an object, and each entry is the set of access rights for that subject to that object.

Access Control Policy: The set of rules that define the conditions under which an access may take place.

Assurance: The grounds for confidence that an entity meets its security objectives.

Attack: An attempt at breaking a cryptosystem. Brute force attack, differential cryptanalysis, and linear cryptanalysis are a few examples of security attacks. An assault on system security that derives from an intelligent threat; that is, an intelligent act that is a deliberate attempt (especially in the sense of a method or technique) to evade security services and violate the security policy of a system.

Audit: The independent examination of records and activities to ensure compliance with established controls, policy, and operational procedures and to recommend any indicated changes in controls, policy, or procedures.

Audit Trail: A chronological record of system activities that is sufficient to enable the reconstruction and examination of the sequence of events and activities surrounding or leading to an operation, procedure, or event in a security-relevant transaction from inception to results.

Authentication: Verifying the identity of a user, process, or device, often as a prerequisite to allowing access to resources in a system.

Authorization: The granting or denying of access rights to a user, program, or process.

Authorized: A system entity or actor that has been granted the right, permission, or capability to access a system resource. See also Authorization.

Asymmetric Key Encryption: A method of encryption that uses two keys: one key, known as the public key, is distributed to multiple users, and the other key, known as the private key, is held by the owner. The public key is used to encrypt messages; only the corresponding private key can decrypt the messages.

Capability List: A list attached to a subject ID specifying what accesses are allowed to the subject.

Ciphertext: Encrypted data.

Confidentiality: Assurance that information is not disclosed to unauthorized persons, processes, or devices. Confidentiality covers data in storage, during processing, and in transit.

Cryptography: The art and science of using mathematics to secure information and create a high degree of trust in the electronic realm.

Decryption: The process of changing ciphertext into plaintext.

Digital Signature: The result of a cryptographic transformation of data that, when properly implemented, provides the services of origin authentication, data integrity, and signer nonrepudiation.

Discretionary Access Control (DAC): An access control service that enforces a security policy based on the identity of system entities and their authorizations to access system resources. (See: access control list, identity-based security policy, mandatory access control.) This service is termed "discretionary" because an entity might have access rights that permit the entity, by its own volition, to enable another entity to access some resource.

Encryption: The conversion of plaintext or data into unintelligible form by means of a reversible translation, based on a translation table or algorithm. Also called *enciphering*.

Hacker: A person who tries (and might succeed) to attack a computer security system for mere fun or other spurious reasons.

Integrity: Preservation of the original quality and accuracy of data in written or electronic form.

Intruder: An individual who gains, or attempts to gain, unauthorized access to a computer system or to gain unauthorized privileges on that system.

Intrusion Detection System: A set of automated tools designed to detect unauthorized access to a host system.

Mandatory Access Control (MAC): A means of restricting access to objects based on fixed security attributes assigned to users and to files and other objects. The controls are mandatory in the sense that they cannot be modified by users or their programs.

Operation: An active process invoked by a subject.

Permission (or privilege): Authorization to perform some action on a system.

Public Key Infrastructure (PKI): A set of policies, processes, server platforms, software and workstations used for the purpose of administering certificates and public-private key pairs, including the ability to issue, maintain, and revoke public key certificates.

Protocol: A set of rules (i.e., formats and procedures) for communications that computers use when sending signals between themselves.

Role-Based Access Control (RBAC): Policies control access depending on the roles that users have within the system and on rules stating what accesses are allowed to users in the given roles.

Role: A collection of permissions in role-based access control, usually associated with a role or position within an organization.

Security Policy: The statement of required protection for the information objects. It defines the (high-level) rules according to which access control must be regulated.

Security Service: A processing or communication service that enhances the security of the data processing systems and the information transfers of an organization. The services are intended to counter security attacks, and they make use of one or more security mechanisms to provide the service.

Security Model: It provides a formal representation of the access control security policy and its working. The formalization allows the proof of properties on the security provided by access control system being designed.

Security Mechanism: A process (or a device incorporating such a process) that is designed to detect, prevent, or recover from a security attack.

Security Threat: A potential for violation of security, which exists when there is a circumstance, capability, action, or event that could breach security and cause harm. That is, a threat is a possible danger that might exploit a vulnerability.

Spoofing: A technique used to gain unauthorized access to computers, wherein the intruder sends messages to a computer with an IP address indicating that the message is coming from a trusted host.

Vulnerability: A weakness in system security procedures, hardware, design, implementation, internal controls, technical controls, physical controls, or other controls that could be accidentally triggered or intentionally exploited and result in a violation of the system's security policy.

X.509: A standard proposed by (ISO) and (ITU) for certificates and CRLs. X.509 defines the authentication framework for global directory services and is globally accepted by companies involved in producing PKI products.

References

[1]

[2] *Computer Networks, Fifth Edition, Andrew S. Tanenbaum, David J. Wetherall, PEARSON.*

[3] Review of "Literary Machines" by Ted Nelson. 1983. *SIG-SOFT Softw. Eng. Notes*, 8(5):34–36, October 1983. Reviewer-Smoliar, Stephen W.

[4] Internet security architecture. *Computer. Netw.*, 31(9):787–804, April 1999.

[5] GENI Design Principles. *Computer*, 39(9):102–105, Sept 2006.

[6] A P Manu and Ankur. Shishodia and V.K. Patle and O.P. Vyas. State of the Art of Cloud Computing and its Research Issues. *Research Journal of Science and Technology (RJST)*, 32(6):147–152, 2010.

[7] M. Abliz. *Denial of Service in Computer Networks*. LAP Lambert Acad. Publ., 2011.

[8] Generally Accepted System Security Principles (GASSP) Version 2.0. Fundamental Limitations of Current Internet and the Path to Future Internet - Draft (ver: 0.9), June 1999.

[9] Defense Advanced Research Projects Agency and Internet Activities Board. Ethics and the Internet. RFC 1087, January 1989. http://www.ietf.org/rfc/rfc1087.txt.

[10] K. K. Aggarwal and Yogesh Singh. Determination of Software Release Instant using a Nonhomogeneous Error Detection Rate Model. Published by Elsevier Ltd., 33(6):803–807, May 1993.

[11] Hamza Aldabbas, Tariq Alwada'n, Helge Janicke, and Ali Al-Bayatti. Data confidentiality in mobile ad hoc networks. *CoRR*, abs/1203.1749, 2012.

[12] M. Allman, V. Paxson, and W. Stevens. RFC 2581: TCP congestion control, 1999.

[13] Ashok Anand, Fahad Dogar, Dongsu Han, Boyan Li, Hyeontaek Lim, Michel Machado, Wenfei Wu, Aditya Akella, David G. Andersen, John W. Byers, Srinivasan Seshan, and Peter Steenkiste. Xia: an architecture for an evolvable and trustworthy internet. In *Proceedings of the 10th ACM Workshop on Hot Topics in Networks*, HotNets-X, pages 2:1–2:6, New York, NY, USA, 2011. ACM.

[14] Oskar Jnsson Anders Dahlgren. *IPsec, the Future of Network Security?* PhD thesis, 2007.

[15] R. Anderson. Why information security is hard-an economic perspective. In *Proceedings of the 17th Annual Computer Security Applications Conference*, ACSAC '01, pages 358–, Washington, DC, USA, 2001. IEEE Computer Society.

[16] Tom Anderson, Ken Birman, Robert M. Broberg, Matthew Caesar, Douglas Comer, Chase Cotton, Michael J. Freedman, Andreas Haeberlen, Zachary G. Ives, Arvind Krishnamurthy, William Lehr, Boon Thau Loo, David Mazières, Antonio Nicolosi, Jonathan M. Smith, Ion Stoica, Robbert van Renesse, Michael Walfish, Hakim Weatherspoon, and Christopher S. Yoo. The nebula future internet architecture. In Galis and Gavras [78], pages 16–26.

[17] Onwutalobi Anthony-Claret. Using encryption technique. pages 1–27, 2006.

[18] M. Armbrust, A. Fox, R. Griffith, A. Joseph, R. Katz, A. Konwinski, G. Lee, D. Patterson, A. Rabkin, I. Stoica, and M. Zaharia. Above the Clouds: A Berkeley View of Cloud Computing. Technical report, University of California, Berkley, USA, 2009.

[19] R. Atkinson, S. Floyd, and Internet Architecture Board. IAB Concerns and Recommendations Regarding Internet Research and Evolution. RFC 3869 (Informational), Aug 2004. http://www.ietf.org/rfc/rfc3869.txt.

[20] GENI Project Homepage. Available:http://www.geni.net/.

[21] Paul Baran. On Distributed Communications: I. Introduction to Distributed Communications Networks. *Volumes I-XI RAND Corporation Research Documents Aug*, 12(1):51, 1964. http://www.rand.org/ pubs/research_memoranda/RM3420/.

[22] E. D. Bell and J. L. La Padula. Secure computer system: Unified exposition and multics interpretation, 1976.

[23] Mary Bellis. ARPAnet: The First Internet, 2012. http://inventors.about. com/library/weekly/aa091598.html.

[24] S. Bellovin, J. Schiller, and C. Kaufman. Security Mechanisms for the Internet. RFC 3631 (Informational), December.

[25] S.M. Bellovin. Security Problems in the TCP/IP Protocol Suite. *ACM SIGCOMM Computer Communication Review Archive.*, 19(2):32–48, April 1989.

[26] S.M. Bellovin. A Look Back at "Security Problems in the TCP/IP Protocol Suite. In *Computer Security Applications Conference, 2004. 20th Annual*, pages 229 – 249, Dec. 2004.

[27] Steven M. Bellovin, David D. Clark, Adrian Perrig, and Dawn Song. A Clean-Slate Design for the Next-Generation Secure Internet. July 2005.

[28] O.P. Vyas Bhawana Rudra, Manu A.P. Service Authentication Codes (SAC) for Emerging Network Architectures. *International Journal on Recent Trends in Engineering & Technology (IJRTET)*, 6(1), Nov. 2011.

[29] Gowtham Boddapati, John Day, Ibrahim Matta, and Lou Chitkushev. Assessing the security of a clean-slate internet architecture. Technical report, 2009.

[30] Ghazi Bouabene, Christophe Jelger, Christian Tschudin, Stefan Schmid, Ariane Keller, and Martin May. The Autonomic Network Architecture (ANA). *IEEE J.Sel. A. Commun.*, 28(1):4–14, January 2010.

[31] Raouf Boutaba and Issam Aib. Policy-based management: A historical perspective. *J. Network Syst. Manage.*, 15(4):447–480, 2007.

[32] R. Braden. Requirements for Internet hosts - communication layers. RFC 1122 (Standard), Oct 1989. Updated by RFCs 1349, 4379, 5884, 6093, 6298.

[33] Robert Braden, Ted Faber, and Mark Handley. From Protocol Stack to Protocol Heap: Role-Based Architecture. *SIGCOMM Comput. Commun. Rev.*, 33(1):17–22, January 2003.

[34] Ian Brown, David D. Clark, and Dirk Trossen. Should Specific Values be Embedded in the Internet Architecture? In *Proceedings of the Re-architecting the Internet Workshop*, ReARCH'10, pages 10:1–10:6, New York, NY, USA, 2010. ACM. http://doi.acm.org/ 10.1145/1921233.1921246.

[35] Michael Burrows, Martin Abadi, and Roger Needham. A logic of authentication. *ACM Trans. Comput. Syst.*, 8(1):18–36, February 1990.

[36] R. Bush and D. Meyer. Some Internet Architectural Guidelines and Philosophy. RFC 3439 (Informational), December 2002. http://www.ietf.org/rfc/rfc3439.txt.

[37] Carlos E. Caicedo, James B.D. Joshi, and Summit R. Tuladhar. Ipv6 security challenges. *Computer*, 42(2):36–42, 2009.

[38] B. Carpenter. Architectural principles of the Internet, Jun 1996.

[39] C. Stephen Carr, Stephen D. Crocker, and Vinton G. Cerf. Host-HOST Communication Protocol in the ARPA Network. In *Proceedings of the May 5-7, 1970, Spring Joint Computer Conference*, AFIPS '70 (Spring), pages 589–597, New York, NY, USA, 1970. ACM.

[40] V. Cerf and R. Kahn. A Protocol for Packet Network Intercommunication. *Communications, IEEE Transactions on*, 22(5):637 – 648, May 1974.

[41] V. G. Cerf. RFC 1052: IAB Recommendations for the Development of Internet Network Management Standards, April 1988. ftp://ftp.internic.net/rfc/rfc1052.txt.

[42] Vint Cerf, Van Jacobson, Nicholas Weaver, and Jim Gettys. BufferBloat: What's Wrong with the Internet? *ACM Queue*, 9(12):10, 2012.

[43] Vinton G. Cerf and Robert E. Khan. A Protocol for Packet Network Intercommunication. *IEEE Trans. on Commun.*, 22:637– 648, 1974.

[44] R. K.C. Chang. Defending against flooding-based distributed denial-of-service attacks: a tutorial. *Comm. Mag.*, 40(10):42– 51, October 2002.

[45] Ranganai Chaparadza, Symeon Papavassiliou, Timotheos Kastrinogiannis, Martin Vigoureux, Emfel Dotaro, Alan Davy, Kevin Quinn, Michal Wdczak, Andras Toth, Athanassios Liakopoulos, and Mick Wilson. Creating a viable Evolution Path towards Self-Managing Future Internet via a Standardizable Reference Model for Autonomic Network Engineering. In *Future Internet Assembly*, pages 136–147. IOS Press, 2009.

[46] A.L. Chapin. Connectionless Data Transmission Survey/Tutorial. RFC 787, 1981. http://www.ietf.org/rfc/rfc787.txt.

[47] E. Chen and J. Yuan. Autonomous-System-Wide Unique BGP Identifier for BGP-4. RFC 6286 (Proposed Standard), 2011. http://www.ietf.org/rfc/rfc6286.txt.

[48] C. Michael Chernick, Charles Edington, III, Matthew J. Fanto, and Rob Rosenthal. Sp 800-52. guidelines for the selection and use of transport layer security (tls) implementations. Technical report, Gaithersburg, MD, 2005.

[49] Brent Chun, David Culler, Timothy Roscoe, Andy Bavier, Larry Peterson, Mike Wawrzoniak, and Mic Bowman.

PlanetLab: an Overlay Testbed for Broad-coverage Services. *SIGCOMM Comput. Commun. Rev.*, 33(3):3–12, 2003. http://doi.acm.org/10.1145/956993.956995.

[50] D. Clark. The Design Philosophy of the DARPA Internet Protocols. *SIGCOMM Comput. Commun. Rev.*, 18(4):106–114, August 1988. http://doi.acm.org/ 10.1145/52325.52336.

[51] David D. Clark, John Wroclawski, Karen R. Sollins, and Robert Braden. Tussle in Cyberspace: Defining Tomorrow's Internet. *IEEE/ACM Trans. Netw.*, 13(3):462–475, June 2005.

[52] "T. Clausen, C. Dearlove, J. Dean, and C. Adjih". "Generalized Mobile AdHoc Network (MANET) Packet/Message Format". RFC 5444 (Proposed Standard), February 2009.

[53] cnn Online: https://sites.google.com/site/secureenterprisel systems/home/journals/j5-cnn-ddos attack explained.

[54] Rafael V. Coelho, Jonata T. Pastro, Rodolfo S. Antunes, Marinho P. Barcellos, Ingrid Jansch-Porto, and Luciano P. Gaspary. Challenging the feasibility of authentication mechanisms for p2p live streaming. In *Proceedings of the 6th Latin America Networking Conference*, LANC '11, pages 55–63, New York, NY, USA, 2011. ACM.

[55] F. Cohen. Computer viruses: theory and experiments. *Comput. Secur.*, 6(1):22–35, February 1987.

[56] European Communities. The Future of the Internet, August 2008. ftp:// ftp.cordis.europa.eu/pub/fp7/ict/docs/ch1-g848-280-future-internet_en.pdf.

[57] A. Conta, S. Deering, and M. Gupta. Internet Control Message Protocol (ICMPv6) for the Internet Protocol Version 6 (IPv6) Specification. RFC 4443 (Draft Standard), March 2006. Updated by RFC 4884.

[58] Marco Conti, Song Chong, Serge Fdida, Weijia Jia, Holger Karl, Ying-Dar Lin, Petri Mähönen, Martin Maier, Refik Molva, Steve Uhlig, and Moshe Zukerman. Research challenges towards the future internet. *Comput. Commun.*, 34(18):2115–2134, December 2011.

[59] D. Cooper, S. Santesson, S. Farrell, S. Boeyen, R. Housley, and W. Polk. Internet X.509 Public Key Infrastructure Certificate and Certificate Revocation List (CRL) Profile. RFC 5280 (Proposed Standard), May 2008.

[60] J. Crowcroft, I. Wakeman, Z. Wang, and D. Sirovica. Is Layering, Harmful? (Remote Procedure Call). *Network, IEEE*, 6(1):20 –24, January 1992.

[61] H.C.Du David. Clean Slate Design of Internet for Supporting Service-Oriented Computing and Applications. In *IEEE International Conference on Service-Oriented Computing and Applications (SOCA07)*, Virginia, 2007.

[62] John Wroclawski-Dina Katabi-Joanna Kulik Xiaowei Yang Robert Braden Ted Faber Aaron Falk Venkata Pingali Mark Handley" "David Clark, Karen Sollins. "New Arch: Future Generation Internet Architecture,FINAL TECHNICAL REPORT".

[63] J. Day. *Patterns in Network Architecture: A Return to Fundamentals*. Pearson Education, 2008.

[64] Bhavya Daya. Network Security: History, Importance, and Future. November 2011.

[65] G. Van de Velde, T. Hain, R. Droms, B. Carpenter, and E. Klein. Local Network Protection for IPv6. RFC 4864 (Informational), May 2007.

[66] S. Deering and R. Hinden. Internet protocol, version 6 (ipv6) Specification. RFC 2460 (Draft Standard), dec 1998. Updated by RFCs 5095, 5722, 5871, 6437, 6564.

[67] Andrea Detti, Nicola Blefari Melazzi, Stefano Salsano, and Matteo Pomposini. Conet: a Content Centric Inter-Networking Architecture. In *Proceedings of the ACM SIGCOMM workshop on Information-centric networking*, ICN '11, pages 50–55, New York, NY, USA, 2011. ACM.

[68] Rachna Dhamija, J. D. Tygar, and Marti Hearst. Why phishing works. In *Proceedings of the SIGCHI Conference on Human*

Factors in Computing Systems, CHI '06, pages 581–590, New York, NY, USA, 2006. ACM.

[69] Sabrina De Capitani di Vimercati, Pierangela Samarati, and Sushil Jajodia. Policies, models, and languages for access control. In *DNIS*, pages 225–237, 2005.

[70] Constantine Dovrolis. What Would Darwin Think About Clean-Slate Architectures? *SIGCOMM Comput. Commun. Rev.*, 38(1):29–34, January 2008. http://doi.acm.org/10.1145/1341431.1341436.

[71] Patrick W. Dowd and John T. McHenry. "Guest Editors' Introduction-Network Security: It's Time to Take It Seriously". *Computer*, 31(9):24–28, September 1998.

[72] Rudra. Dutta, George N. Rouskas, Ilia. Baldine, Arnold. Bragg, and Dan Stevenson. The SILO Architecture for Services Integration, controL, and Optimization for the Future Internet. In *IEEE International Conference on Communications*, June 2007.

[73] P. Mahonen (ed), D. Trossen, D. Papadimitrou, G. Polyzos, and D. Kennedy. Future Networked Society. EIFFEL whitepaper, December 2006.

[74] Mohammad Amin Kheirandish Fard, Sasan Karamizadeh, and Mohammad Aflaki. Enhancing Congestion Control to Address Link Failure Loss Over Mobile Ad-hoc Network. *CoRR*, abs/1110.2289, 2011.

[75] Darleen Fisher. US National Science Foundation and the Future Internet Design. *SIGCOMM Comput. Commun. Rev.*, 37(3):85–87, July 2007.

[76] Rodrigo Fonseca, George Manning Porter, Randy H. Katz, Scott Shenker, and Ion Stoica. IP Options are Not an Option. Technical report, University of California, Berkeley, 2005. http://www.eecs.berkeley.edu/ Pubs/TechRpts/2005/EECS-2005-24.html.

[77] S. Frankel and S. Krishnan. IP Security (IPsec) and Internet Key Exchange (IKE) Document Roadmap. RFC 6071 (Informational), February 2011.

[78] Alex Galis and Anastasius Gavras, editors. *The Future Internet - Future Internet Assembly 2013: Validated Results and New Horizons*, volume 7858 of *Lecture Notes in Computer Science*. Springer, 2013.

[79] Anastasius Gavras, Arto Karila, Serge Fdida, Martin May, and Martin Potts. Future Internet Research and Experimentation: the FIRE initiative. *SIGCOMM Comput. Commun. Rev.*, 37(3):89–92, July 2007.

[80] Gregory Gromov. Roads and Crossroads of Internet History, 2012. http:// www.netvalley.com/intval.html.

[81] EC FIArch Group. Fundamental Limitations of Current Internet and the Path to Future Internet, Draft (Ver: 1.9), March 2011.

[82] FIA Research Roadmap Working Group. Future Internet Assembly Research Roadmap. Towards Framework 8: Research Priorities for the Future Internet, 2010.

[83] E. Djambazova-K. Dimitrov-S. Ioannidis E. Kirda H. Bos, E. Jonsson and C. Kruegel. *Anticipating Security Threats to a Future Internet*.

[84] B. Haberman and J. Martin. Internet Group Management Protocol Version 3 (IGMPv3) / Multicast Listener Discovery Version 2 (MLDv2) and Multicast Routing Protocol Interaction. RFC 5186 (Informational), May 2008. http://www.ietf.org/rfc/rfc5186.txt.

[85] Michael Hafner and Ruth Breu. *Security Engineering for Service-Oriented Architectures*. Springer Publishing Company, Incorporated, 1 edition, 2008.

[86] Michael Hafner and Ruth Breu. *Security Engineering for Service-Oriented Architectures*. Springer Publishing Company, Incorporated, 1 edition, 2008.

[87] M. Handley. Why the Internet Only Just Works. *BT Technology Journal*, 24(3):119–129, July 2006.

[88] Maritta Heisel, editor. *Software Service and Application Engineering - Essays Dedicated to Bernd Krämer on the Occasion of*

His 65th Birthday, volume 7365 of *Lecture Notes in Computer Science*. Springer, 2012.

[89] M. Higuero, J. Unzilla, P. Saiz, E. Jacob, M. Aguado, and I. Goirizelaia. A practical tool for analysis of security in systems for distribution of digital contents based on 'attack trees',. In *Broadband Multimedia Systems and Broadcasting, 2009. BMSB '09. IEEE International Symposium on*, pages 1 –6, May 2009.

[90] R. Hinden and S. Deering. IP Version 6 Addressing Architecture. RFC 4291 (Draft Standard), February 2006. Updated by RFCs 5952, 6052.

[91] P.F. Hingston, L.C. Barone, and Z. Michalewicz. *Design by Evolution: Advances in Evolutionary Design*. Natural Computing Series. Springer, 2008. http://books.google.co.in/books?id=FzJF0sYDvw8C.

[92] Stephen J. Hoch. Hypothesis Testing and Consumer Behavior: "If It Works, Don't Mess With It". *Advances in Consumer Research*, 11:478–481, 1984.

[93] P. Hoffman. Cryptographic Suites for IPsec. RFC 4308 (Proposed Standard), December 2005.

[94] Scott Hogg and Eric Vyncke. *IPv6 Security*. Cisco Press, 1st edition, 2008.

[95] T. Hossmann, A. Keller, M. May, and S. Dudler. Implementing the Future Internet: A Case Study of Pub/Sub in ANA. In *Proceedings of CFI '08*, Seoul, Korea, 2008.

[96] JGN2plus Project Homepage. Available: http://www.jgn.nict.go.jp/english/index.html.

[97] AKARI-Online: http://akari-project.nict.go.jp/eng/concept-design/AKARI_ fulltext_e_preliminary_ver2.pdf.2008.

[98] FIREworks Project Homepage. Available: http://www.ict-fireworks. eu/.

[99] PlanetLab Project Homepage. Available: http://www.planetlab. org/.

[100] Paul Innella. A Brief History of Network Security and the Need for Adherence to the Software Process Model. *Information Security*, 10:1–15, 2008.

[101] D.S. Isenberg. The Rise of the Stupid Network. *Computer Telephony*, pages 16–26, 1997.

[102] ISO/IEC. Information Technology - Open Systems Interconnection - Basic Reference Model: The Basic Model. ITU-T Recommendation X.200, International Telecommunication Union, 1994.

[103] J. Postel. Internet Protocol. RFC 791 (Standard), Sep 1981. Updated by RFC 1349.

[104] Van Jacobson, Diana K. Smetters, James D. Thornton, Michael F. Plass, Nicholas H. Briggs, and Rebecca L. Braynard. Networking Named Content. In *Proceedings of the 5th International Conference on Emerging Networking Experiments and Technologies*, CoNEXT'09, pages 1–12, New York, NY, 2009. ACM. http://doi.acm.org/10.1145/1658939.1658941.

[105] Christophe. Jelger, Christian. Tschudin, Stefan. Schmid, and Guy. Leduc. Basic Abstractions for an Autonomic Network Architecture. In *IEEE International Symposium on a World of Wireless, Mobile and Multimedia Networks*, pages 1–6. IEEE, 2007.

[106] D. Johnson, C. Perkins, and J. Arkko. Mobility Support in IPv6. RFC 3775 (Proposed Standard), June 2004. Obsoleted by RFC 6275.

[107] V. Jonnaganti. An Integrated Security Model for the Management of SOA Improving the attractiveness of SOA Environments through a strong Architectural Integrity, 2009.

[108] J. Jonsson and B. Kaliski. Public-Key Cryptography Standards (PKCS) #1: RSA Cryptography Specifications Version 2.1. RFC 3447 (Informational), February 2003.

[109] Wouter Joosen, Javier Lopez, Fabio Martinelli, and Fabio Massacci. The Future Internet. Chapter Engineering Secure Future

Internet Services, pages 177–191. Springer-Verlag, Berlin, Heidelberg, 2011.

[110] B. Kaliski. PKCS #7: Cryptographic Message Syntax Version 1.5. RFC 2315 (Informational), March 1998.

[111] Dina Katabi, Mark Handley, and Charles E. Rohrs. Congestion Control for High Bandwidth-delay Product Networks. In *SIGCOMM*, pages 89–102, 2002.

[112] S. Kent and R. Atkinson. Security Architecture for the Internet Protocol. RFC 2401 (Proposed Standard), nov 1998. Obsoleted by RFC 4301, updated by RFC 3168.

[113] S. Kent and K. Seo. Security Architecture for the Internet Protocol. RFC 4301 (Proposed Standard), December 2005. Updated by RFC 6040.

[114] J. Kohl and C. Neuman. "The Kerberos Network Authentication Service (V5)". RFC 1510 (Historic), September 1993. Obsoleted by RFCs 4120, 6649.

[115] Teemu Koponen, Scott Shenker, Hari Balakrishnan, Nick Feamster, Igor Ganichev, Ali Ghodsi, P. Brighten Godfrey, Nick McKeown, Guru Parulkar, Barath Raghavan, Jennifer Rexford, Somaya Arianfar, and Dmitriy Kuptsov. Architecting for Innovation. *SIGCOMM Comput. Commun. Rev.*, 41(3):24–36, July 2011.

[116] Butler Lampson, Martín Abadi, Michael Burrows, and Edward Wobber. Authentication in distributed systems: theory and practice. *ACM Trans. Comput. Syst.*, 10(4):265–310, November 1992.

[117] O. Lassila, F. van Harmelen, I. Horrocks, J. Hendler, and L. D. McGuinness. The Semantic Web and its Languages. *IEEE Intelligent Systems.*, 15(6):67–73, November 2000.

[118] Keunsoo Lee, Juhyun Kim, Ki Hoon Kwon, Younggoo Han, and Sehun Kim. Dos attack detection method using cluster analysis. *Expert Syst. Appl.*, 34(3):1659–1665, April 2008.

[119] An Lei and Zhu Youchan. The solution of ddos attack based on multi-agent. In *Educational and Information Technology (ICEIT), 2010 International Conference on*, volume 2, pages V2–530–V2–532, 2010.

[120] Barry M. Leiner, Vinton G. Cerf, David D. Clark, Robert E. Kahn, Leonard Kleinrock, Daniel C. Lynch, Jon Postel, Lawrence G. Roberts, and Stephen S. Wolff. The past and future history of the internet. *Commun. ACM*, 40(2):102–108, February 1997.

[121] Kees Leune. *Access Control and Service Oriented Architectures*. PhD thesis, 2007.

[122] Frank Leymann, Schahram Dustdar, Paolo Traverso, and Michael P. Papazoglou. Service-oriented computing: State of the art and research challenges. *Computer*, 40:38–45, 2007.

[123] Dr. Tony Li. Design goals for scalable internet routing. RFC 6227, May 2011.

[124] Z. Li, X. Xu, L. Shi, J. Liu, and C. Liang. Authentication in peer-to-peer network: Survey and research directions. In *2009 Third International Conference on Network and System Security*, pages 115–122, Oct 2009.

[125] Pete Loshin. *TCP/IP Clearly Explained*. Morgan Kaufmann, 2003.

[126] Georgios Loukas and Gülay Öke. Protection against denial of service attacks. *Comput. J.*, 53(7):1020–1037, September 2010.

[127] Gavin Lowe. A Hierarchy of Authentication Specifications. In *Proceedings of the 10th IEEE workshop on Computer Security Foundations*, CSFW '97, pages 31–, Washington, DC, USA, 1997. IEEE Computer Society.

[128] A P. Manu, B. Rudra, B. Reuther, and O.P. Vyas. Design and Implementation Issues of Flexible Network Architecture. pages 283–288, October 2011.

[129] Michael Menzel, Ivonne Thomas, and Christoph Meinel. Security requirements specification in service-oriented business process management. *2012 Seventh International Conference on Availability, Reliability and Security*, 0:41–48, 2009.

[130] Rodney Van Meter, Joe Touch, and Clare Horsman. Recursive Quantum Repeater Networks. 2011.

[131] E. Meyer. ARPA Network Protocol Notes. RFC 46, 1970. http://www.ietf.org/rfc/ rfc46.txt.

[132] Roger Meyer. *Secure Authentication on the Internet*. 2007.

[133] Michael Bell. *Service-Oriented Modeling (SOA): Service Analysis, Design, and Architecture*. Wiley, 2008.

[134] Jelena Mirkovic, Sven Dietrich, David Dittrich, and Peter Reiher. *Internet Denial of Service: Attack and Defense Mechanisms (Radia Perlman Computer Networking and Security)*. Prentice Hall PTR, Upper Saddle River, NJ, USA, 2004.

[135] Prateek Mittal and Nikita Borisov. Information leaks in structured peer-to-peer anonymous communication systems. In *Proceedings of the 15th ACM Conference on Computer and Communications Security*, CCS '08, pages 267–278, New York, NY, USA, 2008. ACM.

[136] P. Molinero-Fernandez and Zhang N. McKeown, H. Ip going to take over the world (or communications)? *ACM HotNets*, February 2002. http://yuba.stanford.edu/cs244wiki/index.php/.

[137] Refik Molva. Internet security architecture. *Computer Networks*, 31(8):787–804, 1999.

[138] David Moore, Colleen Shannon, Douglas J. Brown, Geoffrey M. Voelker, and Stefan Savage. Inferring Internet Denial-of-Service activity. *ACM Trans. Comput. Syst.*, 24(2):115–139, May 2006.

[139] T. Moors. A Critical Review of "End-to-End Arguments in System Design." In *Communications, 2002. ICC 2002. IEEE International Conference on*, volume 2, pages 1214 – 1219 vol.2, 2002.

[140] Er Moshchuk, Tanya Bragin, Steven D. Gribble, and Henry M. Levy. A crawler-based study of spyware on the web. 2006.

[141] Paul Müller and Bernd Reuther. Future Internet Architecture - A Service Oriented Approach (Future Internet Architecture - Ein serviceorientierter Ansatz). *it - Information Technology*, 50(6):383–389, 2008.

[142] M. Myers, R. Ankney, A. Malpani, S. Galperin, and C. Adams. X.509 Internet Public Key Infrastructure Online Certificate Status Protocol - OCSP. RFC 2560 (Proposed Standard), June 1999. Updated by RFC 6277.

[143] M. Nagaratna, V. Kamakshi Prasad, and S. Tanuz Kumar. Detecting and preventing ip-spoofed ddos attacks by encrypted marking based detection and filtering (emdaf). In *Proceedings of the 2009 International Conference on Advances in Recent Technologies in Communication and Computing*, ARTCOM '09, pages 753–755, Washington, DC, USA, 2009. IEEE Computer Society.

[144] T. Narten, E. Nordmark, and W. Simpson. Neighbor Discovery for IP Version 6 (IPv6). RFC 2461 (Draft Standard), December 1998. Obsoleted by RFC 4861, updated by RFC 4311.

[145] T. Narten, E. Nordmark, W. Simpson, and H. Soliman. Neighbor Discovery for IP version 6 (IPv6). RFC 4861 (Draft Standard), September 2007. Updated by RFC 5942.

[146] Roger M. Needham and Michael D. Schroeder. Using encryption for authentication in large networks of computers. *Commun. ACM*, 21(12):993–999, December 1978.

[147] K. Nichols, S. Blake, F. Baker, and D. Black. Definition of the Differentiated Services Field (DS Field) in the IPv4 and IPv6 Headers. RFC 2474 (Proposed Standard), dec 1998. Updated by RFCs 3168, 3260.

[148] Y. Nir. IPsec Cluster Problem Statement. RFC 6027 (Informational), October 2010.

[149] M. Nystrom and B. Kaliski. PKCS #10: Certification Request Syntax Specification Version 1.7. RFC 2986 (Informational), November 2000. Updated by RFC 5967.

[150] Ola Olsson. Why Does Technology Advance in Cycles? Working Papers in Economics 38, Goteborg University, Department of Economics, March 2001. http://ideas.repec.org/p/hhs/gunwpe/0038.html.

[151] Sean W. O'Malley and Larry L. Peterson. A Dynamic Network Architecture. *ACM Trans. Computer Syst.*, 10(2):594–606, May 2008.

[152] Manu A P. Investigating Service Oriented Network Architecture for Internet Functionalities, Thesis, Indian Institute of Information Technlogy, Allahabad, INDIA. pages 1–123, October 2012.

[153] Homepage Available: http://www.ccnx.com/ Palo Alto Research Center, Content Centric Network.

[154] Jianli Pan, Subharthi Paul, and Raj Jain. A Survey of the Research on Future Internet Architectures. *IEEE Communications Magazine*, 49(7):26–36, 2011.

[155] Krishna. Pandit, Patrick. Stupar, and Wolfgang. Granzow. Service-Oriented Architecture as an Enabler for the Convergence of the Internet with Cellular Systems, 2010.

[156] Dimitri Papadimitriou. Future Internet - The Cross-ETP Vision Document. Technical report, European Future Internet Portal, January 2009.

[157] Michael P. Papazoglou, Paolo. Traverso, Schahram. Dustdar, and Frank. Leymann. Service-Oriented Computing: State of the Art and Research Challenges. *IEEE Computer Society*, 40(11):38–45, November 2007.

[158] Michael P Papazoglou, Paolo Traverso, Schahram Dustdar, and Frank Leymann. Service-Oriented Computing: a Research Roadmap. *International Journal of Cooperative Information Systems*, 17(02):223, 2008.

[159] B. Patel, B. Aboba, W. Dixon, G. Zorn, and S. Booth. Securing L2TP using IPsec. RFC 3193 (Proposed Standard), November 2001.

[160] Subharthi Paul, Raj Jain, Jianli Pan, and Mic Bowman. A vision of the next generation internet: a policy oriented perspective. In *Proceedings of the 2008 international conference on Visions of Computer Science: BCS International Academic Conference*, VoCS'08, pages 1–14, Swinton, UK, 2008. British Computer Society.

[161] Subharthi Paul, Jianli Pan, and Raj Jain. Architectures for the future networks and the next generation internet: A survey. *Comput. Commun.*, 34(1):2–42, January 2011.

[162] Pierre-Yves. DANET: Future Internet Strategic Research Agenda, 2010. http://www.future-internet.eu/fileadmin/documents/reports/.

[163] Louis Pouzin. Presentation and Major Design Aspects of the Cyclades Computer Network. *Proceedings of the NATO Advanced Study Institute on Computer Communication Networks. Sussex, United Kingdom*, pages 415 – 434, 1973.

[164] Roger S. Pressman. *Software Engineering: A Practitioner's Approach*. McGraw-Hill Higher Education, 5th edition, 2001.

[165] Jay Ramachandran. *Designing Security Architecture Solutions*. Wiley, 2002.

[166] E. Rescorla. Diffie-Hellman Key Agreement Method. RFC 2631 (Proposed Standard), June 1999.

[167] Bernd Reuther and Dirk Henrici. A Model for Service-oriented Communication Systems. *J. Syst. Archit.*, 54(6):594–606, 2008. http://dx.doi.org/10.1016/ j.sysarc.2007.12.001.

[168] R. L. Rivest, A. Shamir, and L. Adleman. A method for obtaining digital signatures and public-key cryptosystems. *Commun. ACM*, 21(2):120–126, February 1978.

[169] Alfonso Rodríguez, Eduardo Fernández-Medina, and Mario Piattini. A BPMN Extension for the Modeling of Security Requirements in Business Processes. *IEICE - Trans. Inf. Syst.*, E90-D(4):745–752, March 2007.

[170] George Roussos and Vassilis Kostakos. RFID in Pervasive Computing: State-of-the-art and Outlook. *Pervasive Mob. Comput.*, 5(1):110–131, February 2009. http://dx.doi.org/10.1016/j.pmcj.2008.11.004.

[171] Bhawana Rudra, A.P. Manu, and O.P. Vyas. Security and Authentication Issues in Emerging Network Architectures with Special Reference to Sonate. *Computational Intelligence and Communication Networks, International Conference on*, 0:658–662, 2011.

[172] Chung. Sam, Davalos. Sergio, An. Joseph, and Iwahara. Katsumi. Legacy to Web Migration: Service-Oriented Software Reengineering (SoSR) Methodology. *The Special Issue of the International Journal of Service Sciences 2008.*, 1(3/4):333–365, 2008.

[173] Pierangela Samarati and Sabrina De Capitani di Vimercati. Access control: Policies, models, and mechanisms. In *Revised versions of lectures given during the IFIP WG 1.7 International School on Foundations of Security Analysis and Design on Foundations of Security Analysis and Design: Tutorial Lectures*, FOSAD '00, pages 137–196, London, UK, 2001. Springer-Verlag.

[174] Xavier Sanchez-Loro, José L. Ferrer, Carles Gomez, Jordi Casademont, and Josep Paradells. Can Future Internet be based on constrained networks design principles? *Computer Networks*, 55(4):893–909, March 2011.

[175] Ravi Sandhu and Pierangela Samarati. Authentication, access control, and audit. *ACM Comput. Surv.*, 28(1):241–243, March 1996.

[176] Ravi S. Sandhu, Edward J. Coyne, Hal L. Feinstein, and Charles E. Youman. Role-based access control models. *Computer*, 29(2):38–47, February 1996.

[177] Stefan Savage, David Wetherall, Anna Karlin, and Tom Anderson. Practical Network Support for IP Traceback. *SIGCOMM Comput. Commun. Rev.*, 30(4):295–306, August 2000. http://doi.acm.org/10.1145/347057.347560.

[178] S. Schindler, J. Didier, and M. Steinacker. Design and Formal Specification of an X.25 Packet Level Protocol Implementation. In *Computer Software and Applications Conference, 1978. COMPSAC'78. The IEEE Computer Society's Second International*, pages 686–691, 1978.

[179] M. H. Schonenberg, R. S. Mans, N. C. Russell, N. A. Mulyar, and W. M. P. van der Aalst. Towards a Taxonomy of Process Flexibility, 2007.

[180] Peter Schoo. On the Future of Security in Future Internet, 2009.

[181] Mischa Schwartz and Leonard Kleinrock. History of Communications: an Early History of the Internet. *Comm. Mag.*, 48(8):26–36, August 2010. http://dl.acm.org/citation.cfm?id=1861764.1861769.

[182] Yang seo Choi, Jin-Tae Oh, Jong-Soo Jang, and Jae-Cheol Ryou. Integrated ddos attack defense infrastructure for effective attack prevention. In *Information Technology Convergence and Services (ITCS), 2010 2nd International Conference on*, pages 1–6, 2010.

[183] Ivan Seskar, Kiran Nagaraja, Sam Nelson, and Dipankar Raychaudhuri. Mobilityfirst future internet architecture project. In *Proceedings of the 7th Asian Internet Engineering Conference*, AINTEC '11, pages 1–3, New York, NY, USA, 2011. ACM.

[184] Steven L. Shaffer and Alan R. Simon. *Network Security*. Academic Press Professional, Inc., San Diego, CA, USA, 1994.

[185] Prabhat K. Singh and Arun Lakhotia. Analysis and detection of computer viruses and worms: An annotated bibliography. *SIGPLAN Notices*, 37(2):29–35, 2002.

[186] Joseph D. Sloan. *Network Troubleshooting Tools*. O'Reilly, 2001.

[187] spamhaus Online: http://www.theregister.co.uk/2013/03/27/spamhaus_ddos_megaflood/.

[188] V Srivastava and M Motani. Cross-layer Design: a Survey and the Road Ahead. *IEEE Communications Magazine*, 43(12):112–119, 2005. http:// ieeexplore.ieee.org/lpdocs/epic03/wrapper.htm?arnumber=1561928.

[189] William Stallings. *Cryptography and Network Security: Principles and Practice*. Prentice Hall Press, Upper Saddle River, NJ, USA, 5th edition, 2010.

[190] J. D. Sterman. *Business Dynamics: Systems Thinking and Modeling for a Complex World*. McGraw-Hill, 2000.

[191] W. Richard Stevens. *TCP/IP Illustrated (vol. 1): the Protocols*. Addison-Wesley Longman Publishing Co., Inc., Boston, MA, USA, 1993.

[192] Peter Stuckmann and Rainer Zimmermann. European research on future internet design. *Wireless Commun.*, 16(5):14–22, October 2009.

[193] D. Thaler. Border Gateway Multicast Protocol (BGMP): Protocol Specification. RFC 3913 (Historic), 2004. http://www.ietf.org/rfc/rfc3913.txt.

[194] S. Thomson, T. Narten, and T. Jinmei. IPv6 Stateless Address Autoconfiguration. RFC 4862 (Draft Standard), September 2007.

[195] J. Touch, Y. Wang, and V. Pingali. A Recursive Network Architecture. Technical report, ISI Technical Report ISI-TR-2006-626, October 2006.

[196] Joe Touch, Ilia Baldine, Rudra Dutta, Gregory G. Finn, Bryan Ford, Scott Jordan, Dan Massey, Abraham Matta, Christos Papadopoulos, Peter Reiher, and George Rouskas. A Dynamic Recursive Unified Internet Design (DRUID). *Comput. Netw.*, 55(4):919–935, March 2011. http://dx.doi.org/10.1016/j.comnet.2010.12.016.

[197] Joseph D. Touch and Venkata K. Pingali. The RNA Metaprotocol. In *ICCCN*, pages 157–162, 2008.

[198] Vlasios Tsiatsis, Alexander Gluhak, Tim Bauge, Frederic Montagut, Jesus Bernat, Martin Bauer, Claudia Villalonga, Payam Barnaghi, and Srdjan Krco. *The SENSEI Real World Internet Architecture, "Towards the Future Internet - Emerging Trends from European Research"*, pages 247–256. IOS Press, 2010.

[199] Taner Tuncer and Yetkin Tatar. Detection syn flooding attacks using fuzzy logic. In *Proceedings of the 2008 International Conference on Information Security and Assurance (isa 2008)*, ISA '08, pages 321–325, Washington, DC, USA, 2008. IEEE Computer Society.

[200] S. Turner and L. Chen. Updated Security Considerations for the MD5 Message-Digest and the HMAC-MD5 Algorithms. RFC 6151 (Informational), March 2011.

[201] C. Vaishnav. Does Technology Disruption Always Mean Industry Disruption? In *Conference of System Dynamics Society*, pages 1–25, Athens, Greece, 2008.

[202] Barbara van Schewick. *Architecture & Innovation: the Role of the End-to-End Arguments in the Original Internet*. PhD thesis, 2005.

[203] Barbara van Schewick and David Farber. Point/Counterpoint - Network Neutrality Nuances. *Commun. ACM*, 52(2):31–37, 2009.

[204] Lars. Vlker, Denis. Martin, Christoph. Werle, Martina. Zitterbart, and Ibtissam. El. Khayat. Selecting Concurrent Network Architectures at Runtime. In *Proceeding of IEEE International Conference on Communication 2009*, pages 2124–2128, 2009.

[205] Haining Wang, Cheng Jin, and Kang G. Shin. Defense against spoofed ip traffic using hop-count filtering. *IEEE/ACM Trans. Netw.*, 15(1):40–53, February 2007.

[206] Yang Wang, Chuang Lin, Quan-Lin Li, and Yuguang Fang. A queueing analysis for the denial of service (dos) attacks in computer networks. *Comput. Netw.*, 51(12):3564–3573, August 2007.

[207] Kun Wei and James Heather. A theorem-proving approach to verification of fair non-repudiation protocols. In *Proceedings of the 4th International Conference on Formal Aspects in Security and Trust*, FAST'06, pages 202–219, Berlin, Heidelberg, 2007. Springer-Verlag.

[208] A. Williams. Frame Relay: Back to Basics, Standards and Implementations. In *Frame Relay, IEE Colloquium on*, pages 1/1 –1/3, April 1992.

[209] Tilman Wolf, James Griffioen, Kenneth L. Calvert, Rudra Dutta, George N. Rouskas, Ilia Baldine, and Anna Nagurney. Choice as a principle in network architecture. In *SIGCOMM*, pages 105–106, 2012.

[210] Christian Wolter, Michael Menzel, and Christoph Meinel. Modelling security goals in business processes. In *Modellierung*, pages 197–212, 2008.

[211] Thomas Y. C. Woo and Simon S. Lam. Authentication for distributed systems. *Computer*, 25(1):39–52, January 1992.

[212] Guang. Yang. *Introduction to TCP/IP Network Attacks*. Department of Computer Science Iowa State University, Disponvel em.

[213] Xiaowei Yang, David Wetherall, and Thomas Anderson. A dos-limiting network architecture. *SIGCOMM Comput. Commun. Rev.*, 35(4):241–252, August 2005.

[214] Heng Yin and Haining Wang. Building an Application-aware IPsec Policy System. In *Proceedings of the 14th Conference on USENIX Security Symposium - Volume 14*, SSYM'05, pages 21–21, Berkeley, CA, USA, 2005. USENIX Association. http://dl.acm.org/citation.cfm?id=1251398.1251419.

[215] Jie Yu, Zhoujun Li, Huowang Chen, and Xiaoming Chen. A detection and offense mechanism to defend against application layer dos attacks. In *Proceedings of the Third International Conference on Networking and Services*, ICNS '07, pages 54–, Washington, DC, USA, 2007. IEEE Computer Society.

[216] Xiaoyan Zhu Yun Zhou and Yuguang Fang. MABS: multi-cast authentication based on batch signature. *IEEE Trans. Mob. Comput.*, 9(7):982–993, 2010.

[217] Theodore Zahariadis, Dimitri Papadimitriou, Hannes Tschofenig, Stephan Haller, Petros Daras, George D. Stamoulis, and Manfred Hauswirth. The Future Internet. Chapter Towards a future internet architecture, pages 7–18. Springer-Verlag, Berlin, Heidelberg, 2011.

[218] Theodore B. Zahariadis, Petros Daras, Jan Bouwen, Norbert Niebert, David Griffin, Federico Alvarez, and Gonzalo Camarillo. Towards a Content-Centric Internet. In *Future Internet Assembly*, pages 227–236, 2010.

[219] zdnet-Online:http://www.zdnet.com/blog/security/recent-cnn-distributed-denial-of-service-ddos-attack explained/1054.

[220] Lixia Zhang. Evolving internet to the future via named data networking. In *AINTEC*, page 72, 2011.

[221] Lixia Zhang, Kevin Fall, and David Meyer. Report from the IAB Workshop on Routing and Addressing. RFC 4984, September 2007.

[222] Jianying Zhou and Dieter Gollmann. An efficient non-repudiation protocol. In *Proceedings of the 10th IEEE Workshop on Computer Security Foundations*, CSFW '97, pages 126–, Washington, DC, USA, 1997. IEEE Computer Society.

List of Abbreviations

ARPANET	Advanced Research Projects Agency Network
ANA	Autonomic Network Architecture
ANSI	American National Standards Institute
AH	Authentication Header
AES	Advanced Encryption Standard
ACL	Access Control List
ARP	Address Resolution Protocol
ATM	Asynchronous Transfer Mode
BB	Building Blocks
BGMP	Border Gateway Multicast Protocol
BGP	Border Gateway Protocol
CA	Certification Authority
CCN	Content Centric Network

CI	Current Internet
CIDR	Classless Inter-Domain Routing
CRL	Certificate Revocation List
CRC	Cyclic Redundancy Check
DVMRP	Distance Vector Multicast Routing Protocol
DAC	Discretionary Access Control
DARPA	Defense Advanced Research Projects Agency
DNS	Domain Name System
DRUID	Dynamic Recursive Unified Internet Design
DVMRP	Distance Vector Multicast Routing Protocol
DoS	Denial of Service
DDoS	Distributed Denial of Service
DDBB	DoS Detection Building Block
DFBB	DoS Filter Building Block
E2E	End-to-End
ESP	Encapsulating Security Payload
FI	Future Internet
FIND	Future Internet Design
FTP	File Transfer Protocol

FIPS	Federal Information Processing Standards
FIRE	Future Internet Research and Experimentation
GENI	Global Environment for Networking Innovations
HDLC	High-level Data Link Control
HTML	Hypertext Markup Language
HTTP	Hypetext Transfer Protocol
HMAC	Hash Message Authentication Code
IDS	Intrusion Detection System
IAAS	Infrastructure As A Service
ICMP	Internet Control Message Protocol
IPS	Intrusion Prevention System
IEEE	Institute of Electrical and Electronics Engineers
IETF	Internet Engineering Task Force
IP	Internet Protocol
IPng	Next Generation Internet Protocol (official name is IPv6)
IPv6	Internet Protocol version 6 (also informally called IPng)
IESG	Internet Engineering Steering Group
IGMP	Internet Group Management Protocol
IMAP	Internet Message Access Protocol

IOS	International Organization for Standardization
ISP	Internet Service Provider
IPSec	IP Security
IMAP	Internet Message Access Protocol
IRC	Internet Relay Chat
LAN	Local Ara Network
MAC	Mandatory Access Control
Mbps	Megabits (millions of bits) per second
MOSPF	Multicast Open Shortest Path First
MPLS	Multi Protocol Label Switching
MOSPF	Multicast Open Shortest Path First
MANET	Mobile Ad-hoc Network
NAT	Network Address Translator
NFS	Network File System
NCP	Network Control Program
ND	Neighbor Discovery
NIC	Network Interface Card
NOSS	Networks of Sensor Systems
NSF	National Science Foundation

NIST	National Institute of Standards and Technology
NSFnet	National Science Foundation network
NTP	Network Time Protocol
OSI	Open Systems Interconnection
OSPF	Open Shortest Path First
OCSP	Online Certificate Status Protocol
PAAS	Platform As A Service
PAP	Policy Access Point
PKI	Public Key Infrastructure
PIM-DM	Protocol Independent Multicast - Dense Mode
PIM-SM	Protocol Independent Multicast - Sparse Mode
PPP	Point-to-Point Protocol
PUB	Publication
QoS	Quality of Service
RARP	Reverse Address Resolution Protocol
RBA	Role Based Architecture
RBAC	Role Based Access Control
RDF	Resource Description Framework
RFC	Request For Comments
RNA	Recursive Network Architecture

RSVP	Resource Reservation Protocol
RPC	Remote Procedure Call
SAAS	Software As A Service
SAC	Service Authentication Code
SCADA	Supervisory Control and Data Acquisition
SCTP	Stream Control Transmission Protocol
SIP	Session Initiation Protocol
SNMP	Simple Network Management Protocol
SOA	Service Oriented Architecture
SoC	Service Oriented Computing
SILO	Service Integration and controL Optimisation
SMTP	Simple Mail Transfer Protocol
SONATE	Sevice Oriented Network ArchiTEcture
SONET	Synchronous Optical Network
SSL	Secure Sockets Layer
STD	Internet Standards series of RFCs
TTL	Time - To - Live
TCP	Transmission Control Protocol
UDP	User Datagram Protocol
US DoD	United States Department of Defense

WAN   Wide Area Network

XML   Extensible Markup Language

Index